New Politics

The Conscience of a Moderate Series

New Politics

Moderate Politics for Post 2020 America

Harry P. Martin

Print ISBN: 978-1-09836-337-6
eBook ISBN: 978-1-09836-338-3

Author's website: harrypmartin.com

First Edition
December 2020

Table of Contents

Preface v

Acknowledgments viii

Introduction 1

Part 1: American Politics—View from the Middle

Chapter 1: 21st Century Politics—A House Divided 7

Chapter 2: The Silent and Silenced Majority 19

Chapter 3: Who Are American Moderates? 23

Part 2: Ideology—Where American Moderates Stand

Chapter 4: On Rights—Children First 35

Chapter 5: On Institutions—Family First 45

Chapter 6: On Priorities—Country First 55

Chapter 7: On Politics—Solutions First 59

Part 3: Solutions—Where Do You Stand?

Chapter 8: On Guns 67

Chapter 9: On Immigration 77

Chapter 10: On Education 87

Chapter 11: On Climate 117

Part 4: Agenda—What Do Moderates Want?

Chapter 12:   The American Moderate Agenda..............129

Chapter 13:   Are You A Moderate? 159

About the Author 163

Bibliography 164

Index...165

End Notes 169

For all of the children of America and the world. They deserve a much better deal and future from adults if we Americans are who we say we are. *Doing the right thing* for them is long overdue.

And for all of the liberals and conservatives in America here is a new way to look at politics.

Preface

New Politics[†] is the first in a series of projects to explore *The Conscience of a Moderate*. The series title is modeled after the title of a book from the 1960s, *The Conscience of a Conservative*, written by Barry Goldwater, the Republican senator from Arizona during that era. His book laid out his perspective of what a true conservative is. The series begins with what a true moderate's perspective on politics is and how politicians and media are draining the strength of America and destroying our children's future. Other projects will advocate for children's rights, a new deal for children, and moderate views on policy prescriptions for a number of key national issues in domestic, foreign, and global policy.

New Politics is not a book about politics, it is a book of politics about one simple idea. More moderates create more moderation, better politics, and better outcomes for America. My intent in *New Politics* is to place a badly needed counterweight in the middle of the political scale to counter extreme conservatism and liberalism currently dominating American political debates and media coverage. There is a TV show joke that goes, "If you don't like the people around you, get new people." (Audience laughs.) If Americans don't like the politics and politicians representing them, get new politics and new politicians. (Many Americans are not laughing, especially in the aftermath of the 2020 election.)

Written over the winter of 2019 to 2020, before and during the rise of the global coronavirus pandemic and the very controversial presidential election, this book offers political views, from all places, the middle of America. By "middle America," I do not mean the Midwest or Midwestern values, which are stereotypically considered conservative. Instead, I mean the middle of the political ideological spectrum where moderately minded people think, live, work, and raise their families. The moderate middle is where the author hails from.

I am not a political or social scientist nor am I an academician or politician. My lone qualification in undertaking this book is my belief that I am a moderate in my heart of hearts. Though a registered Democrat most of my adult life, I have considered myself an independent voter. I registered as a Republican at the end of the first Obama term. Constantly dissatisfied with both parties through life, today more than ever, I now realize I have been a moderate all along and have no party that represents me. No longer able to watch the

---

[†] The title of the book, *New Politics*, refers to the notion of a break from the 21st century brand of extreme left and right politics and not a reference to or affiliation with any previous uses of the term.

factions push America toward the ends of the ideological spectrum, I count myself among those who want to push both factions to the center and move America forward.

This book asks hard questions like, "How do Americans unravel the divisiveness and start solving big issues?" For moderates, all the answers begin with "More moderates and more moderation will..." Another question this book will help the reader answer is, "Are you a moderate?" "Or, do you want to become a moderate or become more moderate in your political views?" But you just can't put your finger on why and what that means? By the end of this book, you may conclude you are a moderate or are ready to become a moderate.

This book will also introduce you to a new and different way of looking at issues and politics than the current political lens of "left or right." My hope is it will afford the reader an opportunity to imagine an America if moderates were the leaders at both ends of Pennsylvania Avenue. It also will call out how purposefully prejudiced media led debates and hate-filled partisan "stare-and-glare" political standoffs are undermining and endangering our nation. You will get a glimpse of what people in the middle of America whisper about when extreme liberals and conservatives aren't around. You will read ideas that you will not hear on TV but you might hear in the hallway or on the street when everyday people talk politics.

Moderates need to distinguish themselves because neither faction nor party represent us. Nor are they building a future for America many Americans want. While "political moderates" as a differentiating label has gained some traction in recent decades, the lack of a moderate political ideology has meant eligible voters who label themselves as moderate or independent have to describe their political views along the left-right spectrum. If I have it correct, moderates also see principles, policy, and politics differently that defy description and positioning along the left-right spectrum. The dictionary definition of moderatism is "a political philosophy of avoiding the extremes of left and right by taking a moderate position or course of action." To describe moderate views at times, it may better serve to think of a triangle that yields a diversity of ideas in place of a line spectrum that describes binary choices for positions on individual issues. Given how things have turned out so far with conservatism, liberalism, and socialism monopolizing the debate, it is time for thought leadership based on moderatism. A twenty-first century rendering of an ideology of moderatism will be introduced that goes outside the left-right spectrum to differentiate moderates.

The US presidential election and the coronavirus pandemic of 2020-21 demand our full attention. From a moderate's perspective, it did not matter which candidate was elected, things likely turn out badly for America's future and children. Lack of focus on big issues in addition to the loss in faith that our elections are free and fair, loss of learning time for our children, and the loss of jobs and small businesses, especially for those of all colors in the lower half of our nation, expose our inability to create more economic equality and a stronger democracy. The dramatic economic contraction during the pandemic laid bare many of America's blind spots and systemic vulnerabilities. One more political blind spot will be added for your consideration: children.

As an everyday American with a different point of view, I have one personal hope for you as you read this book. I hope your conscience guides you to keep asking yourself one question, "What will America be like ten years, fifty years from now for your grandchildren and their children, if we do nothing?" May we find a way to build a brighter future for them, and may you find the moderate voice inside of you. May the moderate perspective offered here advance national debates and policy options to address America's blind spots and pressing issues.

Unless Americans pursue more moderate politics the politics of the first quarter century of the twenty-first century will sweep America so far afield that America will forget the core values that made it the great nation it has been.

It is time for at least one voice of the *silenced majority* to speak and the conscience of a moderate to be heard. Please lean in to consider new ideas that change how and what America chooses and who we elect to govern us.

—Harry Martin

Acknowledgments

This book was made possible by the many extraordinary, ordinary people I have met in my life who were willing to talk candidly and civilly about politics and to share their perspective, hopes, and dreams. It was also made possible by the interdisciplinary education, experience, and systems thinking I have acquired over the decades. Thank you to the editorial team at Elite Authors who did a great job editing the book.

Special thanks to my wife for her patience with me as I traveled this journey. Thanks to my older brother and our children for their review and input on the early manuscript. Thanks to the many who shared perspectives and information from the Left and the Right.

Introduction

There comes a time when one must take a position that is neither safe nor politic nor popular, but he must take it because his conscience tells him it is right.

—Martin Luther King Jr.

Older Americans may recall from their early years in the twentieth century, Barry Goldwater, the influential conservative senator and presidential candidate from Arizona. In 1960 he authored *The Conscience of a Conservative*, in which he laid out the principles he believed were timeless and immutable of a true conservative. Notably, among the half dozen or so namesake books that followed his, in 2001, from the other end of the spectrum, the late senator Paul Wellstone wrote a liberal's response to Goldwater entitled *The Conscience of a Liberal*. In 2007, economist Paul Krugman—using the same title—authored a recent history of economic inequality as a counterpoint to Goldwater. He argued that among other factors, government policies have contributed to inequality. And in 2017, former Republican Arizona senator Jeff Flake, a conservative similar to Goldwater, published a contemporary view of conservatism under the same title that reacts to the Trump presidency, which he believes does not reflect conservatism or the Republican Party. While a great deal has been written about what true conservatives and liberals believe, there do not appear to be any comparable books that articulate the principles of a true moderate. Therefore, that is what I will attempt to do here in *New Politics*.

With hardly any inclusion of the views of America's politically moderate people in the national dialogue, the political and media elite have exploited our public forums and legal processes to polarize, weaponize, and metastasize American politics. Gerrymandering, dirty tricks, and handpicked extreme political candidates have created legislatures that respond to the will of the party elites and not the people. The unbridled tribal ambition of politicians and extreme ideological groups to control America's wealth, politics, and civil society is playing out as a bizarre reality show. In the wake of predatory partisan politics, there is a trail of collateral damage that is hard to comprehend:

- Political inaction and stalemates on many key problems

- A staggering federal debt in 2020 of well over twenty-five trillion dollars, conceivably headed to thirty to one hundred trillion dollars by midcentury, depending on the dynamics of the coronavirus pandemic or the lack of fiscal discipline and responsibility both political parties display

• Changes in cultural and human institutions that defy human nature and the will of many Americans

• Widening income and wealth gaps leaving behind many Americans of all colors but especially our citizens of African American descent

• Large numbers of America's and the world's children of all races left behind educationally and economically

• A global carbon-based energy footprint that has us possibly recreating in the short span of several centuries a climate that existed a million years ago

• A global population, migration, and pandemic that are stressing the economics, health, and demographics of our nation and many other nations—potentially to the breaking point

Hearing people from both ends of the spectrum talking about America and a second kinetic civil war in the same sentence is incomprehensible to many of us. Yet it is hard to ignore or deny that we are witnessing a civil war of information and a revolutionary war on culture rolled into one. As liberal and conservative factions compete to prosecute their uncivil war of words on Americans, moderates want our eligible voters and future generations to know for what some of us in Middle America stand, and that there is a great deal at stake. Middle America here means the middle of the ideological spectrum. The people of the future should know that there was another faction, a third option, mostly unheard and unopened in the political dialogue. If we lose certain fundamental debates, future generations of Americans likely lose America's standard of living, quality of life, and the American way of life. The American way is a constitutional republic founded on the tenets of fundamental rights, freedom, family, faith, and optimism for the future. It strives to create a society flourishing and prospering under liberty, justice, equality, opportunity, and trust. All these tenets are at risk.

While the primary goal of the book is to lay out a different way to think about political choices based on moderate ideology, I will endeavor to differentiate a true moderate from a true conservative, or true liberal. To frame political principles and national issues, some content will focus on history, science, economics, law, and political philosophy. There will be a look at the debate about interest or lack of interest in a third major political party. There will be a focus on polls to provide context for what pollsters say the political spectrum and ideological map look like.

While polls are typically designed to help both parties understand swing voters and to hone their messages for them, my interest is about establishing a moderate ideology that grounds people who think moderately about conventional politics. The intent is to draw people who desire real progress on crucial issues toward the center and away from intractable partisan positions at the ends of the political spectrum. The hope is that political standoffs and stalemates can be broken by exploring values, beliefs, principles, as well as views on rights, institutions, and policies. Perhaps a positive unintended consequence of this book will be to depolarize the dialogue around some issues and create more independent swing voters, thus drawing them from the left and the right to the center. The perspective in this book may help you decide how to label yourself politically, ask new questions of candidates, and challenge the media's frequently loaded and biased questions. Perhaps it will help you decide how you vote in future elections. It may also encourage you to challenge the political parties to nominate more moderate candidates.

My hope is this book offers you an opportunity to explore a new way to identify and describe yourself as a modern political moderate and to consider a new vision for America inclusive of an equal voice for moderate views and agendas in twenty-first century politics. This book invites you to consider whether you want to continue to accept party politics as usual or whether you are willing to be part of a third, alternative, constructive, positive point of view founded on moderate principles and ideology. At the end of this book, in chapter 13, there is a simple, one minute self-assessment you can take so you can measure how close you are to being a moderate.

This book aspires to help you decide if you are truly committed to the partisan ideology of the political interests that are currently setting the agenda and future direction for our nation, for our children, and grandchildren—our generation's legacy. If you are not, you may be a moderate. This book will enable you to join in the debate with new moderate views and compelling solutions as a twenty-first century moderate. As a call to action to change the political landscape, answers for many of our nation's challenges start with this simple view: more moderates and more moderation produce less extremism, less tribalism, more civil politics, and better outcomes for America.

Even with more moderates and moderation, getting to better political choices, and a brighter future is fraught with formidable challenges because we are already in the middle of a future-changing turning point. A turning point is a moment in history when a society's historical trajectory is sent in a significantly new direction by one or more of six catalysts: 1) surprise e.g., a pandemic, 2) conflict e.g., wars of nations, factions, or ideas, 3) crisis, e.g., the Great Recession of

2008, 4) causes, e.g., women's suffrage, 5) choices—elections, decisions, and policy, e.g., dropping the atomic bomb to end WW II, 6) agency, people whose actions move history by force of will, e.g., Winston Churchill, Gandhi, and Martin Luther King, Jr. The nature of the current turning point is relative to one's political perspective. A moderate American might characterize the turning point in esoteric terms like liberal humanism, relativism, immediatism, socialism, and others. But the moderate could also describe it by choices politicians are making that are easily understood in these practical terms. America's elites and special interests are 'taking from the future' and 'not preparing for the future' to the benefit a smaller and smaller constituency of adults alive today. They are the winners—at the expense of others, especially America's present and future children. [1]

The first formidable challenge is reuniting America amid a very controversial election of 2020, the pandemic, provocative media, and partisan Washington politics. The second challenge is navigating a long list of trending societal mega-forces and factional interests that will intersect and combine in various ways. They are filled with opportunities and new threats for us depending on how we navigate political choices that are now before us—policy choices, issues, and outside forces. Our beliefs will be challenged by an array of potentially future-altering issues ranging from gargantuan debt, a multipolar political world, the economy, the digitalization and virtualization of life, inequality, population, and the natural carrying capacity of our planet. The future will be enabled by phenomenal and frightening scientific advances in silicon-based microminiaturization, software, and genetics to name just a few.

What do you think America's standing in the world will be ten years, fifty years in the future given how global population is growing and geo-politics are evolving? With China as the most populous nation and emerging as the largest economy and military in the world and executing a coherent, focused strategy to become a leading if not the sole superpower, how do things change for America? Will the United States have its own coherent, focused foreign policy strategy to maintain its position in the world, to protect our people and our shores?

What do you think life in America will be like in ten years, fifty years in the future if domestic politics continue to be as divisive and destructive as they are now? Imagine that the national debt continues to grow? Imagine we never solve social equality, economic inequality, education, health care, immigration, elections, fossil energy use, and many other issues? Can you imagine if we fail to focus on our children and how they are created and prepared for work and family life? Imagine the US has to endure more pandemics perhaps more deadly than Covid-19? What will life be like if politicians accept 100s of millions of new immigrants in the next half a century or less? What will life be like if many jobs and businesses never come back after the pandemic lockdown and big businesses successfully eliminate millions of jobs using automation, artificial intelligent processes, and robots?

The future is coming faster than any of us can imagine. The intersection of the *societal challenges* and *scientific advances* in the twenty-first century present complex political issues, questions, and consequences that require: 1) wise choices, 2) decisive action, and 3) virtuous political leadership. From a moderate's vantage point, we have failed on all three counts—so far. Will we choose wisely for the issues that challenge the collective will and the political and moral sensibilities of many Americans? So far, we haven't. Will Americans rise and respond fast enough to the challenges and advances to confront and cope successfully? So far, we haven't. Will political leadership provide unifying vision and values that lead to a stronger, truly inclusive, and prosperous American future? So far, they haven't. So far, all they (we) have done is disorient, disrupt, and now—decisively—divide our nation.

6 | New Politics

Chapter 1: 21st Century Politics—A House Divided

Those who look for the bad in people will surely find it.
—Abraham Lincoln

The determination to vote out the opposition—and the broader trend of acute polarization within the American political system—has altered virtually every facet of our political life. Negative partisanship is affecting the behavior of voters and reshaping the voting coalitions aligned behind each major party.[2]
—Rachel Bitecofer, political scientist, Christopher Newport University

Abraham Lincoln said, *"A house divided against itself cannot stand."* In today's deeply polarized public arena, liberals and conservatives, their ideologues, and special interests, dominate the national politics with very divisive discourse. They have incessantly looked for the bad in anyone who does not subscribe to their point of view. They condemn anyone who does not support their agenda. Both factions have become more extreme and radical, leading Congress to become tribal, uncivil, dysfunctional, and increasingly irrelevant while the federal courts have been the battlefield for politicized justice by liberal and conservative activism. Financed by deep pocket, dark-moneyed special interests, and obsessively focused zealots at the core of the two deeply divided ideological factions, both are hell-bent on influencing anyone susceptible to their propaganda or convinced by their narrative. Both factions drown out the voice of the majority of Americans who are only interested in living their lives and raising their children best they can, in peace in the natural world. Many Americans are not interested in Progressives' new dystopian world or Libertarians' brave new world of a few rich and a lot of not-rich people, nor do they subscribe to the values, agenda, or ideology of twenty-first century conservatives or liberals.

As the national dialogue has divided us, the political process discriminated us, and powerful economic interests have disem-powered us, polls record that Americans say the two political parties are not doing a good enough job of representing them. A majority of the American people believe that a third political party is needed. Over two-thirds of Americans say they want a third party.[3] Let us call them nonpartisans. Those interested in a third political party, however, don't agree on what that third party should be—moderate, more liberal, or more conservative. Nearly a third of Americans, either liberal or conservative, are partisans and are uninterested in considering a third party. They are interested in either promoting their ideology or voting the other party out of office. According to polling by the Democracy Fund Voter Study Group, partisans are not about to abandon their party. By their polling, over three-quarters of Americans feel better with one party or the other, leaving less than a quarter to bounce between the two.[4]

Furthermore, with the two factions deeply embedded in our political, legal, and electoral fabric, it is hard for Americans to understand or support the reforms needed to change the two-party system. Consequently, addressing the political discord by creating a new, third major political party, equally embedded in the political, legal, and electoral fabric, would be very hard. It has only happened several times in our history successfully. While hard to architect and implement, the notion of a third political party should not be completely dismissed as Americans consider their options today to redress their grievances. While the internet and World Wide Web may create new possibilities, the process begins with the formation of ideology and a platform that people can inspect and consider before they decide which party they want to support.

The current ideological frame spans liberal to conservative with multiple groups in between called independent, undecided, and moderate. Pollsters conclude that the in-between groups are all over the ideological map[5] and that there is not a good definition of an independent, undecided, or moderate voter. Despite some overlap independents, moderates and undecided voters are pretty distinct without a common cohesive ideology within or across the groups, according to the Voter Study Group referenced above. Pollsters have trouble parsing out self-identified moderates from the others because moderates survey across a wide range of choices in the ideological map on any given issue. That finding is not surprising as a key attribute of a moderate is that moderates seek solutions, not political causes. Honest differences in how best to address any issue create a diversity of ideas, primarily when the choices presented by the two standing factions do not provide solution-oriented proposals. As pointed out in "The Moderate Middle Is a Myth" by Lee Drutman,[6]

> There are political scientists (Donald Kinder and Nathan Kalmoe) who have concluded that "the moderate category seems less an ideological destination than a refuge for the innocent and the confused." and a "poor predictor of centrism" (David Broockman).

Pollsters and politicians treat people who self-identify as undecideds, independents, and moderates as the "swing" voters for party politicians to sway. While pollsters will determine who they say a moderate is by the way they categorize the electorate, my book proposes a way for people across the political and ideological spectrum to reclassify themselves based on a moderate ideology that challenges the traditional political spectrum. A key goal of this book is to provide a moderate ideological destination for the reader to consider. The aim is to test whether politically moderate thinking can be transformed from a *refuge* to a *destination* for independents, undecideds, moderate Democrats, and moderate Republicans. They all then become swing voters away from the extreme liberal and conservative platforms. One of the questions this books asks is, "Can politically moderate campaigns and positions be advanced by a new breed of moderately minded people and politicians that attract at least swing voters toward solution-oriented politics and policies?"

One of the reasons so many Americans feel a third political party is needed is because the moderate, nonpartisan view has been ignored by partisan conservatives, liberals, and one-percenters who straddle both parties. Partisans are the ones who are determined to vote the other party out of office. Nonpartisans are the ones who are drawn to the center for civil, moderate dialogue on ways to make progress. They are potential moderates. No one is listening to them or representing their interests. With a great deal of help from media, the voice of America's center has gone silent because it has been silenced by politically elite. With control over well designed agendas and orchestrated media messaging, both factions have made sure that hardly anyone is talking about moderate views or issues in any forum, despite the reality that nonpartisans are the majority of Americans.

How did we get back here? Yes. America has been here before. American politics have been deeply divided before with factional disputes over scandals, elections, and policy. The casual student of American history will recognize the similarity with today's focus on scandal and charges of presidential misconduct during the administration of the 45th president and the 1st president. Even during the time of our first president—George Washington—there was great controversy. An issue that dominated the attention of the nation was the hotly debated John Jay Treaty with England, which aligned the United States with England versus France. President Washington desired to revitalize relations with England and resolve open issues from the Revolutionary War. At the same time, Thomas Jefferson, his secretary of state and a Francophile, fought to align with France and avoid England. At one point, Jefferson accused Washington of treason in negotiating that treaty.

As contentious as the election of 2020 has been it is not the first. It feels like it may be the worst. Only history will be able to judge whether it or one of the other contested elections that preceded it, each with their own dramatic consequences, was the most controversial election. Consider the elections of 1800, 1824, 1860, and 1876.‡

---

‡ Other contentious and controversial elections include 1888 and 2000.

The election of 1800 between Federalists John Adams and Thomas Jefferson (with Charles Pinkney Adam's candidate for vice president and Aaron Burr as Jefferson's vice president) ended with Jefferson becoming the third president of the United States after winning against Adams who got 65 electoral votes and Jefferson's vice presidential running mate, Aaron Burr, who received the same number of electoral votes as Jefferson. Because the Constitution did not distinguish votes for president and vice president who both got 73 electoral votes, it took 36 votes in the House of Representatives to break the tie. The presidential contest between Adams (incumbent) Jefferson was filled with vindictive mudslinging with both sides' partisans making outrageous and enraging claims about each other. Both sides thought the election of the other would be the ruin of the country. The political intrigue of that contest was matched with the infighting in the House of Representatives that ensued as Burr attempted to beat Jefferson in the run-off election. Unintended consequences of the divisive election of 1800 led to the 12th amendment to the constitution to redefine how elections are decided and the famous Supreme Court ruling in *Marbury v. Madison*[7] in 1803. The ruling resulted in the establishment of the Supreme Court principle of judicial review, which has created numerous controversial rulings. The election of 1800 was a catalyst for the major turning point in American history: judicial review.

The election of 1824 between John Quincy Adams and Andrew Jackson was even more divisive. Four candidates ran, and none received a majority. Andrew Jackson and John Q. Adams received the most votes in that order, and at the time, the Constitution called for the top three by popular vote to go to the House for selection. The fourth candidate was Henry Clay, also Speaker of the House, who detested Jackson. The House elected Adams, and Clay became his secretary of state. Adam's election may be the first instance of a political quid pro quo that is so prominently argued today as abuse of power. Unintended consequences were the doubling down by Jackson supporters and the formation of the Democratic Party, which led to Jackson's election in 1828, which then led to the naming of Roger Taney as chief justice of the Supreme Court. The election of 1824 was a catalyst for another major turning point in the direction of the nation: the election of Jackson in 1828 and the selection of Taney. Both political events set the stage for the Civil War, among other catalysts like the publication in 1852 of Harriet Beecher Stowe's widely read book *Uncle Tom's Cabin*; the Southern backlash to the Missouri Compromise of 1820, which limited the expansion of slavery in the Louisiana Territory to the 36°30' parallel; and the Dred Scott Supreme Court ruling by Taney in 1857, that ruled strongly in support of slavery; and the last straw, the election of Abraham Lincoln in 1860.[8]

The election of 1860[9] was filled with vicious politics and led to unforeseen consequences during Lincoln's administration. By 1860 some 25 percent of Southern households held five or fewer slaves, and roughly 3 percent of Southern households held twelve or more slaves. The 3 percent dominated Southern Democrats and in turn dominated Southern politics. Southern Democrats, supported by Northern Democrats, pressed their demand for expansion of slavery into all new territories of the United States. As part of the famous *Dred Scott v. Sandford* Supreme Court decision of 1857, Chief Justice Roger Taney ruled that the Missouri Compromise of 1820 was unconstitutional, along with the denial of recognition of blacks, slave or freedman, as citizens of the United States with any rights. Northern Democrats who supported the Southerners' cause for slavery, nicknamed "dough-faces," resisted and obstructed the new congressional Republican Party majority and newly elected President Lincoln at every turn up to, during, and following the prosecution of the Civil War, very much like what happened in 2016 and 2020 elections.

One consequences of that era was the first full impeachment process of Lincoln's second term vice president, Andrew Johnson a senator for Tennessee, whom Lincoln had selected to help bring the North and South back together. Johnson became president following Lincoln's assassination on April 14, 1865. Johnson, a Southern slave owner from Tennessee, was committed to undoing the North's win and reconstitute the South. He enabled southern legislatures to pass "Black Codes," which intended to establish a low-wage servitude economy in former slave states since the Thirteenth Amendment prohibited slavery. He was impeached following his veto of the Republicans' passage of the Tenure of Office Act of 1867, which Congress then overrode. That act intended to ensure Johnson could not fire Stanton, Lincoln's secretary of state, who fully supported the abolition of slavery and reconstruction. Johnson suspended him using a loophole provision of the law. The eleven articles of Johnson's impeachment failed to achieve the two-thirds majority in the Senate to convict by only one vote after two Republicans decided not to convict. Johnson stayed in office until 1869, pursuing pro-South policies that worked to undo the North's win and the Lincoln legacy of Reconstruction.

The selection of Johnson set the stage for another turning point in American history: the Black Codes. The Black Codes were laws enacted following the Civil War that limited black persons' rights. They would later become fully institutionalized in the Jim Crow laws following the several scandals[10] during President Grant's second term and the confluence of a number of concurrent factors in the 1870s: 1) A deep economic depression of 1873 with 25 percent unemployment diminished northern resolve to keep pursuing Reconstruction; 2) The formation of southern resolve to undermine Reconstruction using an intentional propaganda campaign known as the Mississippi Plan to play on northern racism against the black franchise and misrule; 3) The Supreme Court adoption of a very narrow and prejudiced reading of the 14th amendment "equal protection clause" in the *US v. Cruikshank* ruling(1876); 4) and the outcome of the election of 1876. All these factors among others collectively conspired to create the tipping point that enabled the turning point to return 'toward' a slave-like southern society and economy.

The election of 1876 was the catalyst and may be the most controversial election in US History. Ulysses Grant after completing two terms as president as a Republican, which had been the party of civil rights and reconstruction, contemplated running for a third term. However, Congress passed a resolution stating that no president should have more than two terms. With Grant not running, the candidates were Rutherford B. Hayes for the Republicans and Samuel Tilden, a Democrat from New York. Tilden ran against Hayes on the Whiskey Ring corruption scandal which was one of three major scandals during Grant's presidency. Tilden won the popular vote with about 51 percent but received 184 electoral votes, one short of the 185 needed for a majority. Hayes received 165 electoral votes with another 20 electoral votes in dispute from several Southern states due to accusations of suppression of the Black vote. To resolve the controversy over the 20 electoral votes, the Republicans agreed, in exchange for the 20 electoral votes going to the Republicans, to accept the Compromise of 1877. The Compromise called for the removal of federal troops from the military districts established in the Southern states following the Civil War. The military districts administered those states until they drafted new constitutions and adopted the Fourteenth Amendment to the US Constitution. Grant removed federal troops from all but two southern states before he left office. Hayes, who was awarded the 20 contested electoral votes and won the presidency 185 to 184, removed the troops from the final two states when he took office.

With the Compromise of 1877 honored, Reconstruction was dead. Black Codes enabled by President Andrew Johnson evolved quickly into Jim Crow laws in the southern states and were institutionalized by these two Supreme Court's infamous rulings. In *US v. Cruikshank* mentioned above in 1876 the court ruled that the 14th amendment 'equal protection clause' only applied to state action not to private actors so the federal government was constrained in protecting black citizens. And the "separate but equal" ruling in *Plessy v. Ferguson* in 1896 expanded limitations to public actions and spaces—voting, transportation, education, and more. The tragic legacy of these Supreme Court rulings constricted the federal government's ability to protect black citizens from private violence and actions and public institutional discrimination.

What would race relations be today if Lincoln had not selected Johnson as vice president and Lincoln had not been assassinated and Johnson had been convicted? What if Grant had run for and won a third term? What if the scandals in his administration had not improved Democrats chances of winning in the 1876 election and so on? In summary, the election of 1876 was the catalyst for the crucial turning point that connected all of the key events in the past to the future. It enabled the replacement of goals for Reconstruction with the low-wage sharecropper servitude economy and the "separate and unequal" society in the South that lasted more than another century. The vestiges of which the people of the United States live with to the present day manifest as racism, discrimination, poverty, and violence.

The consequences of the animus during the elections of 1800, 1824, 1860, and 1876 created critical turning points in US history. Will our contemporary era here in 2020 also be a pivotal turning point in US History? Will socialism or capitalism dominate national life going forward? Extreme liberals are aggressively advocating for socialism. Extreme conservatives are advocating a conservative form of capitalism. Both advocate for elite and special interest advantage and privilege. Moderates likely want capitalism with greater individual opportunity, mobility, and fairer distribution of economic wealth and education and as little elite and special interest privilege as possible.

Two additional fundamental social turning points are also shaping—one positive and one negative. The positive turning point is America's hopefully constructive contemporary response to racism and the discriminatory effects on African Americans from government policies and social practices that institutionalized residential segregation.[11] The negative one I call adultism. Adultism is the combined discriminatory effects on children from government policies, social practices, and personal adult choices that started in the mid-twentieth century. Much amplified today the discriminatory effects favor adults fully at the expense of children. Adultism will be addressed in chapter 5.

The turning point for adultism is founded in discrimination based on age rather than of race. I will argue that discrimination starts before conception and continues beyond the age of independence. It potentially affects all children but especially affects children born to America's non-affluent of all colors. The discrimination is founded in at least five areas of modern American life: 1) the formation of the modern American family, 2) accommodative law and court rulings for factional identity special-interest politics, 3) various government policies (e.g., education, health care, housing, and others), 4) content industries' commercial entertainment practices, and 5) fertility, genetic, and other sciences.

Moderates are among those who call for positive resolution to America's political blind spots on racism and adultism in addition to other blind spots Americans have. To highlight this point, I will speculate that creating real, positive change for America's community of African descent may not occur until America pursues not only anti-racism changes but also anti-adultism changes so all children of low socioeconomic households can have successful childhoods and thrive. The point just made may not make sense to you at present. This work will make the case that despite the animated dialogue today about rights for minorities and special-interest groups who advocate for their ideological causes, a key common thread of the political war is about adult privilege at the expense of children's rights and interests. Their rights, dignity, prospects, protections, and outcomes are among the casualties on the political battlefield. The future of our democracy and the foundation of civilization hang in the balance depending on how political choices turn out as various trends and forces intersect. Our children's children are the chips on the table.

As the animus of America's early twenty-first century politics come to a head in the election era of 2016 through 2024, here is a brief narrative on the context driving contemporary political and cultural divisiveness. In my view, the debate is fundamentally about whether the United States commits beyond the point of no return to a new social and world order based on wealth, group identity, and individual choices.

What are the roots of the current deep-seated factional anger and political divide? What persons or groups have the power to weaponize media, entertainment, advertising, and news/social networking industries to prosecute a culture war? Are they all one-percenters? What are the roots of this destructive conflict? Are the origins ideological, political, judicial, something else, or all of the above?

Do they emanate from some long-running, unresolved war of ideas between socialism, communism, and capitalism with origins in the eras of WWI and WWII? Or are they an extension of the counterrevolution of the 1960s to the Vietnam War? Or are they a continuation of the backlash to the Watergate incident of the 1970s? Are they founded in newer progressive special interests pressing and winning on cultural causes with outcomes not held by the majority of Americans creating dissension? Are the roots founded in the power of the richest of the rich (the top .1 percent) owning the economic game through regulatory capture' and political influence? Are income, wealth, and economic inequality so rigged that many Americans are disillusioned and disengaged? Are they based in the new power media, Wall Street, and K Street hold over the nation enabled by digital technology and the control of information and misinformation? Is their ability to influence so great they can rig ideological, electoral, and economic narratives so many Americans feel that their votes and hopes are irrelevant?

Was there a single judicial or legislative tipping point that led to this new turning point in American and human history? Was it one or several recent Supreme Court rulings played and pressed by special interest zealots? Perhaps it was *Citizens United v. Federal Election Commission* of 2010.[12] Did Citizens United enable what is labeled "dark money" to change the electoral process from "one person, one vote" to "one dollar, one vote"? While liberals strongly objected to that ruling, they may have learned to live with it and use it better than those who pressed for it from the right. Liberals seemed to have figured out better than conservatives how to mobilize and organize special interests to politically weaponize advocacy organizations, law firms, and social media funded with special interest dark money. Was it *Obergefell v. Hodges* of 2015 that changed the definition of marriage from natural marriage? There is great, unspoken animus to that. These questions will be left to history to judge.

Whatever the origins, those of us in the middle wonder if our founding fathers and framers of the Constitution could have envisioned the forces of human nature and cunning devices of political and cultural war at work today. Many of us wonder if our republic will survive and endure. Americans are generally optimistic, and most believe that there is always hope. It will take significant effort, and a group of Americans who have not been prominent to date: us—the 10 to 60 percent of voting and non-voting Americans in the middle, the political independents and moderates. Moderates are the ones who frequently react negatively to the political dominance, narratives, and media storylines of both liberals and conservatives.

Given the current state of the national political dialogue between the two dominant factions, neither one cares about Americans in the middle nor America's future so long as they can force your vote and get their future. They both do get what they want in a bizarre tango between party elites dripping in political tension as described by a Democratic writer, T. A. Frank. Frank argues as long as both parties' elites misunderstand the voters, those same elites are safe, because the voters have no good choice, only two bad choices. Liberals get socially liberal outcomes based mostly on judicial rulings, bureaucratic regulations, and media-driven pop influence, while conservatives get lower taxes legislatively—both get the big things they want. They don't have to care as long as they enjoy support from the top 1 percent and the media. Their ideologues work to influence gullible adults and our children's innocent, impressionable minds online and in the classroom unchallenged. Their social rent-seeking creates future believers and exploits megatrends that are redefining civilization. Here are some of the megatrends at work today.

Megatrends: Social Forces and Political Factions

1. **Global challenges:** Climate, population, fertility, food/water insecurity, jobs, poverty, natural disasters, ecology, species, oceans.

2. **International challenges:** Refugees, migrations, pandemics, cyber and kinetic warfare, terrorism, and multipolar global powers.

3. **Institutional challenges:** Health care, education, immigration, family, marriage, children, abortion, equality, judicial and criminal justice, trust, elections, Wall street, K street, Mean Street,[§] others.

4. **Constitutional reforms:** Debates on rights, textual interpretation, balanced budget, equal rights, separation of powers, administrative state, and judicial supremacy/activism.

5. **Cultural wars:** Philosophical battles of the cultural "isms"— racism, adultism, ageism, consumerism, elitism, extremism, feminism, genderism, immediatism, liberal humanism multi-culturalism, nonbinaryism, presentism, relativism.

6. **Ideological wars:** Debates over the legacy and future of "isms" about life, liberty, and property rights—nationalism, globalism, libertarianism, extreme liberalism and conservatism, communism, socialism, capitalism, imperialism, exceptionalism, others.

7. **Economic challenges:** Economic inequality, opportunity, growth, debt, taxes, poverty, productivity, jobs, skills, trade, more.

8. **Science and Technological advances:** Debates over biological, genetic, neuro, computer, data, and behavioral science advances, the new and many addictions, impacts from digitization and virtualization on cognitive, social, and economic life. Impacts of software, automation, artificial intelligence, and robotics on jobs and life.

Unless the current generation of eligible voters pursue prudent politics to address the strategic issues above, the issues will resolve in ways many of us will wish we had convened and intervened. The combination and intersection of various political interests and factions will create unpredictable, unintended, and negative consequences for our posterity. Unless current Americans set a sound

---

[§] Mean Street is the author's acronym shorthand for "all things" associated with commercial information content industries, companies, people, practices, and influence: It stands for *M*edia, *E*ntertainment, *A*dvertising, and social *N*etworking & News.

course for many of the above issues, future generations will be damning and condemning our time on earth similar to the way the contemporary generation damns and condemns America's southern Whites time on earth during the seventeenth, eighteenth, and nineteenth centuries for their pursuit and defense of that "peculiar institution"— slavery.

The intersection of any number and any combination of these forces may well complicate and exacerbate our nation's and the world's condition by catalyzing irreversible changes on the planet's carrying capacity, the nature of humanity, democracy, and the direction of civilization. With a number of these forces and factions intersecting over the past several decades, we are already looking at an epic mega-inflection point in the history of humanity in the rearview mirror. Here are some of the prominent force and faction intersections that have already changed how we live and what many think. Consider the intersection of global forces of population, climate, and pandemics as population has grown from two billion to nearly eight billion since 1900—a span of 120 years. Or consider the implications of technological forces of the internet, artificial intelligence, and robotics on population, poverty, jobs, economic inequality, and food insecurity, given the forecast that perhaps a large portion of jobs will be partially automated or eliminated during the second quarter of the twenty-first century. Or consider the inter-section of adultism, feminism, individualism, and nonbinaryism in the progressive demand for the entitlement of an "individual reproductive right" that is occurring presently to the detriment and dismissal of children's rights. Or consider the outcomes of the ongoing intersection of economic inequality, taxes, debt, poverty, and unequal education that have dramatically benefited the ultra-wealthy over the last half century. The pandemic is exacerbating wealth inequality.

Moderatism is not a panacea, but it can help avoid the negative potential threats of many of the megatrend intersections that neither conservativism nor liberalism or socialism will address. Moderatism may be more effective at harnessing the clever policies that liberals and conservatives employ to perpetuate unequal and unconstrained accumulation of wealth by a tiny segment nicknamed the "one-percenters."[13] The one-percenters are well represented at the top of both liberal and conservative groups with the balance of wealth in the twenty-first century shifting to the liberals as economics evolve from manufacturing to service and from physical to digital. Institutional racism and economic inequality will continue to widen the gap between the races, the haves and have-nots, the rich and poor, unless income and wealth generation are recalibrated institutionally in a meaningful way. This moderate is optimistic America can accomplish a reasonable recalibration without adopting any radical ideology. Rearchitecting various institutional policies and unwinding the US government's favoritism toward the wealthy and large corporations in legislation, regulation, and judicial rulings is central to a recalibration. I am not suggesting any socialist's- or progressive's-like redistribution of wealth.

The current national order is what it is because no one has successfully advanced moderates' views at large scale for decades. Efforts by web organizations like 'newpolitics.org', 'nolabels.org', and coalitions like the congressional 'problem solvers' caucus strive to advance bipartisan leadership. However, the two main factions' activists and lobbyists dominate. They have successfully suppressed any rational dialogue in defiance of the voice and will of the majority of Americans. Essentially the liberal-conservative elites have won. Americans in the middle of the spectrum have lost—lost by exclusion and discrimination by those elites. Moderates have lost because their views are ignored.

To counter this current trajectory, moderates need to articulate their vision and agenda of moderatism. They need to enlist all those who believe in political moderation by developing their three current sources of potential political power in America: 1) their numbers, 2) moderate views a majority of Americans can embrace, and 3) ambition to push stalemate-breaking, unifying solutions onto the national stage and into law. Amid the din of the Public Square and powerful tidal forces of twenty-first century megatrends, moderates are the ones who have to step forward as voices of reason, and may have to shout louder than the shrill political voices that currently dominate the national stage just to be heard. Will you be one of those voices?

Chapter 2: The Silent and Silenced Majority

Rule 11. *If you push a negative hard enough, it will...become a positive. Violence from the other side can win the public to your side because the public sympathizes with the underdog.*
Rule 13. *Pick the target, freeze it, personalize it, and polarize it. Cut off the support network and isolate the target from sympathy. Go after people and not institutions; people hurt faster than institutions.*
— Saul Alinsky, from Rules for Radicals, 1971

The prescriptive guidance in Saul Alinsky's very controversial 1971 book, *Rules for Radicals*, briefly paraphrased above, instructs those ruthlessly and relentlessly intent to win at all costs how to successfully silence and subjugate opposition. Fortunately or unfortunately, depending on your point of view, of the many things moderates have in common these three things stand out. 1) They are <u>not</u> ruthless people. 2) They are people of conscience and moral conviction. 3) They are among the silent majority. President Nixon created that label in 1969. For too long they have chosen to be silent. Many want to be heard now but are among the "silenced majority," silenced by media exclusion, by activists' using political correctness, and by extremists using radical tactics right out of *Rules for Radicals*.

Americans in the middle are not only silent and silenced, but also angry. Angry at the power political, financial, and intellectual elites have wielded in creating the many systemic messes we face. They are also angry at the elites of the new digital economy that own and run the information firms in **M**edia, **e**ntertainment, **a**dvertising, and social **n**etworking industries—nicknamed *Mean Street*. Together they are the 'content establishment'. Today held in low regard by many Americans like Congress is the content establishment deserves a broad-brush nickname as Wall Street and K Street have. They seem to favor industry insiders and content producers at the expense of their consumers. Many Americans see them as amplifiers of cultural friction and inciters of political divisiveness, perpetuating long-festering issues and negative partisanship. At this point many in the middle don't know whom to believe or to trust with good reason.

At present many Mean Street firms produce entertainment and news content heavily laced with intentionally biased propaganda, crafted to shape public opinion to manufacture public consent for their political and commercial agendas. At the same time they deliberately suppress public dissent and reasoned discourse. The concurrent pandemic and election issues of 2020 demonstrated the command Mean Street has through its editorial power to censor and decide what to report and not to report. It may have more power than Wall Street and perhaps more power than either end of Pennsylvania Avenue. They need only the eyes and ears of curious minds to apply propaganda, misinformation, and personal attack (ad hominem) tactics. By leveraging internet technology, Mean Street and the political factions have innovated influence tradecraft to publish or censor information on a massive scale. This tradecraft of effective influence tactics and techniques protected by lax national policy on content seems to have enabled liberals to build a significant influence edge over conservatives—zero advantage for moderates.

The outsized power to influence and manipulate peoples' choices is based on the reach of the infrastructure technology of the internet and began with the death of the "fair and balanced doctrine" policy in 1987.[14] Today, too much of the media's reporting may be more accurately characterized as "unfair and unbalanced." Moderates would agree that among a list of reforms, the "fair and balanced doctrine" needs to be reinstated by the US Government and applied broadly across Mean Street firms with consequences.

Power tradecraft used to manage the national dialogue in politics and the press is enhanced by a long list of social science techniques and propaganda tactics. Manipulating outcomes based on the presenter's preferences is easily doable. For example, social science informs us that perhaps as much as 50 percent of any population of people can be influenced on what choices they make just based on whether the question or story presented is in a negative or positive frame.[15] In the modern world humans rely less on their physical abilities and more on their cognitive abilities to deal with the explosion of sensory and information input. The amount of information challenges the limits and weaknesses in the human brain.

For moral suasion content producers and persuaders rely on proven techniques from neuroscience, behavioral, and data sciences to influence what people choose by getting people to make choices using emotional reasoning and techniques that manipulate natural human cognition biases. Examples from a long list of techniques for emotional reasoning include: over-generalizing hyperbolizing, catastrophizing, white-washing the other person's point; forcing politically correct speech/silence; and putting words in a person's mouth. Technology even now enables the ability to put fake words in a fake person's mouth via videos of a digitally manufactured life-like image and voice of a person to get viewers to believe they are watching a real person speak words that they in fact did not speak—a Chatbot.

More techniques follow from the psychology of natural human bias based on reference dependence** and other key tenets from behavioral economics: confirmation bias, framing, anchoring, and nudging. Propaganda techniques add to their toolbox with manufactured news like intentionally biased polls designed to create the perception of an inevitable outcome to influence voters/viewers choices (wisdom of the crowd), and edited content. Interview, language, and story techniques are used to take advantage of cognitive limits and biases to achieve emotive capture†† of a viewer by eliciting their sympathy or shame. Public blaming, shaming, shunning, shouting, silencing, suppressing, sabotaging (demonizing) to oppose a view enable content produces to harvest broader social acceptance of a position-even if the position is counter to viewers' core values.

One of the biggest weapons in the modern media arsenal is what I call "propaganda power plays." When multiple media channels report about a specific topic or person using cadenced messages crafted with similar talking points, themes, tone, and words it is a coordinated content campaign—a propaganda power play. Liberals are far better at running power plays than conservatives. The following are examples of propaganda power plays successfully run by Mean Street channels in recent years:

- For the liberals: pro-Hillary, pro-Biden, pro–choice, pro–identity politics, pro–gun control, pro-immigration, pro–open borders, pro-feminism, pro–recreational marijuana, pro–Russian collusion, pro–climate change, pro–individual reproductive rights, pro–social justice, anti-Trump, and many other "anti's."

- For the conservatives: Pro-Trump, pro-guns, pro–border control, anti-immigration, anti–Mean Street (fake news), anti–Russian collusion. There are more, but you get the idea.

- For the moderates: None. Moderates don't get to play.

Not all propaganda power plays are bad or negative. The anti–underage vaping and the opioid abuse awareness TV power plays in 2019 are examples of positive plays. Unfortunately, both were undermined by Mean Street's power play support for the pro–recreational marijuana agenda. Hopefully well intentioned, the racial justice and social distancing power plays of 2020 by many media

---

** Reference dependence is a key tenet in prospect theory and behavioral economics. It holds that people evaluate outcomes and express preferences relative to an existing reference point, or status quo. It is related to loss aversion which human nature relies on more than gain and the endowment effect.

†† Emotive capture is the cognitive process of getting someone to believe and accept a narrator's story for political or personal gain by getting the individual to react with sympathy or fear using their emotional reasoning instead of intellectual reasoning.

outlets illustrate media-led attempts at creating messaging to solicit public compliance on an issue. As played, both seem to have created as much disunity as unity but time will tell. This moderate can only hope for the good Mean Street could do if it returned to the fair and balanced doctrine or if producers unmuted moderates or championed moderate themes like those that will be presented in following chapters: children's rights, conception control v birth control, political responsibility v political correctness, a transformational war on racism and poverty through education and health care, non-discrimination of people of all colors, an anti–recreational marijuana stance, American election modernization, global sustainability activism through "*And*-focus" on all of the drivers of climate change—population *and* energy *and* economics *and* climate *and* more.

So all Americans voices and ideas can be heard moderates would likely be among those that call on Congress to enact systemic reforms that put the interests of the American people before Mean Street and its infrastructure—the internet. Reform begins with a call to reinstate the fair and balanced doctrine. Additional reforms are needed to reestablish trust in the first amendment protected industries, rebalance power and advantage between digital producers and consumers, and empower diversity of ideas with balanced coverage of all points of view. Moderates would likely further agree that all four content establishment sectors require new regulation and oversight to improve responsible content and practices and to diminish monopoly power and information market control. Here are a few specific reforms moderates' would likely support:

- Repeal Section 230 of the Communications Decency Act to impose accountability and liability on social media firms.

- Regulate Internet Service Providers as utility providers accountable for national-life-critical infrastructure like electric service.

- Enact and enforce a first amendment internet user bill of rights.

- Innovate a new federal circuit court system designed for speed and volume, dedicated to first amendment internet issues to adjudicate abridgement of consumers first amendment protected content.

- Establish new rules of ownership for first amendment class firms. Change industry structure to address the extraordinary advances in digital technology, use of the Advertising Business Model, the concentration of industry assets, and editorial control.

Addressing Mean Street's outsized ability to define the national political narrative, to influence lawmakers, and to exploit Main Street consumers' perception and perspective is one of a number of American imperatives for twenty-first century moderates.

Chapter 3: Who Are American Moderates?

It is time that the great center of our people, who reject the violence and unreasonableness of both the extreme right and the extreme left...declare their consciences.
    —Senator Margaret Chase Smith, 1950[16]

Even though Republican senator Margaret Chase Smith of Maine walked the halls of Congress more than a half century ago, more as an independent than a conservative, her words ring as true today as they did then. As of May 2020, Gallup polling found that 31 percent of Americans identified as Democrat, 25 percent as Republican, and 40 percent as Independent. While there are over 250 million eligible voters, there are about 150 million likely voters—people who regularly or occasionally vote. The remaining one hundred million eligible voters may not vote ever. To provide some context, in 2020 an estimated 158.4 million voted. In the 2016 presidential election,[17] 136.7 million voted but 41.3 percent of eligible voters did not vote. There also are likely voters in both parties who want their party to be more moderate. So there may be more people persuadable to become moderates than the 40 percent in Gallup's independent category. There may be moderate Democrats, Republicans, and undecideds who may be persuadable. The question comes down to whether or not anyone who is not counted as a die-hard partisan conservative or liberal is open to moderatism.

While those labeled as independents are the largest part of the potentially persuadable population, there is a view held by some polling scientists that argues that only a small fraction—7 percent—of the entire electorate is persuadable because the bulk of independents either lean liberal or conservative by affinity as reported in Pew Center research and in an article entitled "Hate is on the Ballot."[18] In short, the total number of people that may be persuaded by moderate ideology and open to compromise to centrist proposals may fall anywhere from less than one-tenth to over half of all eligible voters.

There is a view held by some pollsters that the notion of a *moderate* is a myth and that the middle is a murky collage of independent, undecided, and self-identified moderate voters[19] who hold very diverse views on issues that land them all over the ideological map. That may well be. But I believe that the moderate middle would be larger and "stickier" if it had a more cohesive and depolarizing ideology that articulates their core beliefs and values more so than the traditional political categories analyzed by pollsters. The political categories typically are based on vote choice, party loyalty, or party elite–defined stances on issues which is the one that causes the greatest dissension.

Pundits and cynics alike portray self-proclaimed moderates as lacking in principles and courage of conviction. However, being a moderate does not mean believing in nothing, having no opinion, or not caring enough about anything to do something about it. On the contrary, moderates care a great deal about politics and the future of their nation and people everywhere, especially children.

Most importantly, while pollsters look at classifying people, this work is about helping people reclassify themselves and move toward centrist solutions and away from causes, special interests, and positions. Moderates are different from either faction and perhaps are not so murky once a cohesive moderate ideology is articulated for people to consider.

Another perspective on America's nonvoters in the current political scene needs consideration. A survey conducted by a group called the 100MillionProject[20] about the one hundred million eligible voters in America who do not vote sheds some light on why roughly 43 percent of people eligible to vote did not vote in the 2016 election. The project reports that the one hundred million identify themselves roughly as one-third Democrat, one-third Republican, and one-third independent. The survey's findings document that nonvoters have less trust in the electoral system, less confidence that elections reflect the will of the people. They do not believe that their vote will matter. They consume less political information and news than voters. The primary reason they don't vote is that they don't like the candidates. Nonvoters are more likely to be less educated, lower-income, unmarried, and non-White. The least engaged nonvoters are the "emerging electorate": eligible voters, aged eighteen to twenty-four years old. America's nonvoters are American's politically disempowered, dis-engaged, and disenfranchised. I wonder if this large portion of eligible voters who do not participate exists because they feel they are being left behind. Would moderatism and moderate politicians attract them to engage and participate?

Moderates and Moderatism

Who are twenty-first century moderates? And where do they fit into the political mosaic? They come from all walks of life. Moderates may vote or may not vote. You'll find them in both Democratic and Republican parties as well as independent and undecided voters. Ideologically, they are part liberal, part conservative, and part *neither one*. The *neither one* part that goes unspoken today is the part that this book will emphasize. Most moderates are likely older than millennials‡‡ though there are self-described moderates who are young and diverse.²¹ They are pragmatic people. They are problem-solvers who debate and make decisions from "*And*-focused" choices more so than liberals and conservatives who debate and make their decisions from "*Or*-focused" choices. By example of "*And*-focused" versus "*Or*-focused" choices, moderates are less interested in binary choices like "prochoice or prolife" and more interested in getting all of the factors on the table for debate and decision. Moderates are tough-minded patriots on foreign policy and international relations. They believe in the pursuit of justice. They support responsible freedom, hard work, self-reliance, fair play, and fair compensation according to each person's abilities. Moderates may be either conservative or liberal on economic matters but are more conservative on social issues. Personal responsibility and accountability as well as empathy and perspective are deeply ingrained in their character.

Moderates' Political Core Is Different

Pollsters and political scientists distinguish the ideology of conservatives from liberals using various paradigms and surveys that measure politics through a "left-right lens." Their methods also rely on some research that indicates peoples' politics are predisposed by genetics, temperament, and personality.²² I am offering a view here that is not based in science but observation and reflection. I propose that moderates' political core and their political lens are different from both liberals and conservatives beyond the left-right spectrum lens in at least the following seven ways:

1) Purpose
2) Philosophy
3) Priorities
4) Values
5) Motives
6) Goals
7) Principles

Purpose

Purpose is defined here as the set of ideas that drives the way a person looks at life and makes sense of a complex world. The ideas also drive a person's political spirits and passions. It is the conceptual framework by which one assesses the political prospects of living a meaningful life—raison d'etre. Political purpose frames a person's political idealism, altruism, and perception of reality. Perception of time, space, social group loyalty, station in life, other people, other

---

‡‡ Millennials, known as Generation Y, are the demographic cohort born 1981 to 1996.

groupings, and such are part of the foundation of how a person measures progress towards achievement of their purpose.

Partisan conservatives' and liberals' identity begins with ideology and party loyalty—moderates far less so. Conservatives' orientation to reality is predominantly anchored in the present, seeking personal freedom. Their idealism is anchored to the ideology of 'economic freedom for all'. The dominant themes that frame their altruism are: *diversity of individuals* and group loyalty to genetic family, country, and property. Liberals' orientation to reality is anchored more in the past and the present, seeking repair of real or perceived injustice. Their idealism is anchored to the ideology of 'social equality and justice for all'. The dominant themes that seem to frame their altruism are *cultural diversity* and group loyalty to genetic family and dominant genetic group membership—race, sex, orientation, others.

Moderates' political identity is different. Moderates' political identity begins with the reality of the human condition and a desire to make things better for the common good. Their orientation to reality is predominantly anchored in both the present and future. Their idealism is hard to pinpoint but may be anchored pragmatically to 'fairness as much as possible given individual genetic differences' and making the foundations of life better for all through democracy, societal institutions, and natural civilization. The dominant themes that frame their altruism are *diversity of ideas* and loyalty to their genetic family, their country, and the human family.

"Diversity of ideas" is a moderate notion I will label as *"Both/ Neither." Both* standing factions' positions may have individual value or may be blended into workable solutions for us all, but as far as moderates are concerned, *neither* faction has the right ideology or right answers. On many issues the positions of conservatives and liberals are not even tolerable because separately their proposals do not solve an issue materially or politically. Moderates look beyond 'black & white' to understand the gray space. They want all aspects of an issue examined so the better solution ideas rise to the top. On many issues you will see moderates discuss merits in *both* party's proposals but support *neither* one. Moderates' ideas are frequently the views missing from the debate.

Philosophy

Here is a comparative examination of core philosophical precepts that set moderates apart from conservatives and liberals.[23]

Conservative. Conservatives believe the human condition is founded in nature more so than culture. Conservatives fundamentally believe rights are founded in nature and the role of government is obligated to protect human rights and individual liberty. Their expectation of government is how it protects deeply held principles they hold. They believe in a constitutional democracy, in which the

Constitution is the nation's foundational document to be interpreted by judicial review as "originalists," conserving the founders' thinking and protecting and expanding individual freedom, amended only by constitutional process. Key conservative goals are: promote individual and national interests; limit government to its enumerated powers; minimize the administrative state; restrain judicial authority to interpret law, not make law; and ensure that the rule of law fosters order and public trust. Conservatives posit that humans are somewhat malleable but not beyond what human nature sets as our species' core. All humans are created equal in law but not equal by nature. Individuals, not government, are the sources of creative vitality of society and enable their spiritual growth through individual liberty.

Liberal. Liberals believe the human condition is founded in culture more so than human nature. Liberals fundamentally believe rights are founded in law and that the role of government is obligated to correct history's victimization of various groups. Their expectation of government is how it ought to improve people's lives. They believe in a progressive democracy in which the Constitution is a living document to be interpreted and informally amended by judicial review to incorporate the prevailing public opinions of a time and passionate beliefs of the majority or a well-connected minority. Key liberal goals are: promote progressive interests as new human, constitutional, civil, and economic rights; expand government; maximize the administrative state; push supremacy of judicial authority, and make the rule of law empower progressive ideals. Liberals posit that humans as blank slates are malleable and the role of human nature is negligible. All humans should be treated equally in law and made equal in life. They believe that science and law should be used intentionally to advance equality by mastering nature and human nature to advance liberal humanism. Government is the source of the creative vitality of society and enables individual spiritual growth through rights.

Moderate. Moderates believe the human condition is founded in both human nature and culture but natural rights must be defended as a foundation of the human experience. Moderates believe rights are founded in nature and the Constitution. The role of government is obligated to ensure all people are treated as fairly and equitably as possible in the present and future. Their expectation of government is how it improves institutions they rely on for living their lives. They believe in a constitutional democracy in which the Constitution is interpreted more as originally or textually written, and amended only by constitutional process. Key moderate goals are: promote human, family, national, and children's interests; ensure national institutions foster common good, peace, progress, equality, justice, liberty, freedom, and trust; balance government authority through separation of powers; optimize the administrative state;[24] and ensure that the rule of law protects all citizens, holds each citizen accountable, and constrains factional rent-seeking. All humans are equal before the law but not created equally in life due to genetic diversity. Each should be treated as equally or least as fairly as possible. People are the source of creative vitality of society, and each person is free to pursue spiritual growth through personal freedom.

Whatever moderates agree to politically with conservatives and liberals must 1) be constitutionally founded, 2) solve real needs and problems pragmatically, 3) not artificially change the essence of humans' nature through science or law, and 4) respect humans' dignity and natural rights, starting with children's natural birthrights and their human dignity.

Priorities

Though purpose driven pragmatism sets moderates' political priorities, they do share some priorities in common with both factions. For example, of the key historical forces that drive human history— continuity, change, conflict, contact, and agency— conservatives and moderates may prioritize historical continuity as a reference point to life more whereas liberals may focus more on historical change. In some other ways moderates think like conservatives because conservative's priority for freedom and liberty is based on the natural order of nature, the reality of human nature, and the duty of any nation-state to protect and provide for its citizens first. Also like conservatives moderates prioritize nationalism before globalism. Unlike conservatives, however, moderates prioritize *all* of the rights of the child, not just the one right that conservatives vigorously defend—the right to life of the unborn once conceived.

Moderates' priorities are also like liberals in some ways. They believe in fairness, justice, equality, and compassion. Moderates view of globalism is somewhat different than liberals. Moderates see globalism as a means to achieve global systems stability and sustainability. Liberals see globalism as a way to achieve human unity on liberals' terms. Unlike liberals, moderates prioritize the rights of children, including all of the rights of the unborn. Liberals seem to believe the unborn have no rights. Unlike liberals, moderates do not see every individual or group constituency interest as an entitled right. They see many of the progressives' calls for new rights as demands for privileged personal power and lifestyle choices, not rights. Moderates pursue fairness for all, not supremacy or special privilege for any group. They respect individual rights but hold that each human is endowed with inalienable natural rights. They put children's natural rights before adults' rights, which makes them socially conservative and anti-liberal by a progressive's judgment. Moderates are pro-children. I will argue both factions are antichildren due to their support for harmful policies in key areas of life—procreation, drugs, education, entertainment, health care, housing, and public safety.

Moderates might be inclined to defend their view on children's rights as follows. To provide freedom, justice, equality, opportunity, prosperity as best our nation can, it is essential to create and raise children—new citizens—in safe, nurturing, and loving families free from the horrors of war, disease, deprivation, tragedy, abandonment, abuse, and trauma. Many nations are far from that ideal, including the United States. Many of our current societal ills and many global problems are due to the numbers and outcomes of children conceived unplanned, and unwanted in some cases. Being born into, deprived in, and raised in traumatizing, dehumanizing, impoverished conditions (economic, physical, or moral) is frequently the foundation for lifelong systemic discrimination and disadvantage. True moderates will go way out of their way to protect children from harm, harmful adults, and harmful experiences and to protect their rights. They want children's safety and rights assured and their innocence protected. They hold that governments and adults owe children protection from discrimination, danger, crime, and exploitative commercial interests as well as adult topics, controversial debates, and confusing behaviors.

Moderates are less interested in change and more interested in results that align with their goals and values. Though less ideologically partisan than liberals or conservatives, moderates are determined to seek win-win-win solutions in contrast to win-lose compromises the factions typically fashion. By their nature, they are dissatisfied with politically accommodative compromise ("You scratch my back, I will scratch yours"). They are less interested in voting the other party out of office and more interested in voting into office the best person(s) of vision and values to produce positive results for our nation. They may frequently conclude the best person(s) may not be in either party.

To achieve positive results, they may be considered politically radical by both factions because moderates are willing to challenge positions and question assumptions and intentions. Some will think outside the box to solve complex problems and resolve contentious political divides. With things so far from a healthy range for so long in key cultural, social, economic, and political institutions, moderates are willing to innovate radical policies that nudge political or social behavior back within healthy ranges. Examples of out-of-range issues include national debt and deficits, marriage, abortion, children's rights, race equality, housing, economic inequality, guns in the hands of the dangerous and deranged, digital and physical addiction, health care, education, defense, foreign policy, immigration and population, poverty, climate, global sustainability, congressional dysfunction, structural institutional prejudice, and judicial activism. These illustrate areas where moderate solutions are likely condemned by both factions.

Values

Moderates are different from partisans of both factions in another way: personal values. Three things that make their civil character unique are their values about virtuous political leadership, civility, and responsibility.

On leadership, moderates approach to leadership is framed by an intent to help as many as possible flourish and thrive. Principles that shape how moderates approach policy design are 1) lead and govern inclusively through statesmanship, not partisanship, 2) bridle special interests' ambition for power and control to dictate social and economic benefits, 3) address issues at the root cause as much as possible, not just promote political causes, and 4) focus on problem-solving as the basis for national policy instead of taking sides or supporting positions of special interests.

On civility, when discussing an issue in the hall or on the street, they work to avoid canned media propaganda narratives or ideological filters to defend a position. They employ America's common bond of respect, integrity, fairness, and trust to debate in good faith the issues of the day civilly, sharing their beliefs, views, experience, and common sense. They seek ways to find common ground to build consensus around common causes with common solutions for the common good.

On responsibility, striving to be morally, fiscally, socially, and personally responsible as best they can is in a moderate's political DNA. They are not defined by political correctness. Rather, they expect themselves and their leaders to be defined by a moral north star of political responsibility that focus them on freedom, fairness, faith, the future, and fiscal accountability. Moderates expect to pay national financial commitments and obligations made as they go as much as possible, not take on debt that cannot be afforded. They expect to know how debt incurred will be repaid on their watch before they relinquish leadership to the next generation. They expect spending to be balanced with income and debt to be incurred reluctantly, and not passed forward to future generations as much as possible. Regrettably, America has moved far from that moderate ideal. America used to borrow from the future to invest in public goods for its future. Now it borrows from its future to spend on present-day individual benefits.[25]

Motives

Moderates' moral reasoning about the political rationale—"doing the right thing" is different from conservatives or liberals. Moderates are less motivated about self-good and feeling good and more motivated about common good and creating good results. When thinking about issues on rights, institutions, and policy they are different from both factions in three fundamental ways. Moderates' notion of "doing the right thing" is about 1) root causes, 2) cost-causers, and 3) systemic institutional improvement.

1) Moderates are about root causes more than political causes or correctness. They are motivated to seek solutions that *address issues and solve problems at their root cause.* This one aspect of their moral approach to politics differentiates them from those who want to promote or defend a cause politically for ideological conformity or the self-interests of a specific constituency. Moderates demand real results that solve issues at their point of origin. Why? Because they are pragmatic. Because that is where the best moral-answer and least-cost outcomes are achieved. That is where negative multiplier effects are designed out of policy and positive multiplier benefits can be designed into policy. By nature they recoil at politics that only deal with optics or symptoms, or kick the can down the road.

2) Moderates are about holding cost-causers accountable for any harm[§§26] they impose on others, society, and the American taxpayer through their social and economic rent-seeking behavior. Moderates are motivated to restrain rent-seekers, to help constituencies that are harmed by them, and to minimize costs they impose on others and future generations. Compare that to those who pursue benefit and advantage regardless of the cost or harm to others. Consider that the standing factions' purposes are frequently solely to advance the interests of their adherents and to persuade government to intervene to modify market or societal outcomes that benefit their constituencies' interests. The more government institutions are used to allocate outcomes, the more likely social and economic wealth is transferred or distributed upward to the wealthy or well-connected minorities who can influence political processes. By nature, moderates' sensibilities about equity, fairness, and justice are offended by those who game the system and the rest of us for their group's or cause's gain.

3) Moderates are about seeking continuous systemic improvement to our national institutions instead of seeking constant constituency approval. Moderates support the evolution of our national institutions toward the ideals and goals of our Republic to achieve *a more perfect union* through constitutional stewardship not social engineering. Moderates do not support the misuse of process and purpose by the political interests of rent-seekers exploiting legislative, administrative, or judicial activism. Moderates are interested in 1) improving national institutions that advance the American way and strengthen the nation, 2) rooting out systemic discrimination, 3) designing out structural institutional biases and inefficiencies in national policy, law, and rulings, and 4) revisiting

---

[§§] *Harm* is used here to mean 1) rent-seeking and 2) negative externalities as an economist uses these terms. See the endnote for more detail.

policy to address rent-seeker corruption of purpose and to adjust policies for unintended consequences and loopholes.

Finally, by way of example of how moderates' "*And*-focused" sets them apart from the two standing factions' "*Or*-focused", consider the theme of future global sustainability. Moderates' political focus on our children's future *and* our nation's future *and* our planet's future makes them morally different from liberals or conservatives. Liberals are focused on the planet's future, as evidenced by their passion for climate impact, but far less so our children's and our nation's future, as illustrated by their lack of discipline for children's rights and debt. Conservatives are somewhat focused on our nation's future but not so much on our children's future or the planet's future, as illustrated by their limited focus on children's rights and climate impact. Moderates' *And*-focus on the future of all three sets moderates apart from partisans of the two standing factions.

Goals

For the standing factions' goals, the definition of success frequently only means achieving a political-win for their constituency. Moderates see success as improvement in the human condition, a core human value, a vital issue, or critical institutional function. Here are goals that reflect success for moderates:

1) Minimize the national debt to be paid by future generations.

2) Reduce the number of children born into and raised in poverty.

3) Reduce the number of children in America and the world dying from in-utero conditions, early diseases, abuse, violence, crime, suicide, starvation, and accident to as close to zero as possible.

4) Increase the number of Americans of all colors, all walks of life, participating, prospering, and flourishing in our economy.

5) Increase number of people volunteering for America and humanity.

6) Reduce the number of our young people who fail at life before they start adult life.

7) Reduce to zero the number of children killed at school by any reason.

8) Increase the number of students who complete degrees or vocational training programs on time and with little or no debt.

9) Reduce healthcare cost from 18 percent of GDP to under 12 percent.

10) Expand the labor participation rate near 70 percent from low 60s.

11) Reduce atmospheric carbon dioxide as far under 400 parts per million as is achievable practically with minimal economic impact.

12) Increase US higher education graduation rates from our current twelfth place standing in the world. Strive for first place.

13) Increase number of African American and other racial minorities on corporate and nonprofit boards significantly.

14) Deploy a new national election system built to federally certifiable security and integrity standards that allows every living, legal US citizen to vote as an eligible voter. Cast and record every certifiably-legal vote accurately on special, hard-to-counterfeit, serial-numbered, auditable paper or digital-certificate ballots. All legal votes securely and rapidly stored, counted, tallied, and validated. Certify and audit in a speedy manner each US citizen's vote.

15) Reduce the number of people addicted (especially children) to harmful drugs and cognitive behaviors (gambling, video games).

16) Reduce the National Debt from over 125 percent of GDP to under 50 percent of GDP in under quarter century.

17) Reduce the contribution to federal revenue from individual income taxes from the current over 50 percent level to 45 percent or less.

18) Increase federal revenue contribution from the US digital economy sources from x percent to xx percent. Digital economy nominal gross output reached $2.05 trillion in 2017, totaling 6.0 percent of total U.S. nominal gross output, according to the Bureau of Economic Analysis.[27] How much tax is collected on the 6.0 percent of output? Is federal income at least 6 percent or more of the 6.0 percent of output? Stop giving digital economy a better deal on taxes than physical economy participants.

19) Increase the number of households with children that are led by two adults. Grow from under one half of households back to at least two thirds of households with children where it used to be half century or so ago. Implement policies that foster longer lasting households, marriages, and commitments to offspring.

20) Increase portion of federal revenue from business income taxes from 7 percent to at least 10 percent. In the 1950s, it was 15 percent.

These are but a few of hundreds of goal and performance metrics that measure real social and economic progress. They reflect success for not just the moderate-minded, but for all Americans, and America.

First Principles

Moderates' views on rights, institutions, and national policy start with "first principles," just like the two standing political parties. First principles are fundamental truths or propositions that are the foundation for a system of beliefs or a chain of reasoning. They are the ideological cornerstones on which policy and political choices are set. Liberals and conservatives both seem to have the same first principle of *us first*—that is to say, whatever they want politically as adults for their ideology, privilege, and special interest agendas. Conservatives and liberals have their core principles that go beyond the *"us first"* label. My purpose here is not to restate their views but to explore what drives the political spirits of people in the middle of the spectrum.

In closing, unlike conservatives and liberals, twenty-first century moderates are not about *us first*. Rather, they are about four key organizing principles that strive to reconcile what it means to be fully human within the miracles and limitations of human evolution in our rapidly populating, technologically advanced, and socially diverse modern world. Moderates believe there are bedrock principles that dictate how being human within the modern political world cannot be forfeited, despite the capabilities and options modern science, technology, social life, and political interests create. Moderate ideology strives to reconcile humans' old brain and new brain, to ensure the preservation of natural rights contrary to the contemporary rationales for cultural, moral, factional, and identity relativism. It works to balance the competing forces and factional interests that span the middle of the political spectrum. The challenge before you in this book is to decide if these principles are dead, artifacts of the past, or alive in the hearts of many Americans and a call to action. I will argue that the way moderates think ideologically about rights, institutions, and policy can be framed by these four first principles:

1) Children first
2) Family first
3) Country first
4) Solutions first

The following four chapters provide a view of each principle.

Chapter 4: On Rights—Children First

There can be no keener revelation of a society's soul than the way in which it treats its children.
          —Nelson Mandela, first Black president of South Africa

Like Mandela's profound insight, Dietrich Bonhoeffer, German theologian, wrote, "The test of the morality of a society is what it does for its children." From my perspective I'd combine Mandela and Bonhoeffer to also say, "The moral test of a society's soul is *what harm it prevents* adults from doing to its children."

All three statements are founded in the idea made by philosopher John Locke in 1689 in his *Second Treatise on Government*, that

> "all mankind...being all equal and independent, no one ought to harm another in his life, health, liberty or possessions...Every man has a property in his own person. This nobody has a right to, but himself."

In the modern world, Locke's pronouncement must include children. A true moderate fully agrees with all four statements and argues that it means children's rights come first. Many biological parents fully understand as part of their very being what "children first" means. Their sacrifice in so many ways to provide the best lives they can for their children embodies the fundamental meaning of being human because the genetic parent-child trust bond is sacred and is the existential foundation of human life and society. The current generation has begun to break that sacred bond.

Moderates hold that children, like adults, have inalienable human and constitutional rights—rights to life, liberty, and property—from the very beginning of life. Moderates hold children also have civil rights. Children of our society are entitled to their rights, just as much as adults are. It is society's and government's duty to ensure children are guaranteed their natural rights. We find constitutional authority for "children first" under originalists' and progressives' constitutional interpretations.[28] Children's rights is an American blind-spot. Both factions and all of government are guilty of prejudice and systemic discrimination similar to the long running systemic prejudice against African Americans in residential housing. I will argue we are all constitutionally and morally bound to honor children first.

Both political factions pride themselves on claiming the moral high ground, justifying their positions as "doing the right thing," defending human rights, dignity, and inclusiveness. They do so, excluding children's rights and ignoring children's dignity in a moderate's eyes. Though children are the largest, most vulnerable, and defenseless minority, the courts, Congress, and media signal children's rights have little meaning or no standing before them. Moderates hold everyone has a duty to guarantee children's natural human rights as citizens. They are to be protected against the willed and ill-will forces of commerce, science, or the political interests of individuals, pairs, or groups in marriage or divorce precisely because they are the most vulnerable and defenseless class of citizens.

Legal Harm to Children before Birth

A true moderate argues that our government and our society have prejudiced children's outcomes by harming their human, constitutional, and civil rights from the start of life and continue through their developing years due to various discriminatory policies. Moderates do not willingly subscribe to any policy, law, or court ruling that entitles a person's or special interest's demand for a right that requires the forfeiture of another's life or their constitutional or human rights. Liberals seem to hold that there are no rights for the unborn. Conservatives argue to protect one right for the unborn, the right to life once conceived. The moderate counterview is there is not just one right to life for unborn persons, but there are no fewer than ten rights of unborn and young persons to be protected. I will argue that the scientific advances in fertility and genetic sciences and progressive political demands of the last half century require the enumeration and defense of *five natural rights to life and five natural rights to liberty and property* because all ten are part of the natural world. Presently, they are being largely ignored, denied, and abridged.

The birthrights were inviolable natural law throughout all of human history as natural conception until 1978 with the creation of the fertility industry.[29] Fertility technology can conceive life in a number of ways. Genetic science can now manipulate the genetic code of humans in ways that make it possible in the near future to not only repair humans genetically once living but to create, clone, alter, and design life through a growing list of manufacturing processes and technologies if allowed. The pursuit of profit from growing commercial markets by the retail fertility industry and publicly traded corporations marketing nontraditional paths to parenthood for anyone[30] demand a defense from people who care about children. Their human rights, dignity, and prospects in life are *legally harmed* by definition the moment natural biological union of conception-to-birth is violated by synthetic means, individual consumer choice, or contractual fiction, or when it is treated as a marketplace of buying and selling humans or human parts for creation. Moderates likely agree there are at least these ten natural birthrights, not just one narrowly defined and adjudicated by liberals and conservatives, and not among any rights a new person, a new citizen, must surrender to enter life in United States of America. Abortion will be addressed in chapter 7 to illustrate how a moderate might look at and solve an important ongoing political issue.

Children's Five Natural Rights to Life***

1) Right to be conceived and born in the biological and relational union of two opposite-sex humans.

2) Right to be conceived under equal protection, free from involuntary servitude to contractual obligations and commercial transactions.

3) Right to be a person, defended and protected, once alive in utero.

4) Right to be born <u>once viable</u>. *The current, judicially defined standard.*

> *Replace with* <u>once conceived and a person</u>. *Reasonable people argue a person exists at detection of first heart beat (~week 6 of gestation). Strive for* <u>once wanted, planned, then conceived</u>. *Moderates hold it is the right thing to do as the new standard for America and all nations whose people claim to be civilized, principled, progressive, or moral.*

5) Right to be conceived with natural nuclear genetic material of two and only two natural biological conceiving opposite-sex humans.

Children's Five Liberty and Property Rights

Each new person is entitled by nature to these two liberty rights. [†††]

6) Right to be carried to birth and nurtured in life responsibly by the opposite-sex humans who conceived unless abridged by natural or compelling moral causes.

7) Right of freedom of association with its biological creators. [‡‡‡]

And these three property rights:

8) Right to know the identity of its biological creators. [§§§]

9) Right to its innate talents.

10) Right to its innate innocence in early life.

*** What is a human right? Every person is entitled to certain fundamental rights, simply by the fact of being human. The author argues the ten are inalienable natural human constitutional rights. A broader explanation and defense of them will be made in future projects.

††† What is Liberty? The state of being free within society, free from oppressive restrictions imposed by authority on one's way of life, behavior, or political views.

‡‡‡ The author argues that rights 7 and 8 also include a new person's biological siblings.

§§§ Each person conceived owns the DNA of its conceivers in reciprocity.

All ten natural birthrights[31] are biologically interconnected by nature and inalienable from a moderate's perspective. All ten rights obligate government and society to uphold the genetic parent-child trust bond sacred as the existential foundation of human life and society. They are obligated to prevent current and future generations from breaking that sacred bond by defending these rights for a child's benefit before any adult interests. All are constitutionally justified under state action tests—rational and compelling—and a third, new scrutiny doctrine I am calling for of "sacred scrutiny."[32] Sacred scrutiny is the claim that the Supreme Court as the guarantor of constitutional rights has a sacred constitutional duty under *a more perfect union clause and seven amendments*[****] to go beyond the strict scrutiny doctrine established in *US v. Carolene Products* in 1938[33] to protect those who have no standing, those who are the most legally defenseless in society, children. Sacred scrutiny doctrine is a claim that there is a constitutional burden on litigants, amicae briefs, and the Supreme Court itself to prove that no claim, interest, remedy, or ruling abridges or harms any new person's ten birthrights to life, liberty, or property.

Each of the ten birthrights place profound moral, legal, and constitutional obligations on the fertility industry and genetic science. Their scientific breakthroughs that decouple reproduction from natural biological union produce a (re/dis)orientation to human creation and of human civilization. The industries have begun to completely decouple and destroy that bond for profit. Commercial fertility and genetic science industries must be restricted, restructured, and regulated through comprehensive legislative and judicial action to constitutionally guarantee these children's rights. The three property rights have significant implications for children's rights in federal policy and court rulings on education, health care, housing, citizenship, divorce, Mean Street behavior, proof of parentage, and the doctrine of State Action. These rights prescribe a mandate for new type of birth certificate issued by the federal government that verifies the DNA of biological conceivers at birth.

Moderates reject the claim by some that an individual right exists to choose to reproduce using non-natural means, such as multiple parties or artificial or scientific or commercial or contractual means. All five means have moral deficits and constitutional prohibitions.[34] The claim for the five natural rights to life argues that each new human has an inalienable, natural human birthright to be conceived by mutual consent choice of two opposite-sex humans through natural (or assisted) biological union. All of the estimated 82 to 108 billion

---

[****] The seven amendments are: 1st, 4th, 5th, 9th, 10th, 13th, and 14th.

humans that have entered life since the beginning of our species[35] (*Homo sapiens*) have owned that birthright except for those denied post-1978[††††] by providers and individuals using assisted reproductive technologies and other people's DNA. Moderates put the question on the table: "What gives anyone the right to deny new persons their natural right to be created by two opposite-sex conceivers and parents?" The claim posits there is no authority or argument that empowers any court to deny new humans these natural birthrights. Nor is there any constitutional or legal right that entitles any person(s) or corporation(s) to deny new humans these natural birthrights. The complexities and indignities that are already occurring to newly created human beings will only worsen with more scientific advances and mandated adult privilege unless we fully recognize and enforce these natural human birthrights as inalienable.

Nine of the ten rights have already been taken from children—denied, canceled, or assigned—by science, political and commercial demands, and judicial fiats. They are gone unless Americans rise to defend them. The only right not surrendered yet is Right #5, the right to be created with nuclear DNA of only two opposite-sex humans. Scientists in the UK have already succeeded in making a human with the DNA of three people using the mitochondrial DNA of a 2nd female, for a good cause, to address a genetic disorder. But, the big question is, "Can or should the nuclear DNA of multiple people be combined and allowed to create a new human as genetic and fertility sciences continue to advance?"

A child's life is not a commodity to be purchased. Procreation-from-conception-to-birth is a biological capability endowed by nature and acted on by the mutual choice consent union of biologically capable opposite-sex humans. For individuals to conceive using commerce is not an individual choice, a special right, entitlement, or adult privilege. Without the protections of the ten birthrights, children can be legally harmed as individuals and as a minority class. Their natural human dignity, their right to the sacred opposite-sex parent-child bond, their personhood, and human and constitutional rights are all denied. Moderates do not concede anyone is sanctioned or entitled to special rights at the expense of legal harm to children's rights. "Blood and roots" may not matter to some adults, but moderates respect and defend a child's rights for many reasons but especially because of the opposite-sex parent-child bond of "blood ancestry"—from whom they came— matters to the child. Which of the ten rights are the 'right thing to do' for you? Will you rise to defend all of them? Any of them? Which ones? May all moderates rise to defend all ten birthrights!

---

†††† Some portion of the estimated 8 million fertility industry assisted conceptions.

Legal Harm to Children after Birth

The denial of children's rights in the United States extends beyond the beginning of life. It continues as they travel the long development period from newborn to independent adult in many areas of life including education, health care, public safety, and more. For example, there is a complex and politically charged debate over parental rights. Part of that debate has isolated the United States with regard to the international treaty on the UN Convention on the Rights of the Child, which articulates twelve specific rights[36] to be recognized universally and entitled equally to all children. Of all the countries in the United Nations, the United States is the only nation to sign but not ratify that treaty. Consequently, the United States is not obligated to legally adhere to or empower the twelve rights. However, the United States has signed and ratified the UN Universal Declaration of Human Rights of 1948.[37] I am arguing here that among the thirty human rights enumerated in that treaty, a substantial number apply to children as human beings. Since the US Constitution empowers the supremacy of the articles of treaties that are ratified as the law of our land, the human rights defined by the UN Treaty on Human Rights also empower the ten children's rights articulated above.

Moderates also believe in putting children's futures first in policy planning. That orientation fosters better national and global futures. By pursuing policy, laws, and court rulings with children's rights and futures in mind, leaders are forced to consider the future and present in balance. It also pushes leaders to prevent and avoid negative externalities and adult rent-seeking behaviors that exploit, harm, and discriminate against children in various ways. A nation that 1) plans on forcing its youth to inherit over $25 trillion of national debt with no end in sight, 2) endures/ensures the early death of tens of thousands of our youth by legal and illegal drugs enabled/exacerbated with government policies, 3) increases the likelihood of about one-quarter (some 18 of 74 million) of all children to a life of disadvantage and poverty, 4) aborts hundreds of thousands of unplanned, unwanted humans every year, 5) fails to adequately educate and prepare its young for healthy and successful adult life, 6) discriminates against many before the law, cannot say it works to provide for its children. It cannot claim that it does no harm to its children and their rights. When children's rights are included in making public policy, leaders are pressed to address issues at their root cause—a better path forward in a moderate's eyes.

Here are examples of how a moderate's focus on root causes and solutions changes the entire political dialogue about harmful national policies on two painful long-running issues. It can be argued that both are symptoms of deeper root cause issues of poverty, poor education, and systemic residential housing racial segregation. I am arguing in view of the deeper issues, these two can be treated as root causes due to the many negative outcomes that follow directly from the occurrence of either one or both together.[38] Consider the root causes of these two early life traumas:

1) Early life addiction—addictive drugs and cognitive behaviors
2) Early life experience—unwanted/unplanned conceptions

Early life addictions. The addiction problem in America is described as an epidemic. And it is. This moderate also claims that it is a children's rights crisis heavily discriminating against children's civil rights in many ways. At the core of America's discrimination of children on the drug front is America's current accommodating attitude, national policy, as well as liberal protections of the illegal drug industry and Mean Street industries' practices. All the above enable the exploitation of children by various government policies and commercial interests hiding behind free speech and other arguments.

Here is a closer look at America's two-headed drug issue: 1) use of opioid painkiller drugs (illegal and ill-advised; oxycodone, Vicodin, etc.), and 2) use of drugs that are illegal by federal law—heroin, cocaine, methamphetamines, marijuana, and others. All of these addictive drugs have one thing in common: they all are capable of hijacking the human brain by rewiring the brain's reward circuitry. Drug overdoses have surpassed car crashes and gun violence to become the leading cause of death for Americans under fifty-five, as reported by the *New York Times*.[39] Well over four hundred thousand deaths due to drug overdoses have been reported since 2000 and over seventy-two thousand per year in 2017. Nearly fifty thousand of those deadly overdoses were caused by either heroin or fentanyl. Between 2011 and 2016, the number of Americans who died from fentanyl overdose increased by more than 1,000 percent from 1,660 to 18,335. In 2018, the Immigration and Customs Enforcement (ICE) agency seized enough fentanyl to kill nearly twice the population of the United States. Most of it is arriving from China and some from Mexico. The drug issue is a domestic health and children's rights crisis. It is also a foreign policy and national security issue.

Children are frequently negatively impacted in many ways when drugs are in a household that has young children and teens. They are affected, whether they are exposed to death or addicted adults in the family. They may become traumatized when exposed to peers committing crimes and gang violence, or overdosing, using, or selling drugs in their neighborhoods or schools. The pervasive presence of negative role models in their lives and the glorification of drugs in pop culture and entertainment are addiction promoters and pushers.

According to Dr. Thad Polk at the University of Michigan,[40] people who experiment with marijuana have about a one in ten chance of becoming addicted. One wonders if that will increase, given that in 2019 an estimated one in five high schoolers have vaped with cannabis-laced vaping oil. Young people who experiment with cocaine or heroin have about a one in five to six likelihood of becoming addicted. Youth who experiment with tobacco use have about one in three probability of becoming long-term tobacco users.

Repeated and habitual use involves social and cognitive triggers, but at addiction's core is the relative genetic susceptibility any individual has to addiction based on the configuration of about ninety different genes.[41] So adults accommodating the use of the products through very weak, liberal, and progressive government regulation as well as practices in entertainment and recreation make it easy for users to be created when they are young, vulnerable, and prone to poor judgment. Today they are getting even younger, with middle school children experimenting with vaping with little consequence from their adults or government enforcement practices. We are failing at limiting the supply of illegal drugs. Attacking the supply of drugs is almost irrelevant at this point because of the volume of drugs in the global supply chain. The only way to slow drug addiction is by imposing demand-side interdiction efforts to reduce access and use.

Today, youth who are drug users (less for alcohol) are more likely to grow up to be less productive, less motivated, lower skilled, less competent in relationships and parenting, more likely to be high school or college dropouts, less likely to care about politics or to vote,[42]. Some are more likely to become physically addicted or die early from overdose. When the drug risk is combined with being raised in a single, female-led household, youth, especially males, are more likely to be incarcerated in their early years.[43]

Illicit drug use is a catalyst in over 50 percent of cases of domestic violence, child abuse, and neglect, which can turn a child negative with low self-esteem, hopelessness, discrimination, disenfranchisement, and anger. The National Institute on Drug Abuse reports that half of those arrested for the serious crimes of murder, robbery, and assault were under the influence of illegal drugs. According to the Bureau of Justice Statistics, 70 percent of state prisoners, and nearly 60 percent of federal prisoners, used drugs regularly before incarceration. Once incarcerated, upon release, young people are more likely to be discriminated against in employment opportunities. As an example, a study of young non-offenders versus ex-offenders incarcerated for drug crime looked at who got called back for a second job interview. White non-offenders were called back twice as often as an ex-offender, and Black non-offenders were three times more likely to get called back than Black ex-offenders.[44]

Drugs have a substantial long-term impact on poor judgment, poor choices that youth make. Unfortunately, if and when youth mature, given the addictive nature of drugs and some cognitive behaviors, it is too hard or too late to recover. Government policy has no business enabling, franchising, legalizing anything that will knowingly discriminate or disadvantage our youth beyond their self-inflicted misjudgments.[45] It is highly discriminatory against children, especially males. Males are more likely to make misjudgments and act on poor choices because their brain's prefrontal cortex, where self-regulating decisions are made, may not fully develop until about age twenty-six. Females have an advantage because their judgment faculties mature neurologically earlier, according to the current understanding of neuroscience.[46] A moderate is perplexed how we as a nation recoil at real or perceived discrimination against females but completely ignore discrimination against males. Moderates are opposed to discrimination against anyone.

A moderate is easily convinced that both supply and demand of drugs must be attacked. The nation must attack the negative externalities that attend demand for drugs. Moderates hold that adult tolerance is the crucial cultural root cause of the drug addiction and is where all levels of government and community need to focus. To reduce addiction we should continue to attack supply and suppliers but also disintermediate demand and users (early in life). This is not about criminality or incarceration. This is about mental health and mitigating negative behavior for our youth before addiction can take hold. Moderates' view is: take away the users/experimenters from the sellers and enablers. The argument is: educate, intervene, and manage young people that are identified as users or those at-risk to become users based on their social, behavioral, or genetic susceptibility.

Moderates likely understand that it is not just the addictive substances listed above that require new policy and legislative treatment but also the addictive cognitive behaviors activated by video games, gambling, digital TV, and smartphone screen or application experiences pushed by Mean Street. Architecting national policy to attack supply and demand sides for both addictive drugs and addictive behaviors is required in a moderate's view. We all have talked for a very long time about how heinous "drug pushers" are, but now how about we expand our condemnation to include "addiction pushers" as well as "drug pushers". "Addiction pushers" include the owners, boards of directors, executives, employees, and on-screen/on-stage performers associated with some of America's large Mean Street corporations. They also ought to be accountable when using digital presentation techniques that manipulate human sensory, cognitive, or emotive brain functions to achieve long-lived consumers through addictive stimulation. If Americans care about protecting children from the root causes of addiction then targeting the interests of addiction pushers in media, entertainment, advertising, and social networking industries is as important as the interests of drug pushers.

As the likelihood that young Americans will experiment with drugs and cognitive behaviors increases, more of them will become addicted. It is simply a numbers game. The way current national law and policy focus on the supply side for drugs and avoid applying effective accountability on cognitive addiction pushers interplays with the policy on crime and children; it all converges to disadvantage children's rights and their futures. The numbers of our children born into and raised in poverty and exacerbated with addictions are rising creating potentially harmful and insurmountable lifelong outcomes for many children. A well-designed "children first" national policy addresses drugs as a critical root cause. It multiplies positive network effect benefits that reduce national security risks and also reduce crime, economic productivity drag, social safety net costs, taxes, cycles of poverty, addiction, mental health issues, broken lives, preventable early life deaths and, discrimination or exploitation by adults.

Early life outcomes for the unplanned/unwanted. Over 70 percent of pregnancies of women under the age of thirty are unplanned and in many cases unwanted.[47] The one bit of good news is that teen births per one thousand teen females has dropped from thirty-four to nineteen since 2010 to 2019 according to AECF 2019 KidsCount Data Book. However, the numbers in general have not improved. In 1950 far less than one in ten children (4 percent) were born out of wedlock. In 1970, about a decade into the sexual revolution, roughly one in ten children was born to unwed mothers. Today the numbers are far higher, at over four in ten. Fewer than two in ten are born to unwed Asian Americans. As many as seven in ten are born to unwed African American mothers and four in ten to unwed European American mothers. Not all but many raised in single-female-led households that are poor, poorly educated, poorly skilled, poorly motivated, poorly supported by family, and supported by government aid have a harder life. Early life experiences for many from unplanned/unwanted conceptions is an example of a negative-multiplier root-cause issue that produces a number of costly outcomes for the—child, parent(s), community, society, and economy. One major negative outcome, fatherless households, that has its own negative network-multiplier effects will be discussed in chapter 5.

Though other root-cause issues impact a child's development (e.g. abandonment, racism, poverty), moderates' vision to improve the lives of many of our young citizens through politics and policies that solve these two issues (each child planned and addiction free) is far better than liberals' or conservatives' vision. For moderates *the right thing to do* for the sake of children is to rise to defend all of children's rights before and after birth to advance social justice.

Children first, adults second.

Chapter 5: On Institutions—Family First

If you want to summarize the changes in family structure over the past century, the truest thing to say is this: We've made life freer for individuals and more unstable for families. We've made life better for adults but worse for children. We've moved from big, interconnected, and extended families, which helped protect the most vulnerable people in society from the shocks of life to smaller, detached nuclear families (a married couple and their children), which give the most privileged people in society room to maximize their talents and expand their options. The shift from bigger and interconnected extended families to smaller and detached nuclear families ultimately led to a familial system that liberates the rich and ravages the working-class and the poor.[48]
— David Brooks, "The Nuclear Family Was a Mistake"

Moderates would agree with most of the above quote from an article in *The Atlantic* by David Brooks entitled "The Nuclear Family Was a Mistake." They would likely not agree with the meaning of the title or the conclusion that the shift from big, extended families to detached nuclear families caused the disintegration of the family or that extended families are gone.[49] By a moderate's sensibility, the nuclear family was not and is not the mistake. The demotion of the natural nuclear family while informal, abandoned, broken, blended, divorced, and forged[50] family structures were promoted to the new normal was the mistake. For moderates the nuclear family is the bedrock foundation of America's strength and vitality. Without a thriving institution of family, moderates believe America's core will continue to weaken. Fortifying it is at the top of the moderate agenda.

The article the quote is from recounts the troubled recent history of the American family. It tracks the disintegration and decline of the nuclear family in modern America, evolving from large, mostly rural extended families to the urban nuclear family structure that peaked in the era of 1950 to 1965. Though successful during that brief time, the article argues that the nuclear family was an anomaly over time. It observes the nuclear family's failings to help the modern family function for any but the more affluent families led to its decline from the 1970s to the present day. It argues that institutional, economic, and cultural reforms and the shift from bigger, interconnected families to detached nuclear families were the driving forces.

The moderate argument on the disintegration of the American family starts from a different place. It posits that various societal trends, science advances, political demands, and government policies converged over the last half century to create internal and external pressures that pushed and pulled the family unit apart. The argument claims the interplay of five forces enabled by government policy is the root cause for the disintegration of the nuclear family to the detriment of our society, economy, democracy, and children. Science drivers in genetics and fertility that impact family formation were discussed in chapter 4. Mega societal forces that frame the economic, cultural, and institutional reforms that impact family formation and function were briefly discussed in chapter 1.

Along with the science and societal drivers in the 1960s and 70s, the American family began to disintegrate from the combined impact of four politically influenced forces[++++] and greatly exacerbated by a fifth, historical political force—American slavery and racism. These five forces powered by government policy and political movements pushed and pulled apart the nuclear family by impacting family norms, values, structure, stability, and sustainability.

The forces are: 1) economic inequality, 2) mass discrimination by and massive dependence on government, 3) progressive social and political activism, 4) adultism (a new word I will define and explain shortly). Together they impose poverty, disadvantage, discrimination, and disenfranchisement on too many of America's households and children. Moderates are likely inclined to agree political action is needed to force change in enabling policies. Without real progress to reduce the compound negative effect of the forces and policies, it is hard to envision that the American family will be a core strength in the fabric of America going forward. Before each force is examined, here is a brief historical context of several key cultural institutions.

Modern Life and Racism Pushing Families Apart

The moderate's perspective on cultural institutions is that family, marriage, religion, and trust are tightly coupled societal cornerstones that provide the strongest foundation for a durable and sustainable democratic society. A strong institution of family is essential for a strong nation. Seventy years ago, around 1950, one thing religion, marriage, and family as cultural institutions had in common was that they were all practiced by a strong majority of American households. Since then all three institutions have disintegrated. Well over six of ten households practiced religion, and nearly eight of ten households had married couples. In the 1940s, five of six marriages endured even in the aftermath of the post-traumatic societal stress of the early twentieth century pandemics, the Great Depression, and World Wars I and II. Today, all are practiced by a declining minority of American

---

[++++] Slavery is a fifth powerful political force that will be addressed separately as it predates the 1970s by over three hundred years. It has substantially exacerbated family disintegration challenges for a significant portion of people of African and slavery heritages.

households. Fewer than one in two practice religion. Fewer than one in two marriages endure,[51] and less than one in two households are headed by two adults. Marriages were between opposite-sex pair bonds, and family formation was based on the natural laws of natural biological union. Today family formation is based on common law, rights law, and contract law for fertility commerce. In 1960, over three-quarters of children lived in two adult households. Today that number has been cut in half to a third of children.

While much can be said about how historical changes in global population, economics, and culture have impacted family formation and disintegration, nothing compares to the trauma and tragedy imposed on the African American family over the history and legacy of African slavery. It is the fifth political force. Here is the story of just one of many tragic injustices to the African American family—forced migration. From the inception of the African slave trade in the fourteenth century by Islamic traders first trading at ports on the Mediterranean and then at ports on Africa's west coast with Portuguese, Spanish, and English slave traders in the sixteenth to nineteenth centuries, over 12 million souls started what is called the Middle Passage from Africa to new foreign lands. About 10.7 million of some 12.5 million landed at sugar and other commodity-based plantation ports in the Caribbean and Americas. Around four hundred thousand were brought to America, starting with twenty-some sold in Jamestown, Virginia, in 1619, marking the beginning of the charter generation. Across every subsequent generation of American slaves, only a small number managed to secure freedom as a family and even then occasionally were broken up as a family by slave brokers who would entice their children away, to be sold into slavery in the South.

Between 1790 and 1860, especially after 1808 when Congress withdrew the United States from the international slave trade, one million slaves were sold from plantations in the Upper South to plantations in the Deep South in a labor migration called the Second Middle Passage. As the Upper South started to move from tobacco to wheat farming, which needed less labor, slaves became more valuable as capital than they were valuable for labor. The Deep South states, formed from purchases of Louisiana and Florida territories, at that same time were adopting cotton as a plantation crop because the invention of the cotton gin made cotton growing a viable, highly profitable crop. Cotton needed a lot more labor to make it viable and cheap labor to make it highly profitable—slave labor. A national business quickly evolved in the sale and speculation of slaves for plantation markets in the Deep Southern states. Twenty five percent of first marriages between slaves and about half of all nuclear families were broken apart. Half of all slave children lost one or both parents to interstate sale. Children faced a 30 percent chance of sale. The long-term trauma and scars of forced separation have created intergenerational stresses that are still visible today.[52] They are also the primary causes for and outcomes from the intergenerational disintegration of the African American family.

The legacy of slavery through Southern state Black Codes, Jim Crow laws, and federal laws were all institutionally designed to exclude, control, or intimidate. For example, in the 1910s to 1950s federal housing[53] practices in zoning, real estate brokering, and federal lending programs very intentionally discriminated against Black families. They worked to create the self-perpetuating dynamics of the urban ghettos and high rise public housing projects in many cities by federal design. Institutional racism is still visible today in various institutional policies and practices in government, housing, banking, public and higher education, health care, criminal justice, media, and entertainment. Moderates would likely be like-minded that policies that perpetuate institutional racism can and should be eliminated. Disintegration of many families of African American descent whose histories originated in American slavery has created a national disgrace and challenge that persists to this day. Moderates would likely be unified in calling on corporations, universities, judges, legislatures, and courts to correct discrimination of people of all colors but especially our African Americans—now.

Forces Pushing Nuclear Families Apart

Economic inequality. While slavery and racism have an immense negative impact on our African American community, a key force pushing apart nuclear families of all colors from the inside are the pressures caused by the sharp increase in economic inequality from the 1970s to the present, as measured by household wealth. Economic inequality is pushing the disintegration of American families through an array of work, education, pop cultural, and personal choice pressures[54] that lead an adult or teen to disengage from blood family or the institution of family. Though economic inequality has existed throughout the American experience, over the past fifty years, fueled by market and technological advances and the outsized political influence of the very wealthy, income and wealth gaps have widened dramatically. Money continues to concentrate in fewer and fewer hands. In 1890, near the height of the Gilded Age, the bottom 90 percent of the US population owned 27 percent of the nation's wealth.[55] Today the bottom 90 percent owns 23 percent. The top .1 percent held 15–18 percent of the nation's wealth until World War II, when a long, slow decline occurred that bottomed in the mid-1970s at around 8 percent. Since then the wealth of the top .1 percent (yes one tenth of one percent) has steadily increased to the present day to greater than 20 percent. During the same period of time, the bottom 90 percent held about 18 percent in 1920, 30 percent in 1970, peaked around 37 percent in the mid-1980s, and has steadily declined to the present day to less than 23 percent.[56] From about 1990 to 2020, the wealth share of the top one percent increased from about 30 percent to over 40 percent of the nation's wealth, an incredible upward redistribution.[57] In 2020, just three people own more wealth than the bottom 50 percent of households in America (Jeff Bezos, Bill Gates, and Warren Buffett).[58] There can be an energetic debate on how much the economic inequality gap is due to families inflicting economic drags on themselves and how much is the result from more affluent households, especially white households, benefitting from better housing, jobs, economic opportunities and better-informed investment choices. A meaningful portion for whites can be attributed to wealth creation from single family home ownership. Some can be attributed to the outsized return on investment some investors received from the new digital economy commercial investments—e.g., Facebook, Google, etc. However, a major portion of redistribution upward is due to government policies in allocation of spending and economic benefits for industry, corporate, and wealthy rent-seekers in the areas of capital, trade, immigration, patents, legislated favors (earmarks), regulation, tax advantages, and rent-seeker-designed legislation. The upward redistribution of wealth over the past thirty to fifty years is undeniable. Economic inequality has expanded. Moderates would be easily convinced that change in a number of policy areas is required. Moderates would also be easily persuaded revamping Wall Street and K Street is needed to improve prospects for the bottom 95–99 percent of US households so they can earn higher incomes and generate real wealth. Addressing policies and politics that have enabled and exacerbated public rent-seeking and economic inequality would do a lot to re-stabilize numerous aspects of our nation—any nation—including the nuclear family.

Mass discrimination by and dependence on the federal government. The second major force pushing nuclear families apart is the combined impact on America's poor and African American households from two massive and pervasive sets of long-tailed federal policies of the modern era (1900 to the present). The first set of federal policies enshrined residential housing racial segregation with the force of law for at least the first three quarters of the twentieth century—arguably to the present day. The second set enabled the rise of dependence on government of America's poor but especially the African American community during the last third of the twentieth century to the present. Historians may conclude that both race discriminatory and dependency policies while sustained across all presidential administrations were created in the administrations of Wilson, FDR, and LBJ to reflect widely held racism and/or to appease Southern Democrats demands for separation of races.

Mass discrimination[59] by government fueled disintegration of American families through the micro and macro effects of government policy (state action) that supported individuals' racist beliefs (private action) that intentionally and officially sanctioned in law racially segregated residential housing. Here is a very brief view of some of the race policies created by federal, state, and local governments. The federal level arguably had the greatest multiplier impact via urban and suburban housing policy around major cities nationwide.

Examples of federal race policies include: racially segregated public housing projects in cities, Depression era (CCC and WPA program segregated projects), and WW II efforts (war industries and GI Bill housing and education benefits for whites only); FHA guaranteed mortgage insurance limited for white-only, single family housing developments; federal highway construction targeted in urban areas that went through African American neighborhoods; tax policy that favored suburban single family dwelling versus urban apartment construction projects.

Examples of state and local race policies include: state courts supporting and ordering evictions of African American families from white-only, federally insured, and zoned neighborhoods (built with race restricted covenants that were supported by local churches, universities, and hospitals); state real estate commissions that licensed brokers whose unethical practices promoted segregation and white/suburban flight (e.g., blockbusting sales tactics on whites to get their houses at low prices to resell to African American families at higher prices); school boards and planning commissions color coding and drawing school location maps to ensure separation of races.

The net effect of a hundred years of discrimination by *de jure* (in law) tax and funding policy fueled African American and poor family instability inter-generationally through lower quality education and economic opportunities; less physical, economic, and social mobility; less ability to generate real wealth; and the threat and/or the experience of real violence. Unfortunately, here in the third decade of the twenty-first century not all of the race policies created during the three democratic administrations have been eliminated or redressed.

Mass dependence[60] on government is fueling American family disintegration, particularly those of low socioeconomic standing, through loss of adult male and female motivation to participate and perform in the workforce and the household. Among the many reasons are government guarantees that de-risk failure and impose very few effective consequences for irresponsible disengagement from household and child development. The greater dependence of households on government for direct benefits was ideologically seeded by Presidents Wilson and Roosevelt (FDR). Dependence really expanded dramatically in the 1960s with President Lyndon Johnson's (LBJ's) War on Poverty and the Great Society vision. Enabled by the Democratic Party Congressional supermajorities in both houses following the historic Civil Rights Act of 1964 and Voting Rights Act of

1965, a number of entitlement programs were enacted that set in motion a process of destigmatizing dependency on the government. The entitlement programs have sprawled to the present day to financial transfers of one-sixth of the federal budget to families in poverty and those deemed "in need." Before LBJ, Social Security was the only major social program and from 1959 to 1965 the poverty rate declined from over 22 percent to under 15 percent. During his presidency, the poverty rate stalled while Medicare, Medicaid, food stamps, disability insurance entitlements took hold.

Today America has moved from destigmatizing to promoting full reliance on benefits as entitlements and as civil rights. There are at least seven income-transfer programs and many antipoverty assistance programs. Despite hundreds of programs and trillions of dollars spent to improve the standard of living and earning power, the social and economic mobility of those defined as living in or near the poverty level is about the same since the Johnson administration. Poverty as a measure of income needed to live, originally designed by Mollie Orshansky[61] in the mid-1960s, is now very hard to measure. Today, it is untethered from any measure of poverty, given that entitlements are redistributed in cash and noncash forms to over one-third of US households. Needs-based entitlement payments have grown from 28 percent of federal spending in 1960s to over 67 percent of the present-day federal budget. Both parties are guilty of expanding the entitlement state especially under various Republican presidents.

As conservatives will argue, coincident with the rise of the entitlement state are the decline in workforce participation rates for males ages twenty and older from nearly 80 percent to below 70 percent, and the decline in marriage participation rates for males. These are both coincident with the rise of children conceived out of wedlock living in single-female-led households. Social acceptance of living together and relaxation of sexual mores have somehow led to some types of males and females of all races to be less committed to their children – males more so than females. The proportion of never-married men today is three times higher than in 1965. Federal benefits are financing the effects of children living in households in poverty, needy, or fatherless conditions. A moderate would likely assign a grade of F to America for not holding uncommitted male conceivers accountable and now is not doing well holding female conceivers accountable either. The financial and opportunity consequences to the taxpayer and benefit recipient households who are dependent on the government as sole- or co-breadwinner are large. The systemic discrimination and disadvantages for at least one-third of America's children raised in low-income households are also large.

Single-adult-female-led households comprise 28 percent of all US households, raising 34 percent of all children (24 million). The alarming statistics and studies documenting the rise of the single-female-led household, the fatherless society, and the negative impact on children are voluminous. Children of all colors, but especially of color, from fatherless homes are also discriminated against by state action because they are more likely to be treated differently or punished more harshly if they are poor, abuse drugs and alcohol, drop out of school, or suffer from health or emotional problems. As teens, boys are more likely to become involved in crime. Girls are more likely to become pregnant. Their children grow up to repeat the cycle. Surrounded by public policies and entitlements that basically hold no one accountable to a high standard for having and raising children, too many of our defenseless youth are the net losers.

Finally, the absence of adequate work-family workplace policy that supports primary wage earners who are also primary caregivers has exacerbated the decline of family and increased dependence on government. It is an issue about which moderates care a great deal. Working women, particularly in the lower-income quintiles, frequently have to choose low-wage jobs due to their need for time flexibility. The need for flexibility makes it harder to develop marketable skills to improve their earning power. Architecting policies that provide support and paths to better opportunities are needed to help the caregivers of America's next generation succeed.

Changing policies and norms to encourage the presence of both adult male and female conceivers as competent, positive role models in children's lives and homes would go a long way to reestablish more two-adult-led households, whether legally married or not. Moderates would likely agree that America and Americans need to face and solve these realities head-on. If we want to reduce the disadvantages imposed on many of America's children's lives and gradually lower the large-scale dependence on government for household life support, then improving their home life is front and center. Moderates get it.

Forces Pulling Families Apart

Progressive social and political activism. The first force pulling nuclear families apart from the outside is progressive activism for cultural and legal institutional reforms that as argued in this book have harmed children legally and materially. It started in the 1960s with the relaxation of marriage, responsibility, and sexual mores. Progressives' political activism then added to the disintegration with demands to structurally embed cultural, moral, and identity relativism in social norms and institutions. Combined, they often untethered and disoriented adults' and children's natural roles in families. Activists' demands to conform to their worldview grounded in individual adult privilege have led to a growing list of adult advantages at the expense of children with many negative outcomes. For example, today, many do not marry when there are children—creating collateral damage and the phenomena of serial conceivers and serial abandoners. Nontraditional marriage, no-fault divorce, no-harm-no-foul abandonment, nontraditional pathways to parenthood among others have created complex outcomes for too many children and society. For the most part, progressives have won the institutional contests, most fought judicially, with no one—not leaders or judges—standing to protect children and their rights. Moderates likely agree with conservatives that the social costs of progressives' grand social experiments are huge and not readily visible, given America's blind spots for children and women alone with children—too many raised at-risk and defenseless. Moderates likely support redesign of the legal foundations of the new social practices and to pursue ways to stabilize and revitalize the institution of family.

Adultism. The second force pulling nuclear families apart, also starting in the 1960s along with progressive political activism, is a social phenomenon of adult discrimination as an expression of adult privilege. The notion feels abstract, is subtle, and is hard to accurately articulate. In simplest terms it is any adult doing what they want despite any risks, costs, or damage to a child or to children as a minority class. For example, would adultists recognize or honor any of the ten fundamental rights claimed for children in chapter 4?

As the social foundations of modern life have become more untethered from human nature, natural evolutionary processes, responsible behavior, and traditional practices, some portion of adults are more self-oriented. They are adults and groups who feel empowered, entitled to take an aggressive stand on "*adults first-me first*" politics. There is no political "ism" label at present as other brands of discrimination have—racism, sexism, ageism, etc. There is no word to name the discrimination by adult privilege so I am naming it "adultism". Adultism is defined as "the creation of intended or unintended legal or material harm to children by acts of individual adults or to children as a minority class of US citizens by the actual or statistical impact of institutional or government policy."

Those adults who are adultists see most everything relative to their personal preferences including when children are involved—family formation, divorce, abandonment, life. For example, what are your sensibilities about family formation using fertility assisted reproductive products and technologies?§§§§ How far should that go? Should there be restrictions? Do you feel it is OK at the expense of a child's birthright, to deny the child its' biological mother and its' biological father, and their participation in the child's life? For a true moderate, it is not OK. That optionality contributes to the decline of the institution of family. Irrespective of anyone's sense of morality or

---

§§§§ Service, products, and technologies that decouple conception and gestation and use commercially transacted human biologic material as conception products

equality, it is unacceptable to a moderate because the child, the new US citizen, is legally harmed by being denied its' fundamental rights. How do you see it?

As a second example, consider blended family dynamics. Where is the line between responsible behavior and abandonment of prior children for an adult who has children by multiple partners? If there aren't enough resources available to children from prior partners is that fair? There are those that see adultism as age discrimination, as social rent-seeking—personal gain at the expense of children's rights and needed resources. How do you see it?

In summary America's institution of the nuclear family, those linked by genetic bloodlines from generation to generation, is in decline while every other arrangement is celebrated and accepted as the new normal. The decline of intact nuclear families; the growth of blended, broken, divorced, never-married-single-female-led families, in addition to promotion of forged families have all converged to dramatically change children's lives. Does your conscience see it as for the better or the worse—on average, in the whole? All five alternative family formation experiments do not seem to be working out very well for children as a minority class. Especially for children of lower socio-economic adults as reflected in many statistics on education, health, crime, drugs, jobs, suicide, mental health, and others. Though any of the five may work well in individual situations, natural, biological-union-formed nuclear families are still civil society's best institutional investment for societal cohesion, stability, and sustainability. What can Americans do to reclaim it as the core of society? Moderates start with advocating for the importance of family, blood relations, and roots[62] in weaving the institutional fabric of our nation, every nation.

The quote at the beginning of the chapter, observing that life is better for adults and more affluent families and worse for children, captures the reality that the institution of American family is broken. For many, especially our poor, the combined impact of slavery-racism and the four political forces of economic inequality, mass government discrimination and dependence, progressive demands, and adult discrimination (adultism) are compromising too many of America's children. A moderate may agree these five are the real root causes disintegrating the American family. Americans as citizens and voters must face them head-on. Can America make real progress on social justice or have a strong future as long as these forces are allowed to negatively impact a significant portion of our children? For moderates *the right thing to do* for the sake of our children is to rise to solve the injustices that weaken the institution of the American family.

Family first, the rest second.

Chapter 6: On Priorities—Country First

Loyalty to country ALWAYS. Loyalty to government, when it deserves it.
—Mark Twain

In the election of 2016, the forty-fifth president established his national policy platform's first principle as "America First." That proclamation created incredible controversy, attacked aggressively mostly by liberals. A moderate would say "America First" is self-evident. On this principle, moderates and conservatives and all who hold country first are aligned. I first heard of the term in Linda Killian's book *The Swing Vote* in 2011, where she labeled a faction of voters in the Democratic Party as "America-First Democrats."[63]

Allegiance of the Governing to the Governed: Citizens First

A modern nation-state (post–Treaty of Westphalia 1648) has three things: 1) a sovereign territory with borders, 2) people governed within those borders, and 3) laws that protect the borders and govern the people within the borders. Every nation's government has a sovereign and moral duty to defend, protect, and serve its people first. Every citizen has a duty to be a patriot and serve its country first so long as its government is just and holds the consent of the governed. Just ask any person from any other nation you visit whom they think is first. The principle of Country First does not prohibit or restrict the globalist view. People can pursue economic, cultural, or humanitarian collaboration internationally. Americans can purse humanitarian aid through our government's policies as well as our individual and collective volunteerism. Americans can support people seeking rescue, recovery from disasters in places like the Bahamas as well as peace and progress in war-torn regions like Syria and Ukraine, to mention a few from a very long list. Country First simply balances the priorities and needs of one's own country and people rationally with those of refugees and people of other nations. Even America has to set priorities with so many of our people left behind and so deep in debt.

Hardly anyone from a moral modern society would deny the humanitarian obligation to assist other peoples enduring extreme hardship from natural disaster, pandemic, or war. But as a fundamental principle of how priorities are set, resources are allocated, and policies are framed, Country First is a clear obligation for all nation-states. Resources, jobs, and opportunities are not unlimited. The reality of international relations and limited resources press patriotically minded Americans to be practical. We are forced to accept the fact that there are countervailing national and cultural forces at work around the world. Some nations are interested in dominating the culture of other nations through various means or arbitraging their economies to acquire their wealth.

Consider the implications of China's size, strategy, centralized planning, and communist party rule. With nearly 20 percent of the world's population, at 1.4 billion of 7.8 billion by 2020 estimate, it also has the largest standing military, 2nd largest economy, and intelligence gathering presence around the world. China may have the ability and the intent to cause a twenty-first century version of a "China Syndrome". The 1979 American movie, *The China Syndrome*, tells the story of a US nuclear power plant that malfunctions and nearly creates a *nuclear meltdown*. If the hot nuclear material in a nuclear reactor super overheats, becomes molten, it can, figuratively speaking, melt a hole down through the earth all the way to the other side of the world.

Its "China First", "Belt and Road", and global presence strategic initiatives potentially enable it to pursue economic and global dominance as it rapidly evolves from an external economy through a peripheral economy to a core economy. China's strategy relies on specialization and imitation tactics leveraging cost-of-labor and intellectual property arbitrage, China-centric regional infrastructure and trade network among many other elements. Imagine China able to impose its will for its interests using economic or military force. Imagine China able to impose its will using its cyber and in-country assets to create a *political meltdown* in a target nation lowering the target's resistance all the way to China's interests. Through internal conflict, chaos, disinformation, and tradecraft, policy and actions favorable to China enabling China to achieve its goals without any direct conflict or confrontation with the target nation. In my view that is a twenty- first-century version of the *China Syndrome*.

America's compelling post–World War II economic dominance and moral leadership as the core economy and singular global superpower are in visible decline. The many reasons for this are well developed in Joseph P. Quinlan's *The Last Economic Superpower*.[64] America is a decreasing portion of human civilization at less than 4.5 percent of the world's population and is headed down to about 15 percent of the world's economy. Our share used to be over 25 percent. Americans have to rethink and recalibrate various domestic, foreign, and global policies accordingly to hold America's position in the global order and to re-establish leadership in a new form.

Notwithstanding the potential impact of China and other global actors, the challenge today is that the cumulative global needs of peoples under stress are overwhelming and leading to migration, refugee, and immigration tidal waves. Current policy approaches are inadequate and ineffective to address the enormous need. For example, nations taking in large numbers of refugees are buckling under the financial burden and societal stress. The United States, Germany, Turkey, Mexico, Italy, and Jordan among others are at the top of that list. Another example is foreign aid, which has fallen far short to address poverty in impoverished regions of the world (e.g., Africa and Central America). Until we are willing to systematically look at the whole interconnected set of global challenges and architect effective solutions, there have to be boundaries, priorities, and hard choices. There have to be some redlines on the number of immigrants, refugees, dollars allocated to nation building, and global defense of other nations because the resources and goodwill of America are limited by our own self-imposed challenges. Moderates fully accept and understand these sobering trade-offs as painful realities.

Allegiance of a Nation to Its Children—Living and Future

As presented in chapters 4 and 5 from a moderate's perspective, the people of the United States are morally and constitutionally obligated as a sacred duty *in order to form a more perfect union* and *to secure the blessings of liberty to ourselves and our posterity* to legally protect and not legally harm its present or future children. In 1872, the Congress established Yellowstone as the first National Park to preserve nature's heritage for future generations. Moderates would likely wonder how there could be a lesser moral obligation to preserve and protect children's rights for future generations of children? If our adults are not morally inclined to care for their own children or support the nurturing of the nation's children, they are still legally obligated by the United States ratification of the UN Universal Declaration of Human Rights Treaty. Every nation has obligations to their children, bound by international treaty, if they ratified either the UN Universal Declaration of Human Rights or the UN Convention on the Rights of the Child.

Allegiance of the Governed to Their Nation—Patriotism

Patriotism is also part of Country First. Most people understand freedom is not free because there are those who would subjugate America for their benefit or to confiscate its wealth. Many of the wars fought through history were prosecuted by one nation's ambition to grow its wealth by taking the wealth of another nation.

To be able to defend our people and our way of life from those who want to take away our freedom or our wealth, Americans have to be ready, willing, and able to serve: "To be strong, America has never needed everyone to serve in the same way. It does need everyone to serve in some way."[65] Moderates agree and hold up the banner "Everyone able serves." If being an American is not part of your personal or political identity, then there is something amiss in your worldview by moderates' sense of patriotism. Moderates are easily persuaded that all able citizens not only owe duties of care and trust in civil society but also a duty of service to their country, community, the common good, and for some portion of us, their faith. For those that do not join the military in the active defense of our nation, moderates see four ways each citizen can contribute to our country through national service: 1) be a good or great parent of or a mentor to or benefactor for children at risk, 2) be a Good Samaritan to those you see in need and random acts of kindness, 3) participate in faith- and civic-based organizations that pursue humanitarian missions of conscience, 4) volunteer for local, state, national, or international humanitarian aid or public works projects. Volunteer as an emergency first responder or for disaster responses—floods, forest fires, hurricanes, tornadoes. Consider various kinds of infrastructure modernization public works projects for communities in deep poverty —water, solar, sewer, more.

Today people of different nations volunteer together, and governments work collaboratively on global policies and investments. The world community is doing a number of things through the United Nations for health, disease control, and other concerns. At present, many nations' and nonprofit organizations' efforts span the world, achieving patchwork progress at best in contrast to the potential results achievable if pursued with systemic solutions to address the causes of human suffering and global unsustainability. Moderates support collaborative humanitarian, peace-seeking, and economic development efforts of the United Nations, but there are two others that moderates likely believe need to be pursued: 1) population, and 2) poverty. Both come into full view for the estimated 80 million of inhabitants in refugee camps as estimated by the UN in 2020. About half of the people living in refugee camps are children. Imagine groups of nations (Nations United) supplementing the charter of the UN, uniting in shared vision and common purpose, providing expertise, resources, and volunteers organized to truly move the needle in the right direction on critical issues of population and poverty in crisis areas of the world? Initiatives of Nations United could provide medical, food security, education, public health, medical health, and conception control programs staffed with a coordinated community of volunteers from all over the world. Other large-scale projects Americans can volunteer for include modernization and recovery-repair for areas destroyed by natural disasters—fires, floods, hurricanes, and typhoons. There are international initiatives in which nations can unite to create a more collaborative and compassionate response that bring the people of the world closer together. For moderates *the right thing to do* for the sake of our children and all Americans is to rise to defend America first before global politics, but serve global humanitarian needs as best we can.

Country First.

Chapter 7: On Politics—Solutions First

Democracy is finding proximate solutions to insoluble problems.
—Reinhold Niebuhr, American theologian

Benjamin Franklin's 1736 adage "An ounce of prevention is worth a pound of cure" captures the same pragmatism moderates hold. Moderates believe policy solutions should serve America's people, problems, prosperity, and progress, pragmatically, before party politics. In other words, moderates prefer to prevent fires more than spend all the time, energy, and money to be great at putting fires out. There are many issues that need real practical solutions that require our government, politicians, and people to come together. In chapters 8 through 11, four hot-button issues will test how moderate you may be. Chapter 12 will test more of your opinions with five additional topics that likely make the twenty-first century moderate agenda.

In this chapter, one hotly contested issue, abortion, will be used to illustrate how a moderate might apply the principle of Solutions First to arrive at a different conclusion, solution, and political position as compared to the standing factions' partisan Party Politics First. It will demonstrate why moderates are frequently alienated by both factions' and the media's treatment of an issue.

Moderates' Solution on Abortion

The question of abortion as a national issue has been vehemently debated by pro-life and pro-choice advocates for nearly a half century as of the writing of this book. They have been warring since the original 1973 Supreme Court ruling in *Roe v. Wade* about the right to privacy for a woman to choose to abort or not abort and that a right to life only exists when the fetus can survive on its own outside a woman's body.

In a moderate's mind, the political debate, the media treatment, and the judicial battlefield have been absolutely Lilliputian and unproductive. The factions are irreconcilably divided. Framed as a binary "*Or*" issue (pro-choice *or* pro-life), the rights war is morally and constitutionally unsolvable because the binary frame only inflames and ignores the core issue. For moderates the behavior of unplanned/unwanted conceptions is the core issue, not a woman's right to privacy or to choose to abort. The issue of avoiding unplanned conceptions is more solvable here in the twenty-first century than it was in the twentieth century. Extraordinary advances in medical and scientific knowledge about the avoidance of conception enable new political and social solutions. But America's body politic and the media are not working on pro-conception avoidance; they are singularly focused on pro-choice.

The rights war ignores the reality that there is not just one right to life but at least five rights to life among the ten natural birthrights into life, as argued in chapter 4 on children's rights. There is not just one person's rights at stake. There are four stakeholders' rights involved: 1) female conceiver, 2) male conceiver, 3) new person(s) conceived, and 4) state action on behalf of civil society representing the collective rights and interests of present and future citizens burdened with tangible and intangible costs.

Here is an example of how a moderate's differentiating *"both/ neither"* view looks at the abortion debate politically. A moderate would say both sides and the Supreme Court have it wrong by only considering one adult's claim to a derived (substantive) constitutional right to privacy. Moderates likely support *both* pro-life and pro-choice but also believe in *neither* because they also believe in pro-children and pro–all positions. Neither pro-children nor pro-all are supported by conservatives, liberals, or the Supreme Court. All three seem to avoid any viewpoint that does not boil down into a binary choice decision. Moderates recoil at binary choices because they want complex issues solved at root cause—which means looking at the whole of the issue.

Pro-life is supportable by a moderate because science proves, and as pro-lifers hold, life begins at conception with the activation of living/developing processes and the formation of new DNA. It is impossible to deny, as science proves once the DNA of the male fertilizes the female egg, the new, unique DNA in the egg is a new human based on the DNA of the two opposite-sex conceivers.[66] Even though nature's abortions (miscarriages) occur in about one in four to five conceptions[67], once the blastocyst attaches to the uterine wall, the probability that the human will survive to birth starts rising with modern nutrition, maternal diligence, and medical care. Moderates would want the pro-life position to be the way of society. But it has to be accepted as an ideal to be sought because of the fact that humans are fallible. Moderates accept the fact and embrace the ideal. Now, we can get much closer to the pro-life ideal with the moderate solution in the twenty-first century. A key question for pro-life proponents for political debate on constitutional grounds is, "When does a new human become recognized and defended as a new person with rights of personhood and citizenship?" Moderates are the kind of people that will work to answer tough questions like this one as part of root cause solutioneering. I will offer an answer in chapter 12, section 5 in the New Deal for Children.

Pro-choice is supportable by many moderates, reluctantly for some, because there is a window of time post conception, getting smaller, when it can be abstractly argued the new human is not yet a new person. While the simple definition of <u>person</u> is a human being regarded as an individual, a much deeper definition may be needed to establish a constitutional foundation. Unquestionably a new person's viability by the current state of medical science is much closer to conception, even by the standard set by Justice Harry Blackmun, who authored the majority decision in *Roe v. Wade*. As Justice Sandra Day O'Connor opined in her 5–4 majority ruling in *Akron v. Akron Center for Reproductive Health* 1983, "*Roe v. Wade* is on a collision course with itself". Advances in medical arts enable viability much closer to conception and protect maternal health better.

Given that males' and females' wills and passions are frail and fallible, undoing unplanned/unwanted conceptions very early in gestation with modern methods available can be an option if society wants to provide one when one or both conceivers are confronted with the reality that they are not ready or suited for a minimum commitment of two decades to each other or their creation. There are five reasons to potentially abort. They are 1) rape,[68] 2) incest, 3) self-choice, 4) saving the life of the gestating female, and 5) ending the life in utero because of profound, unmanageable, or terminal physical, mental, or genetic defects. However, how wide should the window of time be for each of the five different reasons to stop a pregnancy? A potential sixth concern—female and/or male conceiver's intent to abandon a newborn to the state or to adoption, adds to the list of very uncomfortable topics for many. I will argue the sixth concern is not a reason for abortion but for limitations on the conceiver(s) rights and privileges going forward.

Opposing advocates have not engaged in a fine-grained national dialogue on each of the five root causes above. All we have is a binary "for-or-against" debate framed as a rights issue for one participant— the female. And we are nowhere closer to achieving a broadly supportable and sustainable political solution that most Americans can accept for at least two reasons:

1) The coarse-grained binary frame makes it virtually impossible to come to a political consensus.

2) Politics focus on constituency satisfaction through the demand for a privileged right instead of solving the root cause which inflames people of conscience from several perspectives.

Moderates, reluctantly for some, accept limited support for pro-choice but may be inclined to defend it more on pre-personhood grounds than privacy with time and other limits for self-choice abortions.

Pro-children. Moderates advocate to defend and protect children because they are the most vulnerable, defenseless, and least legally protected minority class of American citizens. Moderates' pro-children defense begins with the ten natural birthrights and continues with policy to address whether or not society (by government state action) can trust that the conceivers will perform parenting faithfully and responsibly. Will they respect and safeguard the rights of the new citizen? All humans who make it into life, whether planned or unplanned, wanted or unwanted, constitutional or unconstitutional, are here and have the right to be respected, protected, defended by everyone, like everyone. Moderates make the case that pro-life, pro-choice, and pro-children positions can be fashioned into a consistent policy and serial process. Partisans will claim that one cannot be both pro-choice and pro-life at the same time, nor can all three positions be in the same argument. Moderates disagree. We want a mature dialogue about all ten rights, five reasons for an abortion, and all four participants' rights. Completely different, more elegant, effective, and humane national policies and cultural practices emerge when the debate is pro-all and not just about pro-life versus pro-choice.

Pro-all. The moderate policy design on abortion would be an integrated, legislated national policy solution framed within the broad view of natural reproduction and address head on unwanted conceptions as the fundamental root cause. Moderate policy goals strive to maximize the prevention of unwanted/unplanned conceptions and minimize the need for abortion. In brief the policy approach would strive to reorient America's cultural theme of Planned Parenthood, which can be characterized as abortion-oriented. The new cultural and institutional theme is Planned Childhood, which is oriented toward prevention of unwanted conception and quality of early life for children as a class of citizens. Rather than focusing solely on undoing unwanted conceptions through abortion, moderates advocate policy that institutionalizes and inculcates societal competency at conception prevention and early confirmation. Policy would make widely available very economical conception prevention education, products, practices, health care services, and such. Women and men then are able to enjoy their heterosexuality responsibly with minimal risk of conception until and unless they fully, mutually consent to want to conceive new life, new citizens of the United States. All of this is achievable now with the moderate policies, using existing medical technology, health care and pharmacy distribution infrastructure, and facilitated with the addition of the new national institution mentioned above: Planned Childhood.

Consequently, like the new national social norm of practicing responsible social distancing that evolved during the coronavirus pandemic, practicing responsible conception prevention substantially reduces the number of unwanted conceptions, pregnancies, abortions, heartache, trauma, and cost. This policy avoids many negative emotional costs and consequences for adults and children. For those that primarily care about money, it also reduces government dependence and lowers public costs in a number of state and federal programs: health care, education, child care, criminal justice (legal and penal), addiction, and many other service areas which translate into lower taxes over time.

Also, since a number of Americans cannot agree on the pro-life view that life begins at conception, then national policy should include an abortion component with clear policy solutions for each of the five paths to an abortion event stated above as the democratic will of the American people so choose—not the judicial fiat of nine unelected people. It should also include rules of accountability for both sexes for those who are serial conceivers. There ought to be consequences for those that walk away, abandon, abuse, or otherwise endanger the other adult or the new person (child), or prove themselves profoundly untrustworthy for parenting by society.

Consider the current consequences of men and women who are serial conceivers and serial abandoners. Have you heard any stories about children abandoned to the state for foster care? I am aware of females who have conceived nearly ten children all by different males and abandoned all of them to be raised by the state without societal or legal consequences to themselves. I am aware of a male who conceived nearly twenty children by different females and abandoned them all to the females to raise, condemning the children to lives of hardship and disadvantage. Have you heard stories of fertility doctors using their own semen to conceive with unknowing female clients? I have heard stories of hundreds by a single doctor. Finally, what do you think about the fertility industry's use of repetitive, anonymous (read popular and profitable) sperm donors who have been used to conceive hundreds of new persons? Are you 'ok' with people finding out they have hundreds of blood brothers and sisters at some point in their lives? I doubt most moderates are ok with that. They likely believe that practice is unconstitutional and immoral and must be disallowed.

Moderates' policy would be comprehensive and nationally uniform on conception and abortion, it would also address fertility industry practices, abandonment, deadbeat parents of both sexes, rapists, and pedophiles, and work to fix issues in family court, fatherless children, and children of and by incarcerated adults. America legislated comprehensive environmental protection and climate management policies successfully in the 1960s and 1970s (National Environmental Policy Act NEPA of 1970 and all other related following acts). Today, America enjoys much cleaner water, air, and better environmental practices. America should be able to design comprehensive pro-children national policy and practices for conception instead of a patch-work of constitutional rulings on abortion. Over time the negative societal footprint associated with unwanted conceptions and abortion becomes much smaller and less consequential if moderates' approach to conception prevention is embraced and executed well.

So here you have a moderate's high-level political analysis using a Solutions First approach for just one of the festering issues in American politics, abortion. The moderate position is solution oriented. It attacks abortion at its root cause and ameliorates a number of political issues—racism, sexism, adultism, economic inequality, poverty, government dependence, safety-net costs, broken lives, and more. All these are achievable by pursuing *solutions first* for conception versus *politics first* for abortion.

If we Americans are who we say we are, then the moderate view should prevail in the press and in politics, policy, and practice. If Americans are for justice for all and equality for all, then children's rights must be included and preferably first. Are we willing to give new humans their rights? Will we commit to provide a fairer chance to start life with a decent opportunity to survive and thrive for children of all colors, while reducing the issues that drain our nation and diminish too many young lives from their very beginning?

So far over the past half century with liberals and conservatives leading the debate who we are is only about how much adults' special interests and lives matter. They fight over rights that pit adults against one another with dramatic and negative consequences for children. Since 1973 per *Roe v. Wade* just here in the United States, well over 60 million abortions have been performed. That is more humans than China lost in the famine that followed Mao's ill-conceived Great Leap Forward campaign of the late 1950s when an estimated 15 to 40 million Chinese starved to death. That is more than the estimated 50 to 60 million men, women, and children who died in World War II. With the advances in knowledge and capabilities regarding conception prevention, there are solutions to dramatically reduce the number of unplanned, unwanted conceptions without relying on abortion as the sole unchallengeable issue, unequal right or singular tactic. Moderates insist there be no recrimination for our nation's past on this issue. America needs to grow up, mature as a nation, and become a more perfect union. America needs to move forward. Let us come together to solve abortion as one of the first on a long list of big issues. We can now do much better if we are who we say we are using a Solutions First approach for national policy on the intersection of human heterosexuality, children, and abortion. [69] For moderates *the right thing to do* for the sake of children is to rise to defend all of their rights before birth and after birth. It is time to solve abortion through institutional and individual best practices for conception.

As you now understand, Solutions First as an ideological principle is fundamental to a moderate's political sensibility and thought process because moderates seek institutional root cause solutions, not just constituency benefits alone. The Solutions First principle aspires to break finger-wagging, stare-and-glare political standoffs. It strives to shed light on the root causes of any of America's pressing issues. It also strives to shine a light on workable solutions.

If Americans want real progress, not just change that favors special interests, specific constituencies, or the very wealthy, then Americans have to drive solutions first, political party second. In the following four chapters, four more hotly contested current issues are presented to test how moderate you may be:

1) Guns
2) Immigration
3) Education
4) Climate

Solutions first, party politics second.

Chapter 8: On Guns

A free people ought not only to be armed, but disciplined...
— George Washington, First Annual Address to Congress, 1790

Guns and the right to keep and bear arms are at the center of terrorism and public safety debates here in the United States—especially for schools, government, and public spaces. Can we protect our children and communities, and minimize murders, suicides, and mass shootings caused by people using guns? Is this hope even possible, given how pervasive firearms and dangerous people are? America is among the most violent nations compared to most developed nations. In the World Population Review, the United States is considered the thirty-sixth most dangerous country, with Syria and Afghanistan the most dangerous and Iceland the least dangerous of the 163 nations analyzed. While violent and property crime rates continued to trend down in 2018 from their peaks back in the 1990s, according to the FBI statistics,[70] when it comes to violence involving guns,[71] the United States remains in the violent group along with a group of Central and South American countries.

Americans are avid gun owners. As of 2018, Americans own about nearly half (46 percent) of an estimated 855-plus million guns in civilian hands worldwide. In the United States, the latest estimate is over 390 million guns held in about 50 million of 130 million households with 70 to 80 million gun owners.[72] Over 18.6 million people are legally permitted to carry concealed weapons as of 2019, an increase of over 300 percent since 2007.[73] The vast majority of gun owners in the United States are very law-abiding citizens.

Here are some of the statistics on those who are not law-abiding. Statistics vary by source of the study on suicides and murders by people using guns. In the United States, firearm-related deaths reached 39,773 in 2017. About two-thirds of those deaths were suicides by gun. Compared to the rest of the world, Americans are twenty-five times more likely to be killed by guns than other parts of the world. Brazil leads the world in firearm-related deaths. As compared to several other Western nations in 2017, the percent of total homicides committed by people using guns was 73 percent in the United States, 38 percent in Canada, 13 percent in Australia, and 3 percent in England. While mass shootings currently account for 1 percent of gun deaths, urban violence accounts for the overwhelming majority of homicides, which opens the opportunity for targeted enforcement strategies because urban violence is frequently concentrated in small groups of people and city areas.[74] Unfortunately, it can be concluded that in the United States, access to guns by dangerous or deranged people is a significant factor in causing intentional early deaths and that we are among the most gun-violent nations on earth.

There are at least four root causes of firearm-related violence 1) guns in the hands of dangerous and mentally unstable people, 2) urban violence (gangs, drugs, crimes by desperate people, and others), 3) desperate, disenfranchised, disconnected people—predominantly young males, and 4) violence as a major theme in entertainment. And these social root causes are the root causes of an outsized economic impact. According to studies summarized at the Giffords Law Center, economists estimate that gun violence costs the American economy at least $229 billion every year, including $8.6 billion in direct expenses. The noneconomic cost impacts can be glimpsed through the understanding that each year, nearly fifteen hundred minors are killed by guns, and three million children are directly exposed to gun violence. Young children are most affected by gun homicides in the home—often related to domestic or family violence.[75]

What people in general think about guns can be characterized by public surveys[76] conducted in 2019 by the Gallup Poll, which provides a historical look back on some of the critical questions. In summary, eight to nine out of ten Americans are predominately in favor of background checks to purchase a gun, and the same number are in support of a red-flag process to disarm a gun user if deemed by due process to be dangerous. Roughly five to six out of ten are in favor of banning assault weapons and large magazines (more than ten rounds) for semiautomatic weapons. While a majority are unsure that mass shootings can be prevented entirely, many believe that more can be done to protect schools and public places. Many think we can impact the top seven factors that enable mass shootings by addressing:

1) Failures in mental health detection and monitoring,
2) The means to mass distribute extremist views,
3) Easy access to guns,
4) Inflammatory language of politicians and media,
5) Violence in movies and TV,
6) Drug addiction,
7) Insufficient security.

Liberals label this issue as "gun violence" and focus on guns, new laws, and bans on assault-type guns. In contrast, conservatives and gun advocates across all political factions might label their view of the issue as "weapon abuse" and focus on the individuals and call for enforcing the gun laws[77] already on the books. We may be able to say that some gun laws are ineffective, but we really cannot say there is inadequate legislation because at present there are at least ten major federal gun laws on the books that:.

1) Set age limits: eighteen for shotguns and rifles, twenty-one for all other guns (1968 Gun Control Act).
2) Prohibit (red-flag) a substantial list of people from owning or using guns (felons, fugitives, mentally ill patients, convicted drug users including marijuana, those with restraining orders, US citizenship renouncers, and others).
3) Require *most* gun manufacturers and sellers to be licensed by the Bureau of Alcohol, Tobacco, and Firearms(ATF) in the Department of Justice.
4) Require background checks using ATF Form 4773 conducted by licensed sellers.
5) Establish federal regulations on who can own guns and state regulations on licensing and permitting of where and how firearms may be carried.
6) Create the Gun Show Loophole, which is the most significant gap in regulation. It allows some sellers not to have to be licensed or be required to perform background checks.
7) Set taxation of weapons and ammunition purchases.

Moderates likely agree that modernization and harmonization of existing laws along with some new legal provisions are needed, despite the fact that there are reasonable gun laws in force. There are a few during the Bush (43) era that many would challenge today. An assessment of the laws in place measured against the current realities associated with the four root causes of violence, the potential for terrorism, and the mental state of some portion of our population, have reasonable people conclude some new legislation is needed.

While media characterize the public debate as gun violence and focus primarily on the availability of guns, and the need for new laws and gun bans, there has been little focus in media and entertainment on their own behavior. Media and Hollywood may be responsible for motivating and activating violence in some people. How the media report on violence and defects in law enforcement (policy, process, or personnel) seems to be a trigger for new social phenomena based on news event inspired political movement rioting and violence. The constant glorification of violence in movies, TV shows, and video games desensitizes viewers to violence. Moderates can easily believe that Hollywood's extensive use of graphic and disturbing video images cause or contribute to formation of cognitive disorders related to violence, dehumanization, desensitization, and hatred for some portion of our society. Consequently, the liberal political narrative about limiting guns and access to guns seems disingenuous with their blind spot for the impact of media and Hollywood. And the conservative narrative about limiting mentally deranged or dangerous individuals' access to guns without ensuring ways to identify them also seems disingenuous. Both are parts of the total debate, but the debate

and solution have to include changes in media, entertainment for
viewers, and processes of certifying second amendment fitness for
users. But for now in terms of political dialogue in America today, the
gun debate has boiled down to these two polarizing political positions.

Conservative View

Do you believe that the right to keep and bear guns is a natural
inalienable right of self-defense for the safety of yourself, your family,
and your community? Are you for few restrictions on ammunition and
guns? Do you believe it is the person using the gun who is the problem,
and it is someone else's job to figure out who the bad people are and
to stop the bad people before they do something bad with a gun? Do
you believe a legal gun owner should be able to carry a weapon in any
state by authority of interstate reciprocity laws? Do you oppose
depriving a person's right to keep and bear arms without due process
of law?

Extreme Conservative View

Do you believe that any law that addresses regulation or
limitations on gun owners is to be prevented? Do you believe that
lawsuits against gun manufacturers, serious or not, are to be
prohibited? Do you resist the establishment of federal registration and
licensing of law-abiding gun owners and ammunition? Do you believe
you have the right to use guns to revolt or resist the government?

Liberal View

Do you believe the guns are the problem? Are you in favor of
substantial control over which people can have guns and what guns
people can use, including outright bans on assault guns? Are you
against the passage of a federal interstate gun carry reciprocity law?
Liberals say they can respect the rights of responsible gun owners
while keeping communities safe. Do you favor expanding and
strengthening background checks and close dangerous loopholes in
our current laws? Do you support repeal of current law that provides
legal immunity protections for gun makers and sellers now enjoy? Do
you favor bans on weapons of war—such as assault weapons and large-
capacity ammunition magazines? Liberals resist conservatives' efforts
to make it harder for the Bureau of Alcohol, Tobacco, Firearms, and
Explosives to revoke federal licenses from law-breaking gun dealers
and ensure guns do not fall into the hands of terrorists, intimate
partner abusers, violent criminals, and those with severe mental
health issues.

Extreme Liberal View

Are you for the repeal of the Second Amendment?

Moderate View

Moderates defend the right of law-abiding citizens to keep and bear arms and are opposed to the repeal or evisceration of the Second Amendment. Moderates believe that bad people and automatic and semiautomatic guns can each potentially be a problem. Together they create the bigger problem of enabling mass shootings (four or more deaths by gun in a single event). Moderates believe necessary and proper regulations are appropriate to solve all three issues: 1) the dangerous person, 2) certain kinds of guns, and 3) guns in the hands of dangerous person(s). Consequently, moderates lean right, but we also lean left as well. A moderate will go much farther than a liberal or conservative to solve as many human violence phenomena as we can, which goes far beyond guns alone–that is to say address media, entertainment, video games, and others. Moderates would not support the de-resourcing demands associated with the 'Defund the Police' movement.

A moderate hopes Americans will find the will to work together to make a new America, where at a minimum, no children and as few adults as possible are killed by guns (accidentally or intentionally), especially at home and school, and there are no mass shootings anywhere. You may be a moderate if you can agree as a first step to realize that hope there should be reasonable regulations and laws that modernize and harmonize current state and federal laws:

Certify gun purchases, ownership, qualifications, and fitness (and recertification of personal fitness). Fully record all four transactions in a federal registry (which is currently prohibited by law), and regulate through a uniform set of federal/state laws on gun ownership and carry.[78] Administration should be at the federal level because the Second Amendment and organized militias are national-level rights and should be applied consistently across state borders for interstate reciprocity.

Identify and restrict potentially dangerous people (red and yellow flagging). People determined to be dangerous, convicted felons, or those treated for mental illness or addictions, are prohibited by current law and are red-flagged. Moderates would likely support yellow-flagging with restrictions, which would include those deemed mentally unstable, untrustworthy, or otherwise unqualified by the public record of irresponsibility or untrustworthiness. They would be yellow-flagged (requiring new law) meaning they would be restricted or prohibited from keeping and bearing any gun or certain kinds of guns (temporarily or permanently), until such time deemed safe and trustworthy, as determined by due process.

Establish Second Amendment due process (court system and administration). Moderates propose that due process be conducted in a newly legislated federal administration and circuit court specialized to Second Amendment and militia compliance matters. It would be sized and staffed to handle the volume of cases swiftly, perhaps designed to work with each state's local magistrate judges, judicial processes and facilities (author's idea). Upon due process and adjudication, if a person (gun owner or not) is deemed not to be law abiding or trustworthy with firearms or to be dangerous to others or to himself or herself, guns would be disallowed and removed temporarily or permanently, depending on 1) the expectation of endangerment 2) record of criminal, unstable, or untrustworthy behavior, or 3) level of dangerousness.

Regulate military-grade weaponry. A moderate would further likely agree with liberals that certain guns and ammunition that meet the criteria of "military-grade weaponry", should be regulated to the standards of the military/organized militia as to registering, housing, controlling, and bearing the weapon outside of one's property. (Assault weapons are but one part of a bigger question. See next proposal)

Regulate gun manufacturers more. A moderate would likely support federal scrutiny, regulations, and accountability on gun manufacturers and others as to what kinds of guns/weapons can be made for nonmilitary uses. Who knows what advanced weapons can be innovated that exceed handheld ready-aim-fire? Should smart guns, smart ammunition, or drones weaponized with guns be commercially allowed for private use? Imagine a smart gun/ammo capability that allows a weapon user to fire the weapon miles away from the target and is able to hit the target based on the GPS coordinates of a smartphone on the target—or a smart gun integrated into an off-the-shelf commercial drone that can be aimed and fired remotely. Both of those scenarios go well beyond the current debate of assault weapons, but the author would consider them all military-grade weaponry worthy of rigorous regulation and prohibition from commercial sale and private use. A moderate would likely agree manufacture of military-grade weaponry is subject to authorization by the Commander-in-Chief or the Congress.

Manage gun shows and private gun sales. Moderates would support that all industry participants be licensed and required to comply with uniform regulations and standards—close loopholes. A question moderates would either ask or listen to is, "Should gun shows be allowed at all?" If Americans want a uniform process for purchasing and transferring weapons, would it not be better for all weapons to be bought and sold through certified, licensed entities? We require all cars to be sold through a regulated process with a notary of the public engaged in personal sales to record the transactions for state-level records. For guns, moderates likely will favor state and federal registration of gun sales, private or public, using licensed gun retailers and notaries of the public to record the transaction.

Research into the root causes of violence and gun violence. Moderates would support more academic research and federally funded research to study root causes, triggers, and mental and physical disorders associated with violence in general and specifically gun-related violence on individuals, society, and international relations. Moderates would expect the scope of research to include the influence of all Mean Street industries' of addiction- and violence-related content and any negative effects associated with that content. A moderate might wonder if such research might reveal Hollywood is a key contributor to the level of violence in our nation.

Hold the entertainment industry accountable. A moderate will likely side with anyone in favor of scrutiny, regulation, and disincentives for entertainment industries' constant depictions of sex, drugs, gore, violence, guns, and gun deaths that desensitize people to violence or trigger unstable and dangerous people prone to violence (TV, movies, online videos, apps, and video games). More on this topic in chapter 10, "On Education."

Heighten law enforcement coverage and training for known dangerous areas. A moderate may support building targeted law enforcement and organized peacekeeping strategies for high-violence areas of a select group of urban centers where a disproportionate amount of gun violence occurs (e.g., Baltimore, Chicago, Detroit, St. Louis, others). Moderates would likely also support innovation of consistent, nation-wide programs and protocols for 1) Dangerous encounter training for America's law enforcement on use of de-escalation, mental health specialists, restraint, and weapon force. 2) New 911 supervisory protocol citizens can invoke for real-time audio and visual review and command over controversial situations by engaging a police supervisor in the 911 response chain.

Restrict people deemed dangerous. Moderates would likely advocate mental health laws and practices to yellow- and red-flag people who are either potentially dangerous or untrustworthy and to prohibit them from gun ownership using appropriate links to gun laws as needed. Design and application of mental health and second amendment due process law will have to be integrated and coordinated. This is one of the missing links in solving America's use of guns for violence by dangerous people issue.

Ensure children's safety. There is no federal law that requires gun owners to safely store their guns in their homes or cars, even if children are present. For our children, moderates likely agree government should establish uniform federal and state standards of security and protection for homes, vehicles, and schools.

1) *Home and vehicles.* Apply common-sense gun safety and federal requirements for storage of guns in lockboxes and safes for gun storage. Consider a new loaded weapon standard that requires that the

first one or two rounds of a loaded gun be a very low-charge blank in case it is accidently discharged by anyone –especially a child.

2) *Schools.* Provide security equal to that provided for government spaces, including armed security personnel as deemed appropriate but probably not armed teachers. Why? Unless guns in teachers' possession at school could only be fired by them, arming teachers unfortunately solves the issue for perpetrators of getting a gun into a school for those intent on causing harm. All the perpetrator has to do is coldcock the teacher and take the weapon. Keeping the identity of teachers carrying guns secret will be hard to do.

Perform background checks and standards of fitness. Moderates likely stand with liberals on the need for a process for initial purchase, but we probably go further than they do with respect to periodic online relicensing, repermitting, retesting, and rescreening of the mental fitness for gun owners/users. Online checks would be supplemented with deeper in-person screening and reevaluation of mental fitness for those who are yellow-flagged during the online process. By way of comparison, to ensure the fitness and safety of school bus drivers, state laws require school bus drivers, who carry a huge public safety responsibility, to retest, relicense, and recertify every four years. They must submit to random drug/alcohol testing on demand, and pass a medical exam every year. Moderates are easily convinced that gun sellers, buyers, and owners have a public safety responsibility too. Periodic physical exams are not needed, but like bus drivers, a periodic reexamination of a person's mental fitness for the Second Amendment right is a modest ask of people with public safety responsibility. Also, do we want people who stalk or test positive for drug use (including marijuana?) to be allowed to be gun owners or users? Or should they be limited in some way? I think some moderates would support drug and alcohol addiction testing and certification— at time of purchase and again at retest?[79] Do we want people with impaired self-control (drugs, anger, and personality disorders) to be owners of certain kinds of guns...or any guns?

Extreme Moderate View
Define Second Amendment call to duty. Finally, a moderate would ask, "What about all six statements in the Constitution regarding the institution of the militia and the Second Amendment's reliance on 'a well-regulated militia for the security of a free state'?" Does the Second Amendment mean the right to "keep and bear arms shall not be infringed" *despite a militia requirement* or *as part of a militia requirement*? What did James Madison, the author of the Second Amendment, mean? Madison probably meant both, and it is up to us to apply the dual meaning. The institution of the militia goes back before the founding of the United States. At the beginning of our nation, our founding fathers established the Militia Act of 1792

that obligated all able-bodied White men aged eighteen to forty-five into service if called. The Militia Act as revised and amend in 1903, 1956, 1958, and 1993 still in force today, established 1) an *organized militia* comprised of each state's National Guard, along with various federal reserve military units, and 2) an *unorganized militia* reserve of all other able-bodied people of certain ages. One option to harmonize and modernize laws might be to amend the Militia Act to obligate owners of military-grade weaponry to various regulations, including a mental fitness screening process and other requirements.

In conclusion, a moderate's view is straightforward. Law abiding citizens have the right to bear firearms in compliance with federal and state regulations. There should be federal or military regulations for military grade weapons and ammunition. Those who prove themselves dangerous deranged by act or by background check, or buy/sell weaponry illegally lose or have limited second amendment rights by a new, rapid adjudication process.

Moderate policy view strives to establish a solution that balances the competing demands of keeping guns out of dangerous, deranged hands while protecting the community, and without infringing unreasonably on law-abiding citizens' second amendment right.

If you believe the moderate proposals and views are more reasonable and constructive to address gun management and dangerous people's use of guns, you just might be a moderate. Where do you stand on guns? Are you a conservative, liberal, or moderate? If you label yourself a moderate on guns, give yourself one point on the self-assessment in chapter 13.

Chapter 9: On Immigration

We are a nation of immigrants, dedicated to the rule of law. That is our history—and it is our challenge to ourselves. It is literally a matter of who we are as a nation and who we become as a people. E Pluribus Unum. Out of many, one. One people. The American people.
—Barbara Jordan, Chairwoman, US Commission of Immigration
Reform, 1995

We disagree with those who would label efforts to control immigration as being inherently anti-immigration. Rather it is a right and a responsibility of a democratic society to manage immigration so that it serves the national interest.
—Barbara Jordan, late Congresswoman from Texas[80]

The quotes above from the late Congresswoman Barbara Jordan may capture the spirit of the view of a majority of moderates and perhaps many Americans as well. How much immigration is enough? How much is too much? America has been the most open and generous nation to immigration. America has accepted well over 80 million immigrants since its founding. The percent of foreign-born has run between 5 percent and 15 percent over the last 250 years. One of the major challenges America has faced is how to balance the needs, interests, and values of the native-born, the foreign-born, and immigrants from other lands seeking the opportunity America offers.

We are a nation of immigrants. Everyone's ancestors were immigrants at some point. In a broad sense, virtually all nations are nations of immigrants, with the possible exception of East Africans. It all depends how far back in human history one looks to see where ancestors originated. Evolutionary sciences hold that Homo sapiens (humans—us) evolved from hominids some three hundred thousand to two hundred thousand years ago and began migrating from Eastern Africa some seventy thousand to fifty thousand years ago. The current view is that by twenty-five thousand years ago, virtually every part of the planet was inhabited by small groups of humans except for parts of the South Pacific, New Zealand, and some other islands. Even in North America, Native Americans' forefathers were immigrants via Alaska from what is Russia today.

The movement of human groups has been a constant force throughout human history and a key theme in the story of humans since the time of hunter-gatherers. They migrated constantly for food. Historians estimate that it took about 2.5 square miles of land on average to sustain each person during that epoch.[81] As civilization evolved, crossing natural or territorial boundaries became more than searching for food. It involved the desire for new territory and new wealth. Wealth formation over much of human history has been about subjugating people, acquiring land, and taking things of value from others through force, through conflict.

The basis for modern migrations may involve food security. There are still nearly a billion food insecure people today. However, economic and spiritual imperatives push and pull most of today's immigrants. Migrants are *pushed* from their homeland for relief from population, war, poverty, disease, famine, oppression, or hatred—a horrible life. Some are *pulled* to new places in pursuit of work, tolerance, democracy—a better life. Migrants today are predominantly pulled to stable, modern countries searching for jobs, seeking freedom from physical and economic insecurity as well as striving for political and social freedom.

In the mid-nineteenth century, the difference of the GDP per person in the United States and the developing nations is estimated to have been about 50 percent higher for the United States. Today, with the US GDP per person per year of about \$57,000 (higher pre-coronavirus),[82] is over twenty times higher than the average GDP for impoverished developing nations. That is an extraordinary "pull" migration motivator. Consequently, the motivation to migrate is very high today, even if there is only one "push" factor—poverty or limited homeland economic opportunity. And to which countries will they be pulled? Population scientists say the four dominant "push/pull" migrations of the twentieth and twenty-first centuries are: 1) Latin America and South/Southeast/East Asia to North America (United States has 47 million foreign-born people as of 2019); 2) Mediterranean / North Africa to Europe (e.g., the UK has 8 million, and Germany has 12 million); 3) Central Asia to Russia (11 million); 4) the Middle East to the oil-rich Middle East states (e.g., Saudi Arabia has 10 million). Whether one believes that the "push-pull" dynamics today are different than previous mass world migrations, the stakes for the United States and other advanced societies are likely higher than previous waves because there are hundreds of millions of people around the world willing to migrate someplace else for a better life. Stakes are high because the cost to vet, assimilate, and provide our extensive safety net programs are high. The costs are being paid for with debt that future generations of Americans must cover or repay.

Here are a few examples of twentieth century mass displacement migrations of people seeking a better life. An estimated 60 million were displaced in the aftermath of World War II, with people moving to align with newly drawn borders of conquered and conquering nations. Since World War II, some of the mass migrations include: 1) the migration in 1947 India, as some 14 million people moved as India split into Muslim Pakistan and Hindi India; 2) war displacement migrations of about 10 million during the Bangladesh War of 1971; 3)

6.3 million in Afghanistan during the Russian invasion of 1979; and 4) 5.6 million exiting war-torn Syria from 2013 until now.

Today, immigration is a galvanizing and polarizing political issue. Why do so many Americans today feel so strongly politically about being an open society? Accommodating immigrant populations, globalization, and more closely integrating the peoples and economies of the world are essential priorities for liberals. In contrast, not being an overly open society and serving the current citizenry population first are key priorities for conservatives. Emotions ran high when the Irish immigrated in the mid-nineteenth century during the Potato Famine of 1845-1850 and when Southern Europeans immigrated at the turn of the twentieth century, when the percentage of foreign-born people in the United States was the highest—nearly 15 percent. Today, around 13.6 percent of the US population is foreign-born a substantial increase from a low of about 4.8 percent in the early 1970s.

Emotions are running high because large-scale influxes of new immigrants always create competition for jobs and resources. Typically, people at the lower ends of the economic and education scales are the ones who are affected the most. Social friction also arises from assimilation or integration[83] of new people into economic, cultural, and political life. While ordinary citizens have a general understanding of the impact either from some facts and figures, through media coverage, or experiencing the impact of immigrant populations in their own lives and communities, economists and academics have a factual foundation of the impact of immigration. In a nutshell, economists conclude that over several generations, the net effect of immigration on the receiving US economy is slightly positive for well-educated or professionally trained immigrants, but net negative on average for immigrants who have minimal education in the first generation and over time—more than minus $15,000 per immigrant. [84]

There are probably two reasons emotions run high making this a very prominent political and economic issue today:

Reason 1. Many Americans realize that the problems of the people from the emerging nations are massive and devastating. They are humans that need help. Liberals want American taxpayers to help. Both liberals and conservatives want to contribute some way, but conservatives believe the problems and costs associated with a significant foreign-born population will overwhelm our resources or further disadvantage our own already disadvantaged people. The coronavirus pandemic is current support for the conservative viewpoint, with some 40 million people unemployed as of May 2020—about one-quarter of the US workforce—and trillions, not billions, of new debt being booked that future generations of Americans will have to service and try to repay. Economists report that new immigrants typically impact low-income, low-education workers, low-skill/low-wage jobs the most, along with the previous wave of low-end immigrants. For example, the income of the middle to the top quintile of workers has increased substantially. The income of the lowest quintile of households, the bottom 20 percent of Americans households' share of the nation's income, has dropped from about 4.5 percent in 1975 to less than 3.5 percent in 2005[85] and is approaching 3.0 percent in 2019. Many low-income Americans have negative savings. In 1970 the United States had about 4.7 million foreign-born workers (6.2 percent of the US labor force). In the year 2000, it went over 20 million foreign-born workers (13.3 percent of the US labor force). About one-third of the 20 million did not graduate from a high school, about four times the rate for American-born workers.[86] According to the US Bureau of Labor's statistics, as of 2019 foreign-born workers in the US labor force accounted for about 17.4 percent. Over 20 percent of the foreign-born workforce has not completed high school, over five times the native-born labor force rate of 3.9percent.[87] Some studies and advocacy groups argue that foreign-born workers are essential to the US economy in the coming decades. Conservatives and moderates ask, "What about our young, underemployed, unemployed, and lightly disabled workers?" Should government policy primarily favor immigrant labor first rather than develop, support, and mobilize US-born potential workers first?

Reason 2. The size of whichever problem one is focused on anchors each of us to either of these perspectives: a) the size of their problem, or b) the size of our problem. Liberals feel they can't stand by and do nothing while many humans suffer and strive for a better life. Conservatives believe, as I believe moderates do as well, enabling/encouraging migration will unleash a tidal wave of mass migration that will overwhelm the United States. Some conservatives might say the global tidal wave has started. Consider just one aspect of immigration. According to a projection by the Pew Research Center, under current immigration trend assumptions, immigrants and their descendants are projected to account for 88 percent of US population growth through 2065! In addition to new arrivals, US births to immigrant parents will be the driver of future growth in the country's population. In 2017, the birthrate of immigrant women giving birth in the past year was higher (7.5 percent) than US-born women (5.8 percent). US-born women gave birth to more than 3 million children that year, and immigrant women gave birth to about 780,000.[88]

Here in the twenty-first century, where does any nation draw the line on immigration as *enough*? Here are the problems: 1) staggering numbers of people who are in distress and motivated to migrate, 2) better transportation options, 3) potentially not enough jobs for all those who want or need to work, and 4) the cost to and dislocation of US-born people to assimilate or integrate incoming immigrants. According to the United Nations, 1 percent of the world's population is displaced. There are about 4.2 million asylum seekers worldwide, around 26 million refugees, and an estimated 80 million forcibly displaced persons around the world today![89] There are about 800 to 900 million food insecure persons worldwide today and perhaps as many as 2 billion living on less than $4 a day. The number of adults and children potentially at risk of starvation during the coronavirus pandemic is rising. Would all or most immigrate to any advanced, modern nation if they could? That is the big question. Yet according to the UN High Commission on Refugees (UNHCR), most want to go home if they could make a living at home. In an international Gallup Poll summarized in the book *The Coming Job Wars*, by Jim Clifton of Gallup Poll, a persuasive global perspective on jobs is framed. At the time of that book's publication in 2011, with about 7 billion people on the planet, the poll concluded that approximately 3 billion people wanted a good-paying, steady job of at least thirty hours of work per week. Unfortunately, at that time, there were an estimated 1.3 billion such jobs worldwide—a shortfall of 1.7 billion jobs! Add to that, more people, more people living longer, the emergence of labor-eliminating capabilities from more automation, robots, artificial intelligence software and systems, and more outsourcing and offshoring. One is easily convinced that the shortfall only gets bigger when the rate of population growth, especially in developing nations, is factored in. Where would you draw the line once those motivated to migrate can make it to your nation's border? Are you willing to volunteer to sponsor an immigrant family? Are you willing to put your personal money in one of the buckets for immigrant sponsorship, assimilation, safety-net benefits, education, and health care?

Conservative View

Do you support legal immigration only? Conservatives, like liberals, believe the US immigration system is broken. Conservatives hold that fixing the immigration system is to set limits on entrants and to carefully vet those seeking legal entry and to exclude all who have entered illegally. Do you support English as the official language of the United States? Do you support preservation of heritage languages but favor a requirement for those seeking residency or citizenship to be able to speak English? Are you for substantial restrictions, including merit-based eligibility criteria to immigrate to the United States? Do you support universal use of the E-Verify employment system to verify the legal status of workers and the SAVE system to verify eligibility of applicants for federal benefits? Do you oppose the amnesty executive orders of President Obama? Are you for the construction of a wall on the southern border with Mexico? Do you support interests of workers of US citizenship over foreign nationals? Do you oppose nonfederal jurisdictions declaring themselves sanctuary cities and states for illegal immigrants? Do support restrictions and penalties on those cities that obstruct border control and immigration enforcement? Do you support tougher penalties on repeat illegal immigrant border crossings into the United States?

Liberal View

Do you support both legal and illegal immigrants? Are you for no or minimal restrictions on immigration of anyone from any part of the world to the United States (some form of open borders)? Liberals want to see remedies to enable as many as possible undocumented people living in the United States to get legal documentation and avoid deportation except for convicted criminals. Do you believe repairing immigration law to enable immigrants to stay here is the primary focus of fixing the broken immigration system? Do you oppose a southern border wall? Do you support sanctuary cities and states? Liberals are in favor of foreign nationals immigrating with visas and not through smugglers. Liberals, like conservatives, believe the US immigration system is broken. Liberals defend President Obama's Deferred Action for Childhood Arrivals and Deferred Action for Parents of Americans executive orders to help DREAMers, parents of citizens, and lawful permanent residents avoid deportation. Liberals want to help parents of DREAMers. Do you support efforts to make DREAMers eligible for driver's licenses and in-state college tuition? Are you in favor of culturally appropriate immigrant-integration services, expanding access to English-language education, and promoting naturalization for millions who are eligible for citizenship?

Moderate View

You may be a moderate if you are frustrated by both factions' answer to the issue. Moderates may lean either way, depending on individual differences. In general, they probably lean conservative because of the imperative to take care of US citizens first. A moderate will likely conclude that the potential for large migrations is materially different today than those mentioned above or possibly at any time prior in human history. It is possible to materially and detrimentally impact the economy and society of any receiving nation. Looking through a broad lens, a moderate perceives that immigration is the tip of a significant, complex global population-driven set of problems with deep historical roots and has significant sustainability implications for all nations. A moderate may be inclined to conclude that any political response to immigration requires a modernized and integrated solution of immigration laws, humanitarian aid, and population, foreign, and global sustainability policy actions. The US Congress is only now in 2021 starting to address immigration. Unfortunately, strategic reform appears that it will lack wide bipartisan support that the American people seek.

The liberal view seems to be "let as many in as can make it to our border." The conservative view is that if the liberal view prevails, then the result will dilute our standard of living and destabilize our nation further, which many Americans perceive as already fragile. Moderates likely agree with conservatives that the sum of these immigration issues, along with our internal issues, makes us vulnerable—especially now in 2020, with the pandemic driving the economic recession, wealth destruction, national deficit, and debt at extremes. Impacts of automation and technology on jobs, family disintegration, and growing political instability, a large population living with addictions or in poverty, or both further exacerbate America's risks. Consequently, a moderate likely favor the following:

More border protection. A partial southern border wall as makes sense, and deployment of personnel, sensing and surveillance technology to leverage US border security as appropriate.

Legislate new immigration law. Craft new law based on policy that reflects twenty-first century realities with limits on the number of new people per year and balances merit-based and non-merit-based (family chain, asylum, legal alien, etc.). In pure moderate form, the US could start with a compromise policy of a 50-50 split between merit and non-merit-based quotas against a reasonable annual maximum immigration number. Merit-based entry would be based on a point system of positive factors: profession, job skills in demand, education level, English speaking, wealth, etc. Nonmerit entry would be based on current, traditional UN–US refugee policy and application practices—perhaps enhanced with a requirement for adults have a verified High School diploma at a minimum.

Improve humanitarian care. Find ways to improve the safety, welfare, and humanitarian treatment of those who make it to our borders, especially children, but innovate ways to vet intent and discourage migration before seekers begin their migration for those who will be ineligible for acceptance based on new immigration policy and law. By not modernizing our policies and laws, the US Congress and courts are the ones that cause inhumane treatment because it is an issue of numbers—the numbers of adults and children to be processed, cared for, and adjudicated in due process are massive.

Start private sponsorship. Since the creation of the federal Refugee Resettlement Program by the Refugee Act of 1980, about three million refugees have been resettled in the United States—more than any other country.[90] Moderates might embrace new ideas like some/all non-merit-based immigration be allowed entry only within a voluntary sponsorship program where individual American households of adequate means put their money and homes where their mouths and beliefs are by becoming volunteer sponsors for immigrant families. The sponsor would be responsible for funding and ensuring financial assistance during social and economic assimilation. Today resettlement sponsorship and support for asylum seekers is provided by a handful of religious and civic nonprofits working under contract to the federal government. Without their commitment and networks, the asylum program would be even lower than it is at present.[91] Moderates would not support unrestricted or unregulated entry of asylum seekers, refugees, immigrants, or temporary workers.

Address root causes of migration. Moderates also would call for policy provisions tied to laws that address the root causes of non-merit-based migration (population, poverty, disease, starvation, war, and human rights).

Stop repeat illegal immigrants. Those who enter the United States illegally repeatedly, especially those with criminal records, should be subject to more severe penalties on repeated entry.

Allow regulated temporary workers. However, if the immigration challenge can be put under control, moderates likely would support a well-regulated temporary worker permit system for select industries and occupations. With additional industries and occupations added when jobs are plentiful, and our disadvantaged are substantially participating in the labor force.

Support DREAMers (DACA). Moderates likely support a particular path for people currently categorized as DREAMers (DACA) to permanent resident status and possibly citizenship. Moderates likely agree with conservatives on 'no path to citizenship' and no special/equal rights and no voting rights, or benefits for illegal aliens. Moderates like conservatives would likely support deportation or incarceration of illegal aliens who are convicted of felony crimes.

Prevent all people who are not verifiable US citizens from voting. Moderates likely support a redesign and modernization of policy, practices, and systems used for federal and state election processes to ensure 100 percent reliable voter eligibility, vote casting, and accurate ballot counting for US citizens only. Every eligible and legal US citizen can vote, but Americans are owed the confidence that 1) no one else can vote by mail, in person, or any other way 2) no vote can be counterfeited or corrupted.

Stop state/city immigrant sanctuary. Moderates are probably mixed with some portion not supporting the policy of sanctuary states, cities, churches, or anything sanctuary. The Supreme Court has ruled federal law is supreme over state law in immigration enforcement.[92] States and local governments have a constitutional obligation to support national efforts to protect our borders.

Balance foreign- and native-born US population. In closing, moderates are the kind of Americans who will ask tough policy questions. Here's one. "What ought the maximum percent of foreign-born to be in any given decade?" What answer would a conservative give? What answer would a liberal say? Would anyone respond zero percent? Would anyone say 50 percent? Imagine any nation if 50 percent of the inhabitants were first generation or temporary residents or workers? Can you imagine if America was 50 percent foreign-born with everyone recognized as citizens, entitled with the rights, privileges, and benefits of the nation—including voting rights? What would the chemistry and fabric of the nation be?

How do we determine what is *enough*? Given that the supply of displaced people willing to migrate is far in excess of many nations' ability to absorb the estimated 80 million to many 100s of million willing immigrants, how ought the US set a policy goal? What factors could inform such a policy? Should there be a "formula" that caps the total number of people allowed in until the ratio of foreign-born to native-born people is stabilized at some policy target? If such a method were used what target might liberals or conservatives set?

This moderate would be inclined to set a cap lower than the current 13.9 percent. Why? All of the following US economic metrics would lead a moderate to be conservative for the foreseeable future. The high levels of US pandemic unemployment, under-employment, and structural unemployment along with the high level of the US federal debt and deficit, the high level of small business destruction, the low level of US labor participation rate, the rising trend toward a labor-lite digital economy all indicate the US should increase opportunity for native-born citizens first. If a policy formula were used, here are several factors that come to mind for this moderate that would lower the percent portion of the foreign-born population below the current number of 13.9 percent. 1) The higher US debt to GDP ratio is over xx percent (e.g., 50-60 percent?), or 2) the higher the US-born unemployment rate is over x percent (e.g., 6-7 percent?), or 3) the lower the US-born workforce participation rate is under xx percent (e.g., 65 percent?). Are there others? Should America set a foreign-born target of the midpoint of 10 percent between our historic high of 15 percent and low of 5 percent? What would your criteria be if it were your call? There are no easy answers only hard choices and tough calls. World population of 7.8 billion headed to over 10 billion in the coming decades makes it so.

If you believe that some or all of the moderates' views on immigration are more reasonable and constructive than either the conservative or liberal positions, you might be a moderate. Where do you stand on immigration? Are you a conservative, liberal, or moderate? If you label yourself a moderate on immigration, give yourself one point on the self-assessment in chapter 13.

Chapter 10: On Education

The current set of decisions we have made...have produced a [social] mobility engine that functions incredibly well for a small number of people and poorly for many others. The ones that benefit the most from the system tend to be wealthy and talented and well connected. The ones who benefit least tend to be from families that are deprived or isolated or fractured or all three.[93]
—Paul Tough, *The Years That Matter Most*

American education as a political issue and policy question is quite large and challenging. The moderate assessment starts with a point of view that a nation cannot compete successfully or expect to grow in a globalized digital economy without a healthy and highly educated workforce. A central pillar for improving US economic growth in the twenty-first century has to include education and development of the productive potential of the people of our nation. Consequently, policies that lead to greater educational attainment and better workforce outcomes for as many people as possible is a American imperative for moderates.

While striving to excel in education is common sense for most of us, new insights from studies like "Measuring Human Capital..."[94] make many of us sit straight up! That study concludes that the United States' global rank on education and health care since 1990 has dropped dramatically in the world, from sixth place to twenty-seventh out of 195 countries studied. That finding is at odds with the conventional wisdom that both US education and health care are considered the best in the world. Unfortunately, they both hold first place in terms of the price Americans pay. We get lower results than twenty-six other nations but spend a lot more money—*less for more*. What are the political issues driving the "less for more" narrative for US education?

The Politics of Education
From this moderate's vantage point, here are five key political drivers that are fueling the decline in education. Each is an American imperative for a moderate.

Rights. *The politics of denying, ignoring, and gaming the rights of children.* For decades America has operated under an assumption that material poverty could be cured by government fiat redistribution of money, schools, and jobs, that it is simply a matter of money and resources. It is clearer now that remedies for material poverty do not readily address social drivers of poverty. Attention to children's rights is also require. Moderates likely see education not only as an *expense* like conservatives do or as an *entitlement* like liberals do but also as an *investment* in each new citizen based on each new person's fundamental rights authorized by the US Constitution and the UN Treaty on Human Rights. Moderates are likely to believe education is a right of each new person to own their innate human gifts granted to them by nature. Also, education is explicitly or implicitly protected or obligated in eight of the thirty rights prescribed in the UN Treaty on Human Rights and a number of rights prescribed in the UN Treaty on the Rights of the Child.[95]

Therefore, the development of any innate talents of a new person—be they cognitive or physical—proscribes obligations on adults to avoid harmful behaviors starting before birth and nurture positive development and education actions continuing until a child attains adulthood. As a civil right, Americans are obligated to provide equal access to a quality and safe education for children of all colors, by a moderate's notion of fairness. However, moderates would hold that the obligation is not a blank-check entitlement like liberals demand for students or parents to impose on the taxpayer or their peers. Unfortunately, how education is provided in the United States is very much constrained by legacy issues and attitudes imposed on those in a weak position (by race, income, and sex) by those in a strong position (by intellectual, financial, and political wealth) who are able to set the agenda and outcomes for our society. To achieve equity, enable better outcomes, and address discrimination in all of its expressions, many moderates start with the force of rights and stand with those who call for a transformation in American education institutions and policies to undo the negatives and unleash the positives.

Money. *The politics of crowding out and unfair distribution of education funding for our young, the underemployed, and the unemployed.* Rebalancing and reprioritizing how federal, state, and local tax funds are allocated for education and training are American imperatives for moderates. Moderates likely will support enabling more investment in children's futures. Moderates say, "Stop over spending and under investing on education." For example, federal policy underinvests in adult literacy and workforce development, with programs only reaching about one-tenth of the target community of thirty million adults. Spending for K–12 public education as a local/state government responsibility has made public education structurally uneven, unfair, and discriminatory. Across the states, spending is subject to the wealth and economic strength of one school district versus another. Moreover, the current predominant political focus on "inputs" to education (buildings, teachers' salaries, vouchers, etc.) distracts policy from fully addressing key root-cause success factors. Conservatives believe vouchers and school choice are the solution but that creates competition for the quality schools and teachers leaving behind many students because there aren't enough 'quality seats' for all children to receive a quality education that way. Liberals believe free schools and community college are the answer but their approach has deficits as well because poor students are likely to be less ready and able to learn even if free and/or high quality education are provided. Bottom line is America needs to fix the schools and some significant portion of its students. Moderates likely believe America should spend and invest the amount of money needed to get the United States into the top ten nations internationally, as measured on international comparative education performance studies. To achieve top ten standing, US education money needs to be 1) taxed, 2) sourced, 3) spent, and 4) invested differently. Moderates would insist all four be done efficiently. The question about how much the federal government should be involved in education is a vigorous debate between conservatives and liberals. Moderates would advocate for a different balance between federal and state contributions. Notwithstanding the political debate, the size of federal entitlement programs and chronic overspending creates a "crowding-out effect" for education at the national level. As a nation, the uneven spending on education and overspending on current adult generation's interests "crowds out" future generations needs in a way that a moderate would agree is systemic institutional age and race discrimination.

People. *The politics of prioritizing our nation's people first.* Maximizing the value and untapped potential of our citizens first, especially our children, is an American imperative for moderates. Moderates say, "Stop underutilizing, discriminating, divesting, and dis-investing America's workforce through the various strategies and policies currently in practice." For example, are US policies contributing to our young people (perhaps males more than females at present) becoming less responsible, less productive? Are the effects of drugs and cognitive addictions, distractions, discrimination, disengagement, and disenfranchisement added to any early life learning deficits and disadvantages a person may have a drag on the US economy? This moderate poses the following question: "Would the net economic driving power and participation rate of the US productive population be higher if our youth and workforce were better educated, higher skilled, and less burdened with addictions and distractions?" My answer to that question is yes.

Skills.[96] *The politics of investing in people for productive participation in the economy and society.* Workforce investment to respond to changes in the world economy is an American imperative for moderates. Growing reliance on digital technology makes human capital increasingly crucial for future economic growth. The United States is experiencing a sizable skill gap. Today, it is estimated that 68 percent of jobs require credentials beyond a high school diploma. Roughly speaking, 15 percent of the US workforce is high performing, and about 50 percent performs at or below basic proficiency levels with thirty to forty million performing at the lowest level according to studies conducted by the Institute of Education Sciences. There has also been a marked decrease in workforce investment by the private sector, which has successfully transferred the cost of job training to students and employees over the past several decades. It is quite disappointing that the public sector has not come up with effective policy responses for that.[97] A 2018 report of the World Economic Forum concludes that 54 percent of jobs require reskilling ranging from two months of additional training to over one year of training. The report indicates that employers will likely invest in key jobs and high-performing employees but not in the employees most in need of training. And well over half the employer investment goes to high-performing workers with four-year college degrees. While 53 percent of jobs are middle-skill jobs, just 43 percent of workers are trained to that level. That report illustrates statistical discrimination and racism by a moderate's assessment because the lower half of the workforce has more people of color. Today, four-year degreed people are more Asian, White, and female. According to the National Skills Coalition,[98] an organization working to develop policy solutions for workforce development, over half of the jobs in the United States require training beyond high school but do not require a four-year degree, so not everyone has to go to college to get a decent job. How should America close gaps like these? Those who are studying the skill gap phenomenon believe employers have to be incented to step up to train both current, new, and future workforce entrants. Additionally, for new workforce entrants, preparation for workforce participation and skills training needs to be designed into secondary and postsecondary education.

Mobility. *The politics of incenting people to pursue the American Dream in the twenty-first century.* Of the one hundred million or so eligible voters who do not vote, there appears to be a sizable portion of Americans who are disenfranchised and disengaged from America's productive economy and society. To foster economic growth, prosperity, and participation, reigniting America's economic opportunity and social mobility engines are American imperatives for moderates. How should the United States prepare and reward people to participate in and to produce economically productive results? How should we reward working harder and smarter? The United States has experienced a marked decline in mobility and educational attainment over the past thirty years. Going to college and the decisions made by and about a person in their teens to twenties played prominently in how mobility worked through most of the twentieth century. A college degree used to be a ticket for upward social mobility. Now it is becoming more of a hedge against downward mobility for many. Here in the twenty-first century, prospects for economic opportunity, social mobility, and individual freedom can be positively or negatively impacted at different times in a person's pre-adult years. I argue impacts can occur any time from 1) preconception to prekindergarten (age minus one to five); 2) kindergarten to high school (K–12, ages six to seventeen; and 3) mid-teens to the early twenties.

James Heckman, an economist at the University of Chicago who has studied the economic impact of early childhood development,[99] has found that about 50 percent of the variation of one's earnings potential is determined between birth and eighteen. That means that as much as 50 percent is impacted by an individual's educational choices and actions as an adult. Consequently, investments in pre-K and adult education and the presence of a *lifelong learner attitude* impact individual economic opportunity and social mobility. They are positive root-cause drivers moderates want to improve.

Foundations of US Education

Public education. When looking through the long lens of history, we can see how far America has come since the nineteenth century in both public and higher education as enablers of economic security and social mobility. Leaders like Horace Mann, who in 1837 Massachusetts advanced the idea of the "common school" with universal enrollment, compulsory attendance, and public funding, and philosopher John Dewey, who proclaimed that the purpose of education is to prepare young people for democratic citizenship, illustrate the vision America developed for education. Unfortunately, the history of public education is also a story of discrimination with 1) the separate and unequal education for children of color by the Black Codes in the South and the *Plessy v. Ferguson* "separate but equal" Supreme Court case of 1896,[100] and 2) the education inequity for the poor of all colors across America from the nineteenth century to the present day.

Total US spending on public education was about 1 percent of GDP in 1900 and expanded after the WWII GI Bill of 1944 and Russia's launch of Sputnik in 1957. Sputnik became a defining moment in the United States, with education elevated to a national priority during the Kennedy administration in the early 1960s. After the passage of the Elementary and Secondary School Act in 1965 during President Johnson's administration, spending kept growing to an average of about 5.5 percent of GDP[101] from the 1980s to 2020. A 1983 report during the Reagan administration, *A Nation at Risk*, emphasized the importance of education to the nation's security, and doing education poorly amounted to educational disarmament. It made nearly forty recommendations to reverse America's eroding excellence achieved in education in the 1950s to 1970s. As an update to the Johnson era Education Act of 1965, the 2001 No Child Left Behind Act under President George Bush (43) established a Common

Core curriculum that included federal standards of what a student should know by year. That, along with the divisive debates over school choice/vouchers, more spending, more free education, and more mainstreaming children with special needs, defined the twenty-first century political landscape on public education under Presidents Bush, Obama, and Trump.

In addition to the political issues listed above, school consolidation has been an ongoing theme during most of the last century. The trend of consolidating small schools reduced the number of public schools from approximately 248,000 in 1930 to about 86,000 in 1980. Due to population growth and changes in format from junior/senior high school to middle/high school, the number of public schools has increased from 1980 to 98,000 today. There are over 32,000 private schools.

In 1900, fewer than 17 million students attended public school. By 1970, the population increased to over 51 million, and in 2020, over 56 million (50.8 million attend public school, and about 5.7 million attend private). The percentage of seventeen-year-olds who graduated high school was 6 percent in 1900, nearly 60 percent in 1950, and has increased to over 82 percent in 2017. Also, over time, the high school dropout rate has decreased from over 27 percent in 1960 to about 6 percent[102] by 2016 and continues to decrease. Moderates would want to see the dropout rate get as close as possible to zero percent.[103]

While America is getting some broad benefits from our investment in K–12 public education, it costs American taxpayers a lot, as will be discussed shortly, and it is not equitably distributed with wide variance in spending across some 13,600 school districts in fifty states and four territories. It is evident over the past thirty years at a time when inclusion, equity, and equality are prominent social and political goals that America is failing to provide educational equity for many of America's children under both liberal and conservative control. Fewer benefits and results are accruing from the way the money is being spent, and more children are being left behind, especially males, children of color, children of the poor, and children in poorly educated adult households. Is the decline all the fault of education system policies, practices, and people? Or are there other forces dragging on education?

Higher education. With Harvard College established in 1636 recognized as the first higher education institution in America, the number colleges grew to about two hundred by the mid-nineteenth century. Passage of the Morrill Act in 1862 obligated every state to have a public university for liberal and practical arts. With that and the growing emphasis on education in the second half of the nineteenth century, the number of colleges and universities has continued to grow to over three thousand four-year and about sixteen hundred two-year degree-granting institutions today.[104]

College enrollment has grown from 8.5 million in 1970 to a peak of 21 million in 2011 (about 5.7 percent of the total US population) and now is in decline since 2011 to under 20 million in 2017. In the 1960s, about 60 percent of all college students were male, and about 40 percent were female, up significantly from the first half of the twentieth century when females represented about one-third of undergraduates. Today, females are over 57 percent of undergraduate college students and males are 43 percent. The ratio of males and females has virtually reversed in under half a century. Males are now the minority. The reversal raises the question, "Is higher education actively discriminating against males? Or are males no longer interested in the benefits of a college education—higher-paying jobs and careers, credentialed professions, and being the primary providers for their families?" If it is the latter, what has changed societally that has males less interested in education than females?

As of 2020, America's higher education landscape looks like this. Over 35 percent of Americans have at least a four-year college degree, the highest ever, according to the US Census Bureau. The portion of people over age twenty-five with less than a high school diploma is about 10 percent. College enrollment is about 70 percent of those finishing high school, but the graduation rate in six years or under at four-year schools is just under 60 percent. The graduation rate in three years for two-year schools is about 30 percent but would be similar to four-year schools except that the graduation rate for public two-year schools is only about 20 percent. The graduation rate for Black students is a tragic 20 percent. Females graduate at a higher rate than males consistently. Comparing undergraduate degrees awarded to females in 1930 when they received 30 percent, female undergraduate degrees hit 50 percent in 1980 and has stayed above 57 percent since 2000. According to the US Census Bureau, over 13 percent of US adults have advanced degrees today. Doctoral degrees are almost 180,000 up from under 10,000 in 1960. Master's degrees are about 820,000 in 2016 up from 205,000 in 1970.

In graduate education, the portion of master's and doctorate degrees awarded to international students is quite high. According to the National Science Foundation, in 2015, international students earned 35 percent of science and engineering master's degrees, up from 26 percent in 2000. Their degrees were heavily concentrated in computer sciences, economics, mathematics, engineering, and statistics, where they received about half or more of all master's degrees awarded in 2015.[105] Within engineering, students on temporary visas earned 70 percent of the master's degrees awarded in electrical engineering and more than half of the master's degrees in chemical and materials engineering.[106] At a time when STEM[107] education is so crucial to US economic growth and social mobility, the opportunity of getting an advanced degree for high-paying jobs seems to favor non-US-born students. Why is that? Are there government policies that promote that phenomenon? Or is there systemic discrimination occurring in those institutions of higher learning for financial or political reasons?

Participation and degree rates are not the only aspects of higher education that have risen. Costs have also increased—dramatically. Costs of public colleges grew from $43 billion in 1980 to $365 billion in 2016. Private nonprofit colleges grew from $22 billion in 1980 to $242 billion in 2016. Money granted by the federal government has also increased. Pell Grants awarded to needy students have increased from maximum grants of $450 to over $5,800 per student in 2016. Pell Grants expanded under President Clinton, about doubled during the Bush administration, and tripled during Obama (from $12 billion to over $36 billion) and now are in decline, under $30 billion, during the Trump administration.

Current Landscape of US Education

Public education today. We turn our attention now to the current era for elementary and secondary education. America sees education now less as an investment and more as an expense that is out of control and unfair. For the year 2016, US public education spent $706 billion, or $13,847 per student. Consider that in 2020, for public education, New York has the highest per-pupil spending of all of the fifty states at $23,091 per pupil, about 90 percent above the national average of $13,440.[108] Utah has the lowest per-pupil spending at $7,179 per student.[109] Are the children of Utah and New York getting equitable education? Using the Annie E. Casey Foundation KidsCount 2019 Data Book state by state education well-being rankings, Utah ranked thirteenth, and New York ranked seventeenth.[110] Seems backward? Why isn't New York first or at least in the top five?

The United States has dropped to thirty-eighth place out of seventy-one countries studied for math scores and twenty-fourth place for science as of 2020, according to the Pew Research Center,[111] despite strong spending on education inputs. The United States has doubled the average money spent per student nationwide for public K–12 education over the past several decades.[112] Additionally, there has been an increase in instructional and support staff, from 4.2 million in 1980 to 6.4 million (3.6 million teachers). As of 2016 the public school student-to-teacher ratio has improved from 22:1 to 16:1 (private schools have gone from 10:1 to 12:1). With this perspective in full view, it is hard for a moderate to believe that all American public education needs is more money and more people as liberals would conclude. Moderates would agree new money is needed to invest in pre-K, expanded adult education, twenty-first century support services, and schools that are crumbling and inadequately resourced. But what other factors are driving the decline in education that money isn't fixing? The answer begins with basic skills in reading, math, and science and continues to an important list of social factors.

Today, some thirty two million adults read at about a third-grade level. One in six adults lacks basic reading skills, and one in three lacks basic numeracy skills. Many of those adults are people of color. Adult basic-skills inadequacy is what it is, because the skills are not being adequately learned in childhood. As one measure of early childhood learning, the percent of eighth graders at or above reading proficiency rose from 29 percent in 1992 to 36 percent in 2017. For fourth graders, the percentage of students at or above reading proficiency rose from 29 percent in 1992 to 37 percent in 2017, with females consistently outperforming males by five percentage points or better. By ethnicity, Asian children performed better than children of all other colors. Students of Asian and Caucasian descent performed two to three times better than Latino, African, or Native American populations. The bottom line is that even at 37 percent performance at grade level, American education is under-delivering for about two-thirds of our children and about four-fifths for children of color. Moderates see children and adults not reading adequately as one of the root causes of the decline in the effectiveness of public education. Lack of basic literacy and numeracy is contributing to the decline of America's strength and vitality.

Also reflecting education's decline is the performance of our students preparing for higher education. Using the average SAT math score, here is a comparison of cohorts over time. Since 1972, when the average SAT math score was 530, the SAT math score has declined to the low 500s and 490s through the 1970s, '80s, '90s, poked above 510 in 1997, and ranged from 520 to 510 after 1997; in 2016 it dropped below 510. The SATs were redesigned in 2016, and now math scores are back to 530, about where they were in 1972. Is the recent improvement real or is the test designed now to make scores come out higher without reflecting any real improvement in our students?

Finally, how do American students stack up with other nations' students? There are two tests given periodically to an international consortium of nations that can be used to provide some comparison.

1)   TIMSS (Trends in Mathematical Studies) administered internationally across seventy countries. In the 2015 administration, East Asian countries dominated. Singapore, Hong Kong SAR, Korea, Chinese Taipei, and Japan continue to outperform all participating countries in mathematics at the fourth and eighth grades, maintaining a twenty-year edge. The US was ranked fourteenth in 2015.[113]

2)   PISA (Program for International Student Assessment), in which Singapore shows best, and Hong Kong, Canada, Japan consistently ranked in the top ten. Other strong performing nations include northern European nations. The most recent PISA results,

from 2015, placed the United States an unimpressive thirty-eighth out of seventy-one countries in math and twenty-fourth in science.[114] Will the US standing improve with the 2020 administration of both TIMSS and PISA tests? The pandemic may negatively impact scores not only in the US but in other nations, as schools have been closed or online during the pandemic.

Higher education today. American education is a story of seeking the American Dream of economic opportunity, social mobility, and personal freedom. It is also a story of stratification, discrimination, and broken dreams. The following points from Paul Tough's *The Years That Matter Most* highlight the risky passage in a student's teen years, recounting a study by Raj Chetty, economist at Harvard University. His study came up with four insights about higher education and mobility in America that are quite telling.

1) The chances of becoming rich later in life are tied to the acceptance selectivity of colleges. Students of ultra-selective institutions (Harvard, Stanford, etc.) are much more likely to be rich as adults—one in five. Chances for those who attend "good name" colleges —one in eleven; community college— one in three hundred; and for those with no college—one in one thousand. Quite striking. Even the value of an undergraduate degree declines for those starting from lower-income households.[115]

2) Life outcomes for rich and poor kids at "high-name colleges" are similar.

3) Poor kids attending ultra-selective colleges increase their odds of making it into the top income quintile by a factor of fourteen, even better than rich kids (a factor of four). The poor kids attending ultra-selective schools are typically from the privileged poor group— those who attended private high school but are poor. The rest are the ones who attended public high school and are poor.

4) Rich kids and poor kids do not attend the same schools. Over two-thirds of students at ultra-selective colleges grow up rich, and only about 4 percent grow up poor. Systemic socioeconomic discrimination is quite pronounced at high-selectivity schools, despite their claims of inclusivity. Less-well-off high-performing students self-select themselves from going to high-name colleges for various reasons: money, family, self-doubt, distance, location.

With college enrollment declining from 2011 to 2020 and the cost to attend college continuing to rise, the question has to be asked: "Is College worth it?" The answer is, "Maybe. It depends." In the current model, it depends on who you are, who your parents are, where you go, what you take, how you do, how you apply yourself, and how much debt you take on. It also depends on whether all the above happens in an economic area of the country, or the world, where there are good jobs with better than a living wage. So is college worth it? It still can be even if all the above are not present in a student's life if one has learned "grit" early in life and applies oneself to 1) become a passionate and persevering lifelong learner (more knowledgeable, adaptable, resilient, able to self-learn new things), 2) learn to think in more abstract, critical, complex, and reflective ways, 3) learn to use principled moral reasoning, and 4) develop new cognitive and vocational skills and credentials useful to earn a good living. Like twenty-first century Wall Street investing, American higher education is becoming more like a casino bet. Odds favor the house at all three: the casino, Wall Street, and the college. They win, whether the consumer comes out ahead or not. It is a roll of the dice today. Moderates want to de-rig the house advantages of at least higher education and Wall Street.

Why Is US Education in Decline? Two Sets of Root Causes
What has gone wrong in American education this past half century, and particularly since about 1990 to 2020? Can America do anything to undo the damage and discrimination done to America's children of all colors? According to research, it is not as easy to just blame all the decline on education and educators. But politically, liberals and conservatives have used the education system and teachers as scapegoats for changes occurring in other areas of America. We will see that some education system policies and teachers are key solution levers, but other factors are the bigger issues.

Here are some of the "other factors" that have become root causes of change—some positive and most negative. The other factors span both the context and content of the education process: progressive political activism, court decisions, legislation, pop and online culture, single-parent households, computer-based learning, twenty-first century job skill gaps, Silicon Valley technology driven heavy digital consumption and addictions, institutional education reforms, more deadly addictive drugs, school shootings, discrimination, and more. According to Dr. Alexander Wiseman of Lehigh University, all these changes can be discussed within two sets of factors impacting education success for a child: school factors and non-school factors.

1) School factors. These include anything that can be manipulated to improve how schools work to produce learning success. They cover how learning takes place at school—things like teacher competence and credentials, resources, funding, buildings, classrooms, curricula, technology, and school discipline.

2) Non-school factors (Social factors). These include everything in the environment outside school grounds that can impact a student's ability, willingness, and readiness-to-learn in school. This category includes community, culture, crime, religion, politics, economic inequality, sleep and diet, family (incomes, relationships), parent education level, and parenting skills and style. Drugs, alcohol, abuse, violence, or neglect in the household, among others, can also severely limit a student's ability, willingness, and readiness-to-learn.

There are two crucial findings in Dr. Wiseman's research. First, no one solution will fit everywhere. Each country requires a process to align school and non-school factors that will be the most successful education system in the context of each nation's economic, social, and political setting. For example, what works in Finland or Singapore may not work as well in the United States. Second, social factors (non-school) trump school factors when predicting education success for each student. For example, a bright child of poor parents or attending a poor performing school has a higher probability of underperforming than a bright child of well-educated parents attending a good school.

Contrary to conventional wisdom, teaching is not the key indicator of successful education for a student. The key indicator of education success is student readiness-to-learn. And a measure that precedes readiness-to-learn is ability-to-learn. While teaching indicators of success are related to school factors, learning-related indicators of success are related to non-school factors impacting readiness-to-learn. Here are two lists of factors inhibiting children's readiness-to-learn at school. The first list is five factors that are estimated by the Educational Testing Service to explain 90 percent of the difference in a student's school performance. They all have to do with life at home: 1) number of days absent from school, 2) hours watching screen devices (TV, etc.), 3) number of pages read by the student for homework, 4) number and quality of books at home, and 5) presence of two parents in the home.[116] There is a second list of factors further disadvantaging a student's ability or readiness-to-learn: if they 1) live in unstable families or poor living conditions, 2) have inadequate/unhealthy food, 3) are victims of sexual, physical, psychological, or racial abuse, or 4) endure the presence of alcoholism, drugs, gangs, bullying, domestic violence, and criminal behaviors. Children enduring any negative experience from either list will not do as well as children from stable households or safe communities. They are not as ready to learn. According to various studies, the socio-economic status of a student's family is the single dominant factor defining readiness for learning and education success. Key fact: Students from stable communities or affluent families consistently outperform students from unstable or low-income families and communities.

Consequently, the social context of a child's formative years matters a lot on impacting their ability and readiness-to-learn, both in school and outside of school. Bottom line: No matter how much money, blame, political and judicial activism, and social engineering liberals and conservatives throw at education, research is concluding that school reform does not ensure educational success, nor does it reform society. The reality is that many issues negatively impacting a child's education success come from the family, community, culture, entertainment, politics, screen devices (TV, etc.) and pop culture. Insights on non-school factors help target where to focus politically to attack root causes for real solutions. For moderates, fixing America's education system and outcomes requires a significant transformation to not only improve schools but as importantly, children's lives.

1) Schools. Reform systemic policy design flaws. Neutralize color and affluence discrimination biases. Normalize inputs for elementary, secondary, and higher education institutions across the nation starting with funding. Re-architect education system inputs, processes, and outputs. Integrate preparation for work life in curriculum. Expand focus on pre-K, teen, and adult literacy. Expand skill development and job-training programs significantly. Hold teachers and administers more accountable and incent performance.

2) Children's lives. Enable children and their parents to be better prepared to achieve learning success. Nurture positive, growth minded, lifelong learners. Provide competency programs from preconception to early life for parents and from birth through childhood for children. Reduce all forms of addiction. Innovate investment to seed brighter futures. Hold parents responsible for their competency to support their children's education and hold industry and political cost causers accountable for negative externalities imposed on children, families, taxpayers, and society.

Conservative View
According to the Republican 2016 platform, Conservatives argue that education is not a federal role required by the Constitution, and since 1965 America has spent over two trillion dollars across one hundred federally sponsored programs that have not yielded much progress for America's students. Their philosophy as quoted here is:

> Much more than schooling. It is the whole range of activities by which families and communities transmit to a younger generation, not just knowledge and skills, but ethical and behavioral norms and traditions. It is the handing over of a cultural identity. That is why American education has, for the last several decades, been the focus of constant controversy, as centralizing forces from outside the family and community have sought to remake education in order to remake America. They have done immense damage. [117]

Like conservatives, do you believe in this quote directly from the Republican 2016 platform?

More money alone does not necessarily equal better performance. After years of trial and error, we know the policies and methods that have actually made a difference in student advancement: Choice in education; building on the basics; STEM subjects and phonics; career and technical education; ending social promotions; merit pay for good teachers; classroom discipline; parental involvement; and strong leadership by principals, superintendents, and locally elected school boards. Because technology has become an essential tool of learning, it must be a key element in our efforts to provide every child equal access and opportunity. We strongly encourage instruction in American history and civics by using the original documents of our founding fathers.[118]

Are you for establishment of high-standards, parent-driven school choice for education renewal? Are you for holding down how much taxpayer money is used to fund public education? Conservatives are for the use of school vouchers to allow parents to select and pay for public or private schools of their choice for their children using public funds. Conservatives do not support a national common core curriculum and disagree with "teaching to the test." Conservatives do not see the individual as "human capital" and hold that tenure in education should be replaced with merit-based employment.

Liberal View
According to the 2016 Democratic platform, liberals stand for quality and affordable education and that money ought not to be a barrier at any level of education:

Democrats are committed to making good public schools available to every child, no matter what zip code they live in, and at last making debt-free college a reality for all Americans.[119]

Are you for parents' rights to opt out of standardized testing, rebalancing curriculum so testing informs but does not drive classroom instruction? Are you for expanding after-school, summer, and mentoring programs, especially for students from low-income households? Liberals are for universal preschool programs and good schools for every child and ending what they refer to as the school-to-prison pipeline. For higher education, liberals are for free tuition at public colleges for working families, free community colleges, debt-free college, and relief from current college debt. They are for cracking down on for-profit-college predatory practices, subsidizing historically black colleges and minority-serving institutions, and pushing more colleges and universities to take measurable steps in increasing the percentages of racial and ethnic minorities, and low-income and first-generation students they enroll and graduate.

Moderate View

You may be a moderate if you are frustrated by both factions' broad views on education. Both platforms make some sense on parts of the overall narrative, but neither adequately address the needs of twenty-first century education in America. The negative numbers and outcomes confirm that conclusion. You may be a moderate if you believe that education is one of the cornerstones of civil democracy that enables the development and inclusion of all people into America's economy and society with fairness and equality of opportunity. Consequently, it must be a strategic American imperative like health care.

Moderates are likely persuaded that enabling economic opportunity, social mobility, and personal freedom should start before birth and continue through adult life for each US citizen. You are a moderate if you believe that, other than having good parents or at least being protected from early life trauma, indignity, and discrimination, an excellent education provides each person the best chance to benefit from their innate human potential. It is a person's self-made chance to pursue a productive, prosperous, and purposeful life. It improves the chances a person can participate in civil society responsibly and peacefully and compete successfully in the global economy. Moderates see value in improving education and parenting institutions to improve young citizens' chances and prospects in adult life. Doing so improves societal outcomes for all citizens—a safer and more equitable society, a stronger economy, better economic equality—and diminishes institutional racism and discrimination. Less federal and state spending would be required for safety-net and criminal justice costs because fewer citizens would require negative outcome services. While moderates see education similar to conservatives and liberals on some points, the moderate view of fixing issues at root cause has us looking at education policy very differently than both factions.

Moderates' solution proposal is for a twenty-first century Education Transformation Initiative of innovative policies for pre-K, K–12, postsecondary vocational education, higher education, adult literacy, and job training. In the following section, a partial list of root cause issues and solutions is presented to:

- Improve school factors for 1) public education 2) higher education.

- Improve children's lives addressing non-school factors that impact student learning success and public and higher education preparation.

- Two sets of proposals are presented in chapter 12 in sections entitled 1) Children First: Twenty-first century New Deal 2) Labor Markets: Twenty-first century Jobs and Skills.

Moderate's Proposals for Education Transformation

Improve School Factors Proposal-Part 1

Address public education. The current $700 billion-plus K–12 public education industry is struggling to find solid footing in the twenty-first century to enable education equity and provide a curriculum that delivers the strong foundation all children need to be successful adults. Here are a group of moderate transformational proposals for issues in K–12 public education.

Change taxation, funding, and spending for public education. Funding inequity exists in education systemically across America as funding is set state by state, district by district, public versus private. Currently, the federal government provides less than 10 percent of elementary and secondary education funding, the states provide nearly half, and local government property taxes provide the rest. Dependence on property tax as the core funding method ensures inequity. New taxing and funding approaches are needed to ensure education inputs are more equitably distributed for the benefit of all US-educated children across all states and territories. Moderates' ambition for new approaches is to enable the United States to be in the top ten nations consistently on comparative worldwide education performance rankings. The cost of education is currently dependent on the local economy and the regional cultural and political priority adults put on children's education. In a moderate's eyes, the funding of pre-K, elementary, and secondary education must be significantly re-architected to address education equity and productivity.

Here is a proposal to correct flawed funding. The moderate idea is a new taxation formula based on a combination of federal, state, and local tax sources in different proportions than the current 10-50-40 proportions. The proportions of each of the three levels could be 1) one-third each, or 2) some other proportion that is rational...but whatever it is, it must even out rich and poor states, counties, and districts so that the amount of money spent and the learning opportunities and outcomes per student per district are more equitable for all essential courses and services. If richer districts want to spend more on sports, stadiums, auditoriums, and such, that would be fine but not reading, writing, and arithmetic to say it the 'old way'.

Federal level. The federal contribution for core academic programs would be based on the nations' total wealth and income with a portion allocated to each state based on the number of children to be taught in the state (public and private school). Funding to cover cost of additional new support services (e.g., mental health, drug/

dysfunctional family intervention, etc.) would include revenue sources from dedicated taxes on cost-causing (rent-seeking) industries (Mean Street industries and other). There would be no additional taxes on households to address the expanded 'in-school' support services. These business fees/taxes would be added to compensate the nation and taxpayer for the negative social costs imposed by commercial interests as well as dis-incent education productivity drags, learning distractions, and negative social behaviors those industries create and promote. Also, a general business tax contribution for education would be "on the table" to cover the cost of defining, integrating, and delivering workforce development skills and competency curricula and programs.

State level. 1) Continue use of the current taxation practice in each state with some additional funds for K–12 and vocational education coming from any state-run lottery and recreational drug revenues. The lottery revenue contribution for children's education would be based on the portion of in-state seniors (over sixty-five) to junior citizens (under age nineteen). A portion of lottery revenue is then assured for children's needs, not just the state's senior citizens. 2) Establish a new standardized state funding formula. According to the Education Commission for the States, each state has its own formula for computing how much money the state allocates to fund education in its school districts. Across the fifty states, there are some ten different allocation methods for their formulas (e.g., foundation, weighted, base, block, and census). Basically, their allocation methods are all over the map. A moderate idea would be to modernize and standardize the state methods through federal law under the theme of "all children grow positive" in place of "no child left behind." Presently, many children are not only being left behind but are constrained to move forward, despite existing federal and state education laws.

Local level. Taxation would continue to be based on property value or income or combination as any state prefers, but the goal would be to reduce how much money comes from property tax to pay for education because property taxes are dependent on the economics of an individual municipal area. Property value reflects the wealth of property owners in a school district during their working years. It unduly burdens retired households. One goal of lowering the property tax contribution for education is to reduce the burden on senior citizens so they can remain in their homes longer as they choose. Perhaps the local tax contribution to education could be reduced by at least one-quarter, one-third, or one half?

Improve education inputs (efficiency, effectiveness, and productivity). To reverse America's current "less for more" education result and to ensure the United States "gets more for less," new policies and approaches are needed to lower the cost, increase the value, and improve equitable distribution of the inputs for K–12 education. Inputs include buildings, teachers, classrooms, curriculum (e.g., books, learning aids), computers, transportation, learning support, other services, and more. Here are two example proposals for the education transformation initiative.

Standardize education assets. It is time to modernize– to build much better and safer schools–and to do so at as an efficient cost as possible. Reducing cost starts with standardizing assets and processes as practical to get a better bang for America's education money invested. Here is just one idea for school districts to hold down cost and time to build new schools. Rather than every school district building new schools as a custom project, can US education policy enable state-of-the-art, highly standardized prefab modular-classroom and building-design options that enable faster, lower-cost construction of the classroom and laboratory areas of the school? The standardized national approach would deliver state-of-the-art computer, communications, networking, security, health safety, comfort, fire-proof, and in-class and online learning aids for schools so the children in aging schools and rural and poor school districts can learn safely in new, state-of-the-art schools.

Improve student readiness-to-learn with new coping services. Today, teen and tween students' day-to-day lives are more stressful, with digital and physical distractions and potential mental health risks. Diminished students' readiness-to-learn calls for a rethink of how we help our young have better mental health and focus during their formative years. The growing level of dysfunctional families, progressive activism to change how young people grow up, cyberbullying, suicides, drug use/addiction, and mental and social disorders our young face, all call for the need for excellent in-school coping support services to disintermediate abnormal or development-limiting situations. As part of a comprehensive education trans-formation initiative, it is time to have available services like testing, medical, mental health, character development, and vocational development in addition to security, special education, fitness, food, counseling, drug, and dysfunctional family intervention.

Improve development, accountability, and selection. American education is leaving more children behind, locked in lower levels of academic achievement. The coronavirus pandemic is exacerbating that state of affairs. Part of that is due to social factors, but some of it is due to the state of the US teaching profession. As pointed out earlier, American students' comparative performance results (TIMSS, PISA) on average and in sum have not benefited from doubling the money spent on inputs per student, smaller class sizes (from over 22 to around 16), nor higher teacher credentials or salaries. According to the Nation's Report Card as administered by NAEP,[120] between 2003 and 2019, the nation made gains in both mathematics and reading at the fourth-grade level and mathematics at the eighth-grade level. The nation made no gain in reading at the eighth grade. However, most of the gains occurred between 2003 and 2009 under the Bush administration. From 2010 to 2019, mostly during the Obama administration, there was a significant divergence between the highest- and lowest-achieving students. Education policy must incent and hold teachers accountable for education success in their training and classrooms. Here are two illustrative moderate proposals.

Rethink teacher selection, development, and certification. While the vast majority of America's K–12 teachers and administrators are fully qualified and committed to teach America's children, it is a hard fact that many of America's children are not getting an adequate education. The growing divergence in learning for high-achieving and low-achieving children is quite troubling. As US education is modernized, changing and/or increasing teacher qualifications and credentials have to be on the table too. Most of America's public school teachers have undergraduate and master's degrees in education. There are limited requirements for subject-matter credentials for those teaching at the secondary level or technical specialties. Should the United States model our credentialing system after those nations that rate in the top ten? At a minimum, should America's education schools' curricula include best practices from the countries that are showing excellent results from their teachers? Finland is an example of those nations that establish high academic and subject-matter requirements for their teaching profession. Should America's teaching profession requirements be redesigned so prospective teachers are more subject-matter capable? For example, rather than have teachers major in education as an undergraduate, have them major in one or more subject-matter specializations (math, science, chemistry, etc.) and minor in education, followed by a master's of education degree or certificate that teaches them how to teach. Or if the current bachelor's degree in education approach continues, require a master's in the discipline that they will be teaching.

Expand teacher performance accountability. Some education experts recommend benchmarking teacher performance for comparative evaluation with a portion of their pay based on performance (say 10 to 20 percent). They recommend performance accountability reviews using various teacher value-add, student performance, and outcomes-based metrics. Also, hold teachers and administrators accountable to stop "teaching to the test," promoting at-academic-risk students, and other student harming practices.

Expand skill development. To close the skill gap, America must craft national policy that builds and matches skills needed to fill twenty-first century jobs with US workers and citizens. I believe the policy root causes of the skill gap are: 1) inadequate and ineffective preparation of our nation's youth for workforce participation and jobs,

2) inadequate obligations on or incentives for employers to train or help prepare the US workforce, 3) ineffective policy to right-size and align the US workforce to technology, economics, and population changes, and 4) no national policy to address commercial and social behaviors that distract or demotivate our youth from developing marketable skills. Here are two moderate proposals.

Address youth preparedness for workforce participation. One key issue associated with the US skill gap is that there are students (whether they are disadvantaged, disengaged, or immature) who come out of high school—and all too often, out of college—not knowing what they want to do or what they are qualified or skilled to do. Nor do they have a good awareness of what opportunities and jobs there are. US education has to do a better job of getting our young people prepared for employment. If processes are provided before young people get to workforce age to help them discover what they are good at, what they are interested in, and what jobs are available that are a good fit for them, America can help them shape a direction and focus on their livelihood faster and more accurately. Consequently, US education and workforce development policies should be linked by adding aptitude, vocational awareness, and skill development along with academic achievement curriculum content. The program could start as early as middle school and continue through college and vocational schooling so that youth are better prepared and aligned with the current and future skills and jobs employers need. Moderates would be easily convinced that America needs to broaden workforce development focus as part of our education systems and institutions.

Address low employer participation in national workforce training and development. Over the past two to three decades, the business sector has successfully pushed the responsibility and cost to be trained for existing jobs to students, applicants, and third parties (e.g., for-profit schools). While students and job seekers should be responsible for some of their skill development costs, the specialized skills needed for various job specialties should be shared with employers, as they know exactly what skills are needed and are in a good position to help design the training curriculum. US workforce development policy should pursue a comprehensive approach to close America's skill gap by integrating skill and vocation development into secondary education and expanding the public and private investment in skill training programs in postsecondary and higher education. See the chapter 12 section "Labor Markets: 21st-Century Jobs and Skills" for more ideas and proposals.

Improve School Factors Proposal-Part 2
Address higher education. The current $650 billion-plus higher education industry seems to have not only abandoned its primary mission of educational excellence but also has ballooned costs and

made a fine art of subtle but powerful systemic discrimination based on race, income, and testing skill. The reliance on admissions criteria that discriminate against broad segments of our youth and mission-scope creep from universities to "multiversities"[121] are just two from a long list of criticisms laid at their door. Since the 1970s, leadership and policy changes at many colleges and universities have resulted, not only in a reversal of the ratio of females to males accepted, but also, priorities that trade off education performance for political interests. They have prioritized ahead of students, policies that promote revenue, tenured faculty, an unhealthy reliance on part-time and graduate assistant teaching, an overemphasis of research, oversized bureaucracies and sports programs, alumni giving,[122] and "multiversity" scope creep. Multiversity scope-creep reflects the addition of any number of missions, programs, institutes, think tanks, ventures, causes, and medical schools under an institution's oversight and cost structure—diluting focus and increasing costs. Here is a list of the actionable issues in higher education that are driving price, quality, and outcomes in the wrong direction from a moderate's perspective.

Require alternative college admissions criteria to remove socioeconomic discrimination. (From the Admissions Industrial Complex.[123]) At least two systemic practices are keeping low-income students, especially of color, from being accepted at many colleges:

1) The need for tuition revenue for the college provides an edge for those who can pay full price. A significant number of low-income students are denied access to "high-name" schools because the schools optimize who is accepted on several criteria. The colleges need prospects who can pay enough tuition to balance the school's budget—certainly a real and pragmatic concern.

2) The reliance on standardized tests for comparison and the unbreakable relationship of test scores and household income. Higher-income households achieve higher SAT/ACT scores (e.g., for a $200,000 household, there is a one in five chance a student scores over 1400 on SAT. For a $20,000 household, there is a one in fifty chance a student scores over 1400.[124] In place of test scores, imagine an admissions process that relied on the academic achievement record based on grades, character trait assessments, and other ways to assess and compare students' motivation and likelihood of academic success. Or imagine a national anti-systemic discrimination admissions policy that requires higher education institutions to have a substantial portion of their students come from US lower-income quintile households by national policy? Should Congress enact anti-socioeconomic discrimination policy requiring the top quarter to half of all four-year-degree schools to select a larger portion of their

students from US households from the bottom two to four income quintiles of the US income distribution?

Lower tuition cost of an undergraduate degree. The cost of tuition, room, and board, and the amount of time it takes to earn a degree are financial factors limiting students seeking economic opportunity and social mobility. The moderate view is that American taxpayers could subsidize some portion of tuitions in some situations but completely tuition-free schools with the student having no skin in the game is a bad idea. Before national policy is used to pay, America's higher education institutions should be pressed to reduce the cost and price of at least an undergraduate degree using national policy that inhibits higher education's penchant for overspending and ability to pass those costs onto undergraduate students and their families in the tuition rate and fees. According to the College Board, between 1988 and 2018, the costs of tuition per semester has risen two and three times: from $17,010 to $35,830 for private nonprofit colleges and from $3,360 to $10,230 for public colleges. Costs of higher education are rising for many reasons, including the cost of amenities, research, sports, tenured faculty, large administration budgets, highly paid coaches, and presidents.

Reduce/prorate cost of oversized administrative bureaucracies in tuition. From 1976 to 2007, the ratio of administrators to students doubled from thirty-two per one thousand students to sixty-three per one thousand. That labor expansion reflects some of the costs of becoming a multiversity. Too many administrators and special programs impact the cost of college if they are factored into tuition. Are all the additional jobs needed? Are they supporting core academic missions, or are they supporting brand, prestige, political agendas, or dynasty competitive advantage of the institution? If the costs are not supporting core missions, the costs should be prorated or excluded in the tuition.

Reduce/prorate cost of competitive sports programs in tuition. There are about eighteen thousand teams across more than one thousand colleges. Roughly a half million of twenty million students play. Half of the coaches are paid over a quarter of a million dollars per year. That is around double what professors are paid on average. Colleges are cutting low revenue generating sports during the pandemic but some of those sports programs feed America's national, international, and Olympic athletes so addressing cost of sports is a double edged sword.

Reduce/prorate fully loaded cost of full-time faculty. Improve teaching. Replace tenure. Unbundle some research. College instruction is a five-tier teaching caste system: 1) full and associate professors, 2) assistant professors, 3) instructors and lecturers, 4) part-time adjunct teachers, and 5) teaching assistants (TAs). Tiers 3 to 5 are the contingent teaching force. Much of the undergraduate teaching and broad student engagement is relegated to tiers 3 to 5. In 1975, 43 percent of higher education teachers were classified as contingent, and now over 48 percent are contingent of the 1.45 million categorized as instructional as of 2018.[125] Many tier 5 teachers (TAs) are foreign-born and lack strong English language skills, making it very hard for students to learn from people they cannot understand. The use of contingent faculty for teaching students may contribute some to colleges' dropout rates. Imagine administrators and department heads accountable for instruction quality assurance. Also, professors and associate professors (tier 1) and assistant professors (tier 2) are the only faculty eligible to be granted full tenure at schools that use tenure. Tenure is a career-long commitment to an academician by the institution. The only profession that has a better deal than tenured faculty are judges. Tenured faculty get full pay until they retire, during sabbaticals, and possibly during research periods. It is a major element in the budgets of many higher institutions. The percentage of faculty with tenure has declined since 1993–94 from 56 to 46 percent[126] but only because the number of higher education institutions has increased due to the emergence of for-profit colleges, which typically do not use tenure.

Reduce cost of first-year undergraduate degree courses. Earning an undergraduate degree usually requires taking a number of survey courses in the first year of college. Why should students pay full tuition rate for courses that have many students—frequently hundreds—in the class—that are taught by contingent teachers (lecturer, adjunct, or TA)? Considering that many students are vulnerable to second-guess their course and degree choices in their freshman and sophomore years and are likely borrowing money to just start college, a moderate would be inclined to bully pulpit higher education to lower the cost of first-year courses to reduce the impact in case a student drops out or realizes the initial direction they chose is not the direction they should take going forward.

Reduce time to undergraduate degree completion. An undergraduate degree typically requires completion of 120 to 128 credits or semester hours with a set number of credits of specific set of courses relevant to the general degree and to the specific major.[127] Most bachelor's degree programs will require a minimum of four years of full-time study—longer for part-time study. Imagine getting a higher-quality and more marketable degree on time or in less time and hopefully at a lower total cost when a student has a clear goal and is highly motivated? Some schools are experimenting with faster time-to-completion options.

Improve undergraduate degree completion rate. At a 60 percent on-time graduation rate, the United States is twelfth in graduation rates worldwide. South Korea is first, at about 65 percent. Most undergraduate degree programs require four years of full-time study.

America's students are exceeding the two- and four-year standard time to graduate for a list of reasons including dropping or failing courses, changing majors, or attending part time. Consequently, the costs and time consumed to get an undergraduate degree are higher for many who are challenged to complete a degree on time. One way to assist students in completing an undergraduate degree closer to on time is with better design of core course content to reduce the number of additional courses needed as prerequisites when students change their minds or change their majors. Colleges should reimagine and redesign their survey and major core courses to help reduce the number of additional courses needed when students change majors. US higher education should strive to increase graduation rates toward 70 percent or higher from the current 60 percent graduation rate.

Decrease dropout rate. One additional way to help students and their families is to press higher education institutions to work aggressively to decrease dropout rates. Dropouts are a root cause in the explosion in student loan debt. It is indirect discrimination and it disadvantages students of lower socioeconomic status. They are more likely to drop out or fail to graduate on time. Schools should be pressed to provide more individualized learning and course support services for the "hard" courses to enhance students' ability to succeed and graduate on time. Also, consider ways to hold colleges accountable for dropout rates and graduation rates. Finally, explore other ways to reduce cost and improve earning power, value, and marketability of an undergraduate degree.

Student debt and financing college. Over four out of five full-time undergraduate students receive financial assistance (grants, loans, work study, or aid). The vast majority of the assistance comes from federal and other non-school sources. As of 2020, student debt is about $1.5 trillion—an astounding amount. High interest rates and no forgiveness repayment contract provisions for many education loans are troubling financial industry practices. There also is no accountability on the educational institution with respect to the marketability of any particular degree or assurance that the student's earning power of the degree/credentials will be adequate to repay their education loans. For example, in 2012, the for-profit college industry was educating 12 percent of college students but was the root cause of 44 percent of the student debt defaults at that time. For-profit colleges have been all about selling the prospect of skills to get a job as a promise, not a result. Here are two illustrative moderate proposals.

Update federal Pell Grant program criteria to limit the use of Pell Grants only to pay towards degrees/courses that have demonstrated marketability. Also, authorize use of Pell Grants for reputable vocational and skill development programs.

Reduce cost of borrowing and total debt. Restructure private and public education lending programs so that maximum interest rates that can be charged for student loans are capped at a low interest rate, say 3 to 4 percent, regardless of whether competitive rates are substantially higher. This approach reflects the reality that spending on students' vocational and higher education must be a strategic, long-term human capital investment by them and society. Disallow any loan instruments that charge higher rates. Perhaps require lending institutions to provide a set portion or number of loans to students without regard to race or other criteria at a low rate as part of their regulatory obligation as an authorized lending institution. They should be investing in America(ns) too.

Improve Children's Lives Proposal-Part 1.
Address parents' and students' readiness for learning.
While there has been considerable public controversy and political debate over whether America's educators are getting the job done, America needs to face the fact that there are too many students and parents who aren't getting the job done. Many students are not ready to learn, and some number of parents are not ready or able to do an adequate job of preparing their children to be curious and motivated learners. America's education and social policies have to address the non-school factors that under develop or disable natural learning interest and curiosity. Due to the many reasons discussed previously, children from families that are poor, broken, or under duress are more likely to underperform academically, even if they are in an affluent school system. Also, students from households where stimulation by entertainment drowns out stimulation from curiosity and learning are likely to be less learning ready. Are there policies that can improve learning readiness for children from low socioeconomic households and poorly educated parents? Moderates say yes.

Invest in children. The United States has increased the cost of raising and educating a child to dramatic levels over the past three decades. Though the United States currently provides a number of methods for families to invest and save for education, the methods are primarily used by affluent, better-educated households. Over one-half of households with children do not use any savings vehicles for their children—no cash, savings bonds, CDs, or accounts.[128] Beyond the financial realities for parents about the cost of raising children, Americans do not believe societally that we ought to invest in others' children or children of low socioeconomic standing individually. America's unwillingness to invest in its children as a class of citizens reflects a national attitude, one that has negative consequences that largely deprive education options and opportunity to children of color, children of all colors from poor communities, or parents with low educational attainment. Moderates likely see changing America's attitude on this one aspect of life a policy opportunity to structurally improve economic equality and advantage over time. Here are two ideas: 1) implement a national investment program, and 2) change America's attitude about children. Moderates challenge Americans to be personally responsible to change these five antichildren attitudinal root causes for America's blind spot on children:

1) *Cultural*. A deep-seated attitude that children are more like a property of the parents/guardians instead of a responsibility of the biological parents first but also for all adults *and* society.

2) *Social*. Discrimination of children of color and low socio-economic status. Poor parents and educators silently infer to a child that a good education is not available for them or going to make a difference in its life. The child loses hope and stops trying.

3) *Political*. Misaligned and adversarial factional and sectional visions for the education of America's youth. Aggressive adults and various special and commercial interests want to make children believers of their ideology with idea placement in children's formative years. These players want to replicate the success achieved by the tobacco industry that hooked smokers in the twentieth century as young as they could with product placement in entertainment. America must constrain such advocates.

4) *Economic*. The economic root cause is poor people don't have the money or discipline to set aside money for education. They may not believe they can afford an education or accept the responsibility for paying for their child's education.

5) *Financial*. There are national funding policy flaws. The current policy is "Schools are the states' job, not the federal government's job." Moderates hold both must share the job in a new and different ratio for social justice, equity, and national economic interests.

Moderates do not believe all education should be self-pay, as extreme conservatives hold, or free, as extreme liberals hold. Each family and individual should have "skin in the game" to motivate the individual to apply themselves and appreciate the opportunity. However, there has to be an American imperative to fix the nation's attitude on the two national funding policy flaws on 1) better education equity and 2) funding each child's future for success.

The moderate idea is to offset the high cost of education and the low socioeconomic starting point for children born to poor or minority parents with investment programs that enable the nation to join along with parents, family, states, employers, and students to "group-save" for a child's teen/young adult education expenses. The moderate proposal expands use of the 529 account method to "group-fund" a child's education starting before or at birth. The chapter 12 section "Children First: Twenty-first century New Deal" has more detail.

Improve students' abilities—preparedness for learning. There are many reasons any student may not be prepared to commit the time and effort to excel at learning at any level. Some are due to self-inflicted poor self-regulation, lack of self-discipline, immaturity, distractions, addictions, insecurity, character flaws, low self-esteem, and plain old youthful laziness. Others are from the limits of a student's innate learning capabilities like cognitive weaknesses, attention deficit disorder, and autism. Others are imposed by deficits in parents' relational and educational competencies, any of which can limit a child's interest in learning. Examples of relational deficits in a child's life are the parents' character or the absence of any stable adult or a stable male role during adolescence[129] or the inability of the parent to teach their children positive character traits, basic literacy, or self-regulation. One finding in early childhood development research is that children who can internalize self-control and self-regulation early and well are more likely to be more successful later in life. Designing national policies that improve children's preparedness in early childhood, K–12, and beyond is on the table for moderates.

In addition to good preparation in early childhood, policies and services are needed for both high school and college that enable and empower preparedness-challenged students to succeed. Policies designed to foster better opportunities and eliminate systemic discriminatory employment practices are necessary but still not enough. Policy must also require youth to be prepared to qualify for the good-paying jobs, like jobs in engineering, computers, and the sciences—no entitlements. They have to be willing and prepared to take the "hard courses" like calculus or chemistry. If a college does not provide its students support services to succeed in the hard courses, many students do not take the tough courses that lead to higher achievement/more marketable degrees. Today, some schools pursue a "steer and avoid" strategy.[130] Counselors steer the students perceived as unable to handle the hard courses away from those courses to avoid the risk of failure or dropping a course. A moderate solution would incent or require higher education institutions to provide "support and teach" student services instead of "steer and avoid" advice.

Improve parents' abilities—preparedness as parents. Students of affluent families on average are better prepared for education at all levels, according to researchers. Because of either their good parents or good homes or good schools, these students are able and ready to learn. Since socioeconomic status of the household in which a child is raised is the key factor in determining the likelihood of any student's educational success, there are a number of family and home conditions that moderates would put on the table as politically addressable. The two main issues impacting student readiness-to-learn are beyond the reach of reforming US education: 1) the absence of one or both biological parents in the student's formative years, and 2) the income, wealth, health, and education levels of the adult(s) present in the household. A moderate would address those two factors in national family and economic policy.

There are at least five parenting competencies that research is finding that impact a child's readiness and preparedness for learning that could be addressed through public education policy. Parent(s) or guardian(s) by nature or by training them to teach these five competencies as positive childhood experiences improve a young person's abilities and readiness for education at all levels. Positive character skills starting in early childhood may be among the best set of personal skills young children can acquire that have lifelong positive payoffs. Imagine a public policy that formalizes a national parenting skill development program for prospective and current parents available online or in class. It could include information on health, care, diet, medical, addiction avoidance, current known best practices, critical success factors, and highlight current state-of-the-art "what-to," "what-not-to," and "how-to" content. At a minimum it would include these *five positive parental competencies (5Ps)*:[131]

1) Positive character development (how to give your child a growth mindset)

2) Positive parenting style (how to be authoritative, not authoritarian)

3) Parents' literacy (to ensure a child learns basic literacy early in life)

4) Positive presence in your children's lives

5) Positive conversing (children who hear and speak more words early in life do better)

Moderates likely see political value in fighting to create policy linkage between quality parenting, childhood development, and children's civil rights as one way to lessen or eliminate trauma, disadvantage, and discrimination against a child of any color due to parents' lower economic and educational standing.

Improve Children's Lives Proposal-Part 2.

Address student learning culture. Reduce and regulate commercial distractions and substitutions for learning. In 1970 people had radio, TV, and movies for non-reading leisure activities. Today people have so many more options. The rapid adoption by the United States and many nations of the internet, Mean Street, and Silicon Valley products and services is a seismic social change. We have become an addicted "screen society." Screens are now large parts of the way people of all ages live their lives and spend their time. Screen products so dominate the digitalization of our economy, virtualization of our society, and the acculturation of our children that the term *digital life* is now part of our vocabulary. Digital life is becoming a substitute for physical life for some—including a concerning portion of our young people. Moderates are incline to believe the amount of screen time in young lives is excessive by design.

For moderates solving root causes and holding rent-seekers accountable for the harmful effects of content generated by "screen society" producers is an American imperative. Systemic Mean Street "digital-practices" that condition consumer attention and interest also generate a lot of collateral damage on young digital consumers. There appears to be a growing body of research finding that they can desensitize, depress, demotivate, discriminate, disengage, distract, and possibly disable some portion of US children from applying themselves to academic and cognitive-based learning. Given Mean Street's domination of America's screen society in recent decades and the coincident decline in academic performance of US children, the answer has to be yes. We are learning that a digital consumer and a digital learner are two different things. The enormous amount of cognitive and emotive stimulation from fast-paced, digitally altered or enhanced content delivered at subliminal and near-liminal speed may be creating addicted digital consumers by rewiring our elastic brains[132]—especially young, developing brains. The question of whether or not application and content producers intentionally suppress curiosity and cognitive-based learning using entertainment-delivered social- and emotive-based learning capability for their commercial interests is of political interest to moderates. The question should be of interest to our science and defense communities too. Anything that harms or arrests the natural learning abilities of our children should be a national concern.

How should our society manage and mitigate the direct and indirect negative social costs and consequences of Mean Street practices? I would not be surprised if moderates broadly support substantial regulation on Mean Street behavior to control their pervasive and invasive impact on digital life. Moderates likely will support that Mean Street and Silicon Valley industries should pay their fair share of taxes *and* also cover some portion of the government costs their negative externality behaviors and capabilities impose. Costs incurred include: 1) economic productivity drag for dis-enfranchised youth; 2) incremental government services for cyber-defense, -security, -crime investigation, election fraud protection, and more; 3) corporate censorship regulation; 4) arbitraging government service; and 5) services needed to address children's special needs and social disorders partially or totally caused by online/onscreen interactions—screen addictions, cyberbullying, depression, etc. Here are seven ideas to start the regulation conversation.

1) Industry-specific taxation on the amount of online commercial sales that occur through digital versus physical commerce.

2) Corporate license fees for use of government-provided or government-innovated services.

3) Financial disincentives placed on specific industries and products that use addictive, abusive, or manipulative capabilities.

4) Limitations or prohibitions on various digital presentation and manipulation methods and search policies known to be harmful.

5) Regulations on practices deemed to corrupt the morals of minors or harmful to their physical, psychological, or social development.

6) Age-based time and access controls imbedded by law in the devices children use to limit how long and where they go online.

7) Laws to limit use of the Advertising Business Model (free subscription in exchange to access to your device and your information for free) to generate their revenue. Address contracts that require users to relinquish their right to privacy and ownership of their information in exchange for free subscription. Address industry practices of aggregation, long-term storage, and sharing of personal search and profile information about users.

In summary, child development and education policy topics are of political interest to moderates because they are key early life determinants that influence a person's chances of success later in life. They are crucial to real social justice. There is also a societal responsibility to protect children from trauma, discrimination, disadvantage, and abuse. America cannot ensure every child has the benefit of being born to and raised by two loving, reasonably educated, committed, responsible, trustworthy, law-abiding, affluent, mentally stable, pair-bonded opposite-sex adults. But America can provide training for parents, guardians, and teachers and better preparation for learning with the moderate's Education Transformation Initiative. It is hard to find policy in conservatives' and liberals' party platforms that prescribe elimination of the root causes of broken children with meaningful results in education.

If you believe that some or all of the moderate proposals and ideas above are more credible than either the liberal or conservative stance on education, you just might be a moderate. Where do you stand? Are you a conservative, liberal, or moderate? If you label yourself a moderate on education, give yourself one point on the self-assessment in chapter 13.

Chapter 11: On Climate

Humankind is challenged, as it has never been challenged before, to prove its maturity and mastery—not of nature, but of itself.
—Rachel Carson, 1962, author of *Silent Spring*

Climate Change and Earth's Energy Balance[133]

Biologist Rachel Carson wrote well over a half century ago on environmental topics sounding the alarm that some of humans' choices could alter and harm nature. Since her early warnings, environmental and climate sciences have advanced our understanding of the natural world and humans' impact on the natural world. So much so that questions of science are now questions for politics. There are no easy answers.

Current climate politics revolve around one question: "Is Earth's climate and environment changing due at least in part to the impact of human activity?" This question took shape in the middle of the twentieth century as scientists in different fields, like biologist Carson, started studying and questioning phenomena in the natural world that could not be explained by natural laws and processes. By the early twenty-first century, an overwhelming majority of the scientific community (a ratio of thirty to one in one vote of climate scientists) has concluded that the world's average temperature is not only rising but is rising faster than explainable by energy imbalances caused by natural forces and Earth's natural greenhouse effect. Here are two simple facts. Over the past 140 year history of temperature records, 2016 was the warmest year recorded and 2019 the second warmest, as compared to the twentieth century average temperature.[134] Are these record average world temperatures part of a natural phenomenon or something else? Today concern over questions like these has grown to a full chorus across the world. It has taken center stage for the world's political and economic leaders with the Kyoto Protocol of 1997 and the Paris Climate Agreement of 2015–16. Business leaders at the Davos World Economic Forum of 2020 emphasized the potential climate impact on the global economy as people now better understand humans' role in contributing to climate and environment changes. The nations of the G20[135] produce nearly 80 percent of carbon emissions. China is estimated to produce nearly half of all of the world's carbon dioxide emissions—48 percent.[136] The United States accounts for about 14 percent of the total global emissions.[137] China's population and carbon footprint are central to the whole debate.

The UN International Panel on Climate Change has concluded that if we continue to consume fossil fuel and emit carbon dioxide based on current consumption and population run rates, the average global temperature will rise by about 3.2° Celsius by the end of the twenty-first century. They conclude a rise of that magnitude over that period will likely cause substantial negative changes to both coastal and hinterland living (e.g., migrations and moving cities), ocean-level rise, food production, aridity, severe-weather-event loss of life and property damage, and much more. The Paris Climate Agreement resolved to hold the increase in global temperatures well below 2° Celsius, or 3.6° Fahrenheit. In 2018, a United Nations–backed panel of scientists said the safer limit was to keep it to 1.5° Celsius.

Unfortunately, while the Paris Climate Agreement set a noble goal for the world to be carbon neutral by 2050, a recent study[138] concluded that governments in the Agreement are estimated to produce about 50 percent more fossil fuels by 2030 than would be consistent with a 2°C increase pathway and 120 percent more than would be consistent with a 1.5°C increase pathway. So the Paris Agreement is already in jeopardy of ever realizing its primary goal. The gap is larger than the current global emissions gap, in part from all governments' minimal policy focus on reducing fossil fuel production. There are at least five reasons: 1) the world is awash in cheap oil and ubiquitous fossil-based energy and infrastructure, 2) ambitious national plans continue to drive economic growth based on fossil fuels using government policies and subsidies, 3) financial markets continue to make investments in carbon-based energy producers, 4) legacy investments continue in coal, the most plentiful, cheapest, densest, and dirtiest source of carbon-based energy, and 5) consumers' energy-related investments have been mostly in fossil-fuel-based technology. Consumers have to have enough discretionary income to afford to switch. Many can't afford to modernize their energy use products. Some have to wait until they are at major life transition points (e.g., need to buy a new car, move to a new home, etc.). The way the world addresses the use of coal over the next ten years is critical to tackling climate change[139]. According to recent analysis reported by carbonbrief.org, global use of coal must fall by around 80 percent this decade (2020–2030) if warming is to be limited to less than 1.5°C above preindustrial temperatures.[140] All of these factors will continue to reinforce many nations' reliance on the production and consumption of coal, oil, and gas perpetuating fossil fuel lock-in for their economies unless some rational transition path can be crafted.

The United States withdrew from the Paris Agreement in 2019 under President Trump based on the following rationale: What is the point? Other governments[141] that are still in the Paris Agreement are planning to produce much more fossil fuel than needed to achieve the reduction in global average temperature and the economic costs to the US economy are great. Newly elected President Biden has put the US back in the Agreement as of 2021. Will he adopt carbon policies that enhance America's already declining carbon footprint? The key question is this, "How does the world achieve a goal virtually no nation is fully committed to achieving—yet?" There are recent signs as of 2021 that more nations are increasingly focused and committed to the goals to which they agreed. It is meaningless if one or some nations achieve their stated Paris Agreement commitments without the G20 nations achieving their commitments broadly since they produce 80 percent of all carbon emissions. Is it possible for the nations of the world to limit the average rise in temperature to 1.5–2.0°C without the international cooperation intended in the Paris Agreement? Possibly. But it will be almost impossible unless several critical levers on pressed in common by key nations—at least the nations of the G20, especially China.

How will the Paris Agreement play out politically? While there have been activist movements and demonstrations in past decades, the issue is entirely political headed into the third decade of the twenty-first century. America is at a point where liberals and conservatives can be identified as taking somewhat opposing positions on the question along party lines according to pollsters. In 2017 a Gallup Poll survey regarding climate change indicated the following: 1) fewer than one in five Republicans said they worry about climate change, as compared to more than three in five Democrats, and 2) more than eight of ten Democrats considered that the effects of climate change are visible and due more from human activity than natural causes, while Republicans reported fewer than four out of ten. Independents were about five out of ten on those questions. The net view is that well over half of adults believe climate change is happening. Differences exist by age, where younger adults are more concerned about climate change, as are adult women than men. Better-educated people were more likely to be concerned about human-caused climate change, but that is less so for well-educated Republicans. In 2020, a recent poll conducted by Climate Nexus, a nonpartisan nonprofit group, as reported in *The Atlantic*, concludes climate change is one of top five issues for all voters and number two for Democratic respondents.[142]

The issue has been more a debate between those who feel they are informed and educated on the body of scientific knowledge about climate and environment (believers) and others (skeptics). Skeptics are either 1) not well informed, or 2) don't believe humans can impact something as big as Earth, or 3) don't see or sense the changes in their immediate day-to-day living, or 4) do not believe climate change is happening due to human activity, or 5) believe all climate variations are natural. Both believers and skeptics, if they identify somewhat strongly with a political party, are influenced by the views and positions of the party's elites. Republican Party skepticism seemed to spin negative on climate change somewhere in the 1990s in counterpoint to the importance of energy production/independence, so more Republicans are skeptics. In contrast, Democratic Party elites' positions were/are concerned about climate, so many more Democrats identify as believers.

There is more than enough evidence that forces a rational and reasonable person to conclude there is a net change effect on Earth's climate over the past several centuries in general, and that these changes are most noticeable over the most recent half century. Science can measure carbon dioxide and confirm that it correlates with human energy consumption behaviors (anthropogenic). Consequently, believers, including many moderates, would conclude that climate change is happening by both natural and human-made forces, and the only forces we can impact are those caused by us. Finally, the basis for skeptics' disbelief or denial of climate change and global temperature rise is limited to these: whether or not 1) the impacts and costs of human-made change are significant enough to care about or control, 2) the governments, people, or the carbon dioxide producers of the world are willing or able to cooperate in global solution policies and programs, 3) specific solutions proposed or required may be more or less desirable than others due to national cost effectiveness or politics.

So what does the future hold? Can we do anything about making Earth's future climate and environment more sustainable for future generations to flourish and thrive? Based on the computer modeling and simulation work of the United Nations International Panel on Climate Change, they believe they have a good feel for what Earth's future climate holds for those alive at future times based on different assumptions of human behavior—energy sources, conservation, fossil fuel use, and population growth. Their conclusion is, at least for the present, there appear to be no behavior or solution scenarios that reverse the amount of carbon dioxide in the atmosphere or hold it down below 500 ppm of CO_2 over the next fifty to one hundred years *unless* we change our reliance on fossil fuels. This is not good by most any one's assessment, since most of us can see some observable changes at the current level of the low 400 ppm CO_2. To put these two numbers in perspective, science has concluded that at the dawn of the Industrial Age in the late 1700s, atmospheric CO_2 was about 280 ppm, and during the time of the dinosaurs CO_2 was in the area of 900–1,000 ppm. What does daily life look and feel like at over 500 ppm CO_2?

A key question for believers is this: "Will it matter, or is it even possible for one nation to reduce its CO_2 emissions dramatically—to near zero—through conservation or innovation to make a significant global impact?" The only nations that matter as a single player are China, followed by the United States, the European Union, and India. A key question for skeptics who believe we should "do nothing" is this: "What if you are wrong and temperatures rise to a point where it is too late to fix it fast enough to avoid disastrous outcomes that inflict mass human deaths or require mass movement of people living near coasts or rivers and stranding large chunks of our assets and economy?"

Conservative View

Some skeptics might say the climate change issue is just a hoax, only propaganda. The rest of the skeptics challenge the believers: "Won't nature just fix the climate on its own, so we don't have to do anything?" After all, the planet has evolved by its natural forces over the past 4.6 billion years. A believer's response is: "It will fix it, but not in time and maybe not the way humans will like (hotter, less land, more ocean, more severe weather, fewer species...possibly fewer humans, involuntarily)." The normal evolutionary time Earth takes to rebalance atmospheric energy at some new level based on 500–1,000 ppm of carbon dioxide is counted in thousands of years, not tens of years, as we humans are hoping for here in the present day.

Liberal View

Believers rebut and rebuke skeptics with this: "Politicians and governments should come up with policies and laws that just make the 'polluters' stop emitting so much carbon dioxide and consuming so much fossil fuel or make all of us do some things that reduce the problem." Perhaps this is so, but it is naive. It turns out that almost all of us are the polluters. We use fossil fuels to drive, fly, and keep our homes comfortable in summer and winter. Also, many of the things industry, commerce, and agriculture make for us depend on fossil energy. Governments can come up with programs if they have the knowledge and will to mandate and enforce such policies, but it may be at substantial cost and can be a potential drag on economic growth and strength if done poorly or tailored for special political interests. Unfortunately, debt, deficits, drugs, and discrimination, among other things, are already dragging on economic growth. So skeptics say we don't need more drag. Also, one size does not fit all when it comes to energy use. Using wind, solar, hydro, nuclear, coal, gas, oil, biomass, or hydrogen fuel cells may vary depending on the climate, geology, level of modernity, state of the science, and economics of one geographic region compared to others. And where does that leave any nation if the other countries or the huge CO_2 emitters don't join in? Think China. Then India. The United States and European Union are not increasing as rapidly as the emerging nations with large populations of poor people are, even though their people are generally very low energy consumers—for now.

Skeptics push back, saying, "Science will save us." Science and technology will innovate us out of the CO_2 emission growth problem. They have done it before. They improved gasoline so it did not require lead. They innovated nuclear power plants, along with solar and wind usage, which have nearly doubled in use since 1980. Together they still only produce about 20 percent of America's energy.[143] Science has gone big at times. For example, by the end of the twentieth century, the agriculture genetic science work of Norman Borlaug[144] saved an estimated billion lives from starvation and political instability in India and Pakistan during the 1960s as both nations faced considerable shortfalls in food production for their rapidly growing populations. By introducing genetically modified strains of semi dwarf wheat that could thrive in their challenging climates,[145] his work was a future changing scientific contribution to food security. To skeptics' claim that "science will save us," there may be a way to reduce the amount of carbon dioxide released into the atmosphere at power plants at a manageable cost using hydrogen-fuel-cell-based carbon capture technology.[146]

Moderate View

Most moderates are believers. Moderates likely lean liberal on this issue but believe liberals' anthem of 'save the planet' is wrong-minded. Rather moderates think more like Rachel Carson's quote of 'save humanity – from ourselves'. The planet will continue at whatever energy equilibrium exists. It just may be quite inhospitable for humans and other life forms. Moderates lean in with those who want to see government and consumer actions to reduce carbon use and emissions rapidly, but, also, as pragmatically and cost effectively as possible. Moderates say, "The only way to save the planet (humanity) is for the governments of the major emitting nations to collaborate on an optimal strategy because we just can't stop using carbon-based energy, especially coal, fast enough to prevent carbon dioxide emissions from growing." Coal is in wide use — nearly eighty countries still rely substantially on coal.

There are many carbon emission mitigation solution proposals scientists have advanced, ranging from tinkering with nature to tinkering with humanity, and a number of options in between that rely on science and technology. They fall into two categories: 1) reduce fossil-fuel energy production and consumption, and 2) expand/not decrease natural carbon dioxide absorption systems. Moderates will support those in either category that are effective, cost-effective, pragmatic, and do not significantly disrupt or destroy nature, economic activity, or quality of life. All these ideas are in addition to best practices for consumers protecting their local environments by conserving energy and recycling waste responsibly using the current state of scientific methods. Like selecting energy sources, each energy solution carries trade-offs, some positive, some negative. There is no silver bullet to reconcile humans' energy use and climate change quickly, completely, or safely. Some carry considerable risk, like tinkering with global climate on a grand scale. That approach may have unintended or unforeseen consequences. Here is a list of optional approaches. Moderates will focus on those that are practical and productive in generating measurable results.

Seed—tinker with nature. The first two ideas below are examples of solutions scientists propose that tinker with nature on a grand scale with unknown, unknowable, and potentially unintended consequences. Some have proposed that if the climate gets near the point of no-return inflection points, the world can:

- Seed the upper atmosphere with sulfur dioxide to create a thin aerosol layer that blocks incoming infrared radiation to rebalance atmospheric energy, or
- Seed the ocean with iron to stimulate carbon dioxide capture sending it to the ocean floor.

Switch—replace existing utility infrastructure. Move from high-carbon-dioxide-emitting systems to lower- or zero-carbon-dioxide-emitting systems that do the following:

- Switch power plants from fossil fuel to nuclear-energy that emit almost no carbon dioxide. Trade-offs include long construction times, a larger base of enriched uranium convertible to weapon-grade plutonium, a sizable radioactive waste issue, potential life-altering hazards to people in the vicinity of nuclear plants if there are nuclear accidents, and large volumes of water needed unless thorium reactors are used. Fusion reactors are still far in the future.
- Switch coal-fired power plants[147] to lower carbon content fossil fuels because coal is the most critical energy source to reduce carbon emissions. Convert coal-fired power plants to natural gas, which produces far less carbon dioxide than coal, and retire coal-based plants and replacing them with cheaper-to-build renewable-energy-sourced power plants. While coal use has plateaued since 2014, it is not clear whether the use of coal is peaking or not. Compared to the year 2000, global coal-fired power capacity has doubled to around 2,045 gigawatts (GW) after substantial growth in China and India. Of the seventy-eight countries that still rely on coal, the top ten coal users operate over 85 percent of current production and over 80 percent of planned additional capacity. In addition to about 480 GW retired in recent years or are planned for retirement, there are aggressive efforts to reduce or eliminate coal in a number of countries like the UK and Germany. While national plans for coal use are changing rapidly headed into the third decade of the twenty-first century amid strong calls to eliminate any new coal-based capacity, another 570GW is being built or planned across the 78 nations still using coal. China is the world's largest coal user, accounting for nearly half (48%) of global production primarily from its 2,300 plus coal-fired power plants. [148] Unless there is a

dramatic shift in China's energy strategy, they plan to expand to over 3,500 coal-fired plants in the coming years. Then there is India as well, further back on the modernization curve, but growing in energy consumption for its 1.1 billion-plus people. India has nearly 600 coal-fired power plants with plans for almost 500 more as of 2018. In the US as more natural gas and renewables-based power plants have been deployed, electricity generated from coal in the US has dropped from 52.8 percent in 1997 to 27.4 percent in 2018. In 2017, there were about 350 coal-powered plants in the United States down from over 1,000 in the year 2000. Still, the total nominal coal-fired capacity has stayed about the same at 256 GW today compared to 278 GW in 2000.[149]

Replace—substitute fossil-fueled active generation infrastructure with passive generation technology. Build any new energy capacity with technologies that do not use carbon-based energy sources.

- *Deploy solar and wind energy farms on a massive scale.* Both are now cost-competitive with natural gas and coal. Negatives for wind are that it doesn't always blow or blow everywhere, so advances in large scale electricity storage are needed. Negative for solar is the substantial amount of land solar requires dedicated to collection farms, which is costly and impacts land for living or growing food (unless rooftop solar approaches are used on a massive scale, which would be a great answer except the effort and liability involved to get millions of building/house owners to participate and pay).
- *Deploy hydroelectric power generation as much as possible.* Negatives: Many of the cost-effective dam and flow sites have been developed and environmental issues exist—wetlands, fish, wildlife.
- *Deploy biomass based power generation.* Biomass is supposedly a green, renewable energy source. Negatives: It produces a lot of carbon dioxide. A significant portion of the current biomass fuel source is deforestation. Forests are being clear-cut to create wood chips as burnable biomass fuel instead of other biomass forms like organic waste. Consequently, biomass power based on wood is part of the problem.[150] The world community ought to dis-incentivize wood-based biomass as a power plant fuel.
- *Move personal ground transportation to electric and hydrogen fuel cells* from gas- and diesel-fuel-based vehicles, which is a market transition under way. Expand mass high-speed rail. Maximize the use of autonomous driving vehicles. Negatives include the cost to switch and to deploy refueling station infrastructure. Electric vehicles (EVs) would still have to rely mostly on fossil-fuel-based power plants for electricity until

enough renewable energy sources and storage capacity can be deployed—years away at a large scale.

- *Conserve energy use.* Avoid new capacity required by reducing energy consumed using more efficient (smart) infrastructure, appliances, and manufacturing equipment. The United States has reduced energy per person by about 50 percent since 1975. Some of the US reduction has been due to energy efficiency and conservation, but some of the reduction is due to outsourcing of manufacturing to other countries. Technology advances are enabling the continued improvement in energy efficiency of lighting, heating, communication devices, operating computer data centers, and transportation systems.

Absorb—expand natural carbon dioxide absorption.

- Plant more trees to absorb CO_2 as part of the carbon cycle.[151]
- Stop deforestation. (Brazil's Amazon forest is the most important to save; it absorbs a significant amount of all carbon dioxide absorbed by the earth's plant carbon cycle.) Consider ways to deter Brazil from burning down the Amazon forest for economic growth.
- Adopt other nature-compatible methods, such as composting.

Transform—tinker with humanity. Transform America's or the globe's carbon footprint dramatically by government mandate through reengineering existing infrastructure and human economic, environmental, and social behavior.

- *Incent commercial and consumer choices.* Proposals to impose taxes on carbon use or production in various forms. Negatives include costs and slow time to produce measureable impact, others.
- *Political proposals like the Green New Deal (GND)* from America's liberal politicians which attempts to unify social, economic, political as well as climate justice under one federally led and funded grand plan. It places very aggressive goals and requirements on US industry, business, and people. To a moderate's read, some of that proposal looks noble and useful. Unfortunately, on the whole, it spends a lot of money and changes a lot without clearly improving the United States' social justice or economic strength, or reducing global carbon footprint. On a worldwide scale, it weakens the United States against any who do not implement at least the "green" portion of the Green New Deal. Nor does it likely move the needle much for carbon dioxide emissions, which are predominately generated by China and increasingly India in future decades while the United States and Europe are presently slowing their carbon emissions.

The challenge for all nations is finding solutions that reduce carbon emissions such that drag on economic growth is minimized.

This moderate would predict the net result of liberals' GND on climate in future decades is that carbon dioxide levels will continue to rise globally, despite the Green New Deal. Liberals might feel less guilty that the future rise is less the fault of the United States, but America would be much deeper in debt and weaker relative to at least China. Moderates want some of the same results the Green New Deal liberals want, but the way those results are achieved needs to be accomplished very differently than their approach of the federal government enforcing draconian mandates on consumers and providing massive sums of money for state, local, and special-interest projects with what appears to be minimal accountability.

Capture—Implement carbon dioxide capture/storage technology. This option is now becoming possible and less costly as new hydrogen fuel cell-based carbon capture is being innovated here in the United States. It would take out a large amount of the carbon dioxide produced by power plants where the technology is deployed.

- *Capture and store carbon dioxide* from existing fossil-fuel powered utilities before it gets released into the air. Carbon capture at the point of emission at coal, natural gas, and oil-fired power plants would address the most widespread uses of energy at a root-cause point of leverage. While the primary benefit is to reduce CO_2 emitted into the air, it also enables the option for rapid growth of electric vehicle (EV) use since the fossil-fueled powered sources would not emit more carbon into the atmosphere as more electricity is used to refuel EVs. Another benefit of such a project is that renewable energy solutions can continue to deploy at an economically justified pace. An additional benefit for consumers is that they would not have to buy an electric vehicle and replace their gas or oil furnaces, etc. in the next five to ten years, as liberals are proposing in the Green New Deal. Negatives include the fact that hydrogen has to be produced because it does not exist standalone in nature. Secondly, to rapidly refine the capture platform, a large-scale project and legislation are needed to fund, fast-track, and coordinate engineering, construction, and deployment. Finally, carbon capture can't be used at present for air transport, which is a large producer of carbon dioxide. The challenge for this strategic transition solution is achieving large-scale deployment internationally. Deploying it here in the United States is not enough. Nations including China, India, and some others would need to deploy if they are not going to deactivate a large portion of their coal-powered power plants. For more detail on this proposal, see chapter 12, section 9 ("Energy Policy and Climate Impact—Manhattan Project 2.0").

If one were to boil down the whole climate issue into one thing as a predictor of the future, it would have to be the measure of atmospheric carbon dioxide content, which is currently measured at about 413 parts per million mid-pandemic 2020.[152] It seems that the global community needs to work to reduce carbon dioxide production to as far under 400 ppm as we can get it to create a sustainable, livable world, notwithstanding the onset of the next Ice Age cycle. Before we get back under 400, we may well go over 500ppm with our current population, energy use, and economic reliance on fossil fuel energy. Atmospheric carbon dioxide is growing at several parts per million per year so if we do nothing the world hits 500ppm in 25-50 years. Believers predict that as long as we continue to use fossil fuels in the same or larger quantities we are using today, the amount of carbon dioxide we put into the atmosphere will go up.

In conclusion, to 'reduce atmospheric carbon dioxide to under 400 ppm', moderates likely are negative on the Green New Deal and neutral or mixed on the pluses and minuses of being part of the Paris Climate Agreement. But moderates are likely fully committed to support ways to reduce carbon emissions and build a bridge from our high-carbon-emission trajectory toward a sensible carbon-emission-reduction goal much more cost effectively than US liberals' Green New Deal or the commitment approach of the Paris Agreement. Moderates likely support ideas like: 1) fast-tracking carbon capture true-in and deployment of hydrogen-based fuel technology; 2) expanding use of solar and wind; 3) moving in an economically justifiable way to non-fossil-fuel powered transportation as possible but over a timeframe that consumers can afford and America's electric grid infrastructure can accommodate. There may be distribution issues that must be addressed like the amount of amperage and number of EV cars any neighborhood can handle before upgrade investments are required. 4) investing and improving electric energy storage system technology; 5) eliminating coal- and natural-gas-fired power plants in a phased and as rapid and economically orderly manner; 6) continuing to improve and incent energy efficiency and conservation in industry, commerce, government, and home consumption; and 7) dis-incentivizing fossil fuel exploration and production capacity, including corn- and wood-based biomass.

If you believe that some or all of the moderate positions are more credible than either the liberal or conservative stance, you just might be a moderate. Where do you stand on climate? Are you a conservative, liberal, or moderate? If you label yourself a moderate on climate, give yourself one point on the self-assessment in chapter 13.

Chapter 12: The American Moderate Agenda

We the people of the United States, in order to form a more perfect union...
                              - Preamble of the Constitution of the United States

To understand what drives moderates' political spirits the question implied in the Preamble of the Constitution may say it best, "What will it take *to form a more perfect union*?" To differentiate moderates, we have looked at the chemistry of modern moderates through their beliefs, values, and ideology that ground them and define who they are. We have looked at seven ways in which their political sensibilities are likely different from conservatives and liberals. To see where they stand, we have looked at how a moderate might assess a number of political issues and what imperatives drive them. Now it is time to ask the political question, "What do moderates want?" In a sentence, moderates want liberals and conservatives to be more moderate in their demands, their positions, and more inclusive of moderate-minded people, ideology, and policy ideas. And, if they won't, then moderates want new politics and new politicians.

Recall from Chapter 1 that even though the potential size of the moderate faction is somewhere between 7 percent to over 50 percent of America's electorate, they are not a political party. But, if moderates were a political party, they would need a name and a party platform to articulate their vision, values, and proposals. Let's nickname it the American Moderate Party. Democrats are blue. Republicans are red. Though white would be a logical color for the moderate party (red-white-blue colors of our flag), it holds potentially controversial connotations. The American Moderate Party color can be gold. The American Moderate Party Platform is gold for America because it solves long-festering issues. The platform would be quite large because the list of issues on their Agenda is long.

While some big ideas and goals of both factions are noble, a fair number of their solution proposals won't get the job done. Their proposals are frequently bounded by ideological principal or special interest demands that diminish the value or effect for the whole of the American people. Here are some of the author's high-level proposals for modernizing various aspects of America and American governance in the twenty-first century as a discussion starter. Additional proposal will be made in a future project.

What do 21ˢᵗ-century American Moderates want?

A government that is right-sized for the contemporary needs of the nation during any era and governs through policies that:

1) Protect the *people* of the United States, our democracy, rights, and America's way of life through a strong economy and defense, the rule of law, and fair elections—provably the will of its legal citizens;
2) Foster *prosperity* for as many as possible and our posterity;
3) Achieve *progress* toward equality, fairness, and justice for all, but especially for children of all colors by eliminating as many early life causes of discrimination, disadvantage, deprivation and trauma;
4) Pursue *peace* and the general welfare amongst ourselves and peace-loving people everywhere; prevent ill-willed powers from acts of war, terror, crimes against humanity, or authoritarian rule;
5) Ensure *liberty* to pursue freedom, happiness, faith, and purpose;
6) Sustain our *planet's* carrying capacity for future generations.

To achieve these six goals, what do American moderates want? We want a lot of issues addressed and messes resolved that can't be covered in one introductory work. But here are five additional American Moderate Agenda Domestic Policy Proposals, so you have a total of ten issues in this book to assess. The point of this exercise is to see if moderates can build a common ideological foundation to get air time using political focus on root causes, cost-causers, and continuous institutional improvement. This section puts new, out-of-the-box ideas on the table for all to inspect. Will these ideas help moderates build a consensus on critical issues that are stalemated by party politics and media play? Will these ideas help moderates stop being silenced and 'all over the ideological map'? You decide.

Sample Moderate Agenda on U.S. Domestic Policy

1. Institutional reform. Dangerous People and Guns.   *Chapter 8*
2. Institutional reform. Immigration.   *Chapter 9*
3. Institutional reform. Education.   *Chapter 10*
4. Sustainability policy. Climate Impact.   *Chapter 11*
5. Children's policy.   21ˢᵗ-century New Deal   *Chapter 12*
6. Labor markets.   21ˢᵗ-century Jobs & Skills
7. Institutional reform. Health Care & Health Care Insurance
8. Institutional policy.   American Service & Volunteerism
9. Energy policy.   Carbon Capture Manhattan Project 2.0
10. Fiscal policy.   Budget, Deficit, Debt, Fair share, New revenue

If you agree with three or more of the following five ideas, give yourself one point on the 'Are you a moderate?' Self-Assessment in Chapter 13.

American Moderate Agenda[153]

5. Children First: Their Human Dignity, Rights, and Bright Futures

Humanity owes the child the best it has to give.
        —Eglantyne Jebb, Founder, Save the Children Fund, 1919[154]

Moderate's View

`   *We are America. Here, just like adults, every child is entitled as a citizen of the United States to their dignity, their rights, and the best start in life we can provide as parents and as a nation.* As FDRs' New Deal was plain English for a changed concept of responsibility and duty of government toward economic life, the Moderate Agenda calls for a New Deal for all children of all colors within the jurisdiction of the United States and hopefully the world. We call for a changed concept of responsibility and duty of society and government toward new life and young life. In the twenty-first century their rights, protections, prospects, and preparation for education and adulthood require a transformational focus. Moderates seek equality and social justice for children by eliminating or minimizing negative root cause issues and cost-causers' impacts on children's dependent years.

To achieve those goals, a number of national institutions need to be reformed spanning national policy and practices in conception, family, marriage, education, health care, workforce development, cultural, and social institutions. Additionally, reforms and new rules on various commercial practices spanning entertainment, social media, pop culture industries, and others are needed. America must strive to dramatically improve America's childhoods and increase the value, quality, and relevance of their education and health care as preparation to become responsible contributing members of American society. As articulated in the Annie E. Casey Foundation 2019 Data Book preface, *"Children make up one-quarter of this nation's population and all of its future."*

Moderates' Proposal for a New Deal for Children

At the beginning of this work, I claimed that a new age of discrimination is at hand based on America's blind spot for children and their rights. The argument presented is that America's blind spot exists because of adult discrimination, cultural practices, structural institutional discrimination, advances in genetic, computer, neuro, decision, and sciences and technology exploited by Mean Street firms and political constituencies. Policies pressed by political interests for progressive values and adult privileged rights have rendered children legally and politically defenseless in some aspects of their lives from pre-conception to adulthood. Before I leave it to your conscience to decide whether or not I have made the case, compare your political sensibilities with those in this section that advance a new legal and cultural deal for children based on children's natural human rights. Will our children's children, America, the world, be better off if some or all of the New Deal offered below becomes the new normal? Which parts would you support?

Goals for the New Deal span state actions, changes in adult culture, and systemic societal institutional reforms that establish from pre-conception to the age of independence ways to: 1) Honor children's dignity and inalienable human rights starting with the conception of their lives. 2) Protect and guarantee children's civil and constitutional rights. 3) Foster brighter futures especially for those conceived to people of modest to low socio-economic standing. 4) Improve education, health care, and workforce preparation. 5) Minimize the occurrence and long term effects of un-trustable or abusive parentage. 6) Eliminate root causes of in-utero and early life trauma, death, discrimination, or disenfranchisement that in turn create so many costs for our children, families, communities, and nation. 7) Reduce the number of unintended conceptions to as close to zero as possible. 8) Eliminate unconstitutional conceptions. 8) Attack Adult Privilege, negative adult preferences, and political choices that cause harm to children. 9) Reduce the cost of raising children in America as possible. Here is one moderate's view of a new deal for children. What would yours include?

Universal Public Policy Proposals

1) The US Government, the Congress, and Supreme Court, recognize and uphold children's ten substantive constitutional birthrights to life, liberty, and property[155].

2) The Congress, States, and Public consider the merits of a 'Children's Bill of Rights' constitutional amendment.

3) The Supreme Court honors US obligations to the UN Universal Declaration of Human Rights Treaty in rulings that impact the rights of children.

4) Congress ratifies the UN Convention on the Rights of the Child.

5) The United States, United Nations, and all Nations United attack all forms of child trafficking, slavery, sex slavery, starvation and life-insecurity aggressively on all fronts.

6) All branches of government and society uphold children's human, constitutional, and civil rights.

7) Americans strengthen the American way by crafting domestic policies that successfully address how children are created, raised, educated, and franchised into adulthood.

8) Establish a non-profit organization called Planned Childhood whose mission is to promote and implement federal programs to achieve *Children First* goals.

9) Congress by Statute or President Executive Order by or the Supreme Court by modernization of Roe v Wade declares a pre-born human conceived by US citizens as a legal person and US citizen entitled to all constitutional rights, privileges, and immunities at a biologically definable pre-born moment within the first nine weeks of gestation. *Moderates' proposals for debate are: conception, uterine implantation, first heartbeat [about week 6], and maturation from embryo to a fetus [about week 9].*

10) The United States Congress, Courts, and States uphold equality for children in conception, early life, marriage, divorce, family court.

11) Legislate policy that: 1) Dis-incents unplanned conceptions. 2) Promotes nuclear family formation. 3) Incents the increase of two-adult-led households with children toward a national goal of two-thirds of all households.

12) The Congress, Courts, and States uphold the birthright of each new human to 'conception by two, mutual choice, consenting opposite-sex humans' as the sole means of human creation. Place restrictions on fertility and genetic industry to limit conception services to qualified legally married opposite-sex pair bonds exclusively. All others can adopt.

13) Promote pathways to foster or adoptive parenthood for all those fully committed to parenthood. There are nearly half million in the US. Tens of millions worldwide.

14) Foster ways and means to protect children as United States citizens from being conceived in unwanted-unplanned conceptions.

15) Address the whole of genetic science with respect to gene editing, new discoveries and innovations, on their possible uses in the conception and design of human beings and manufactured tissues.

16) Expand research to pursue solutions for neo-natal genetic, congenital, and early age onset physical and mental disorders, diseases, and disadvantages (e.g., autism, cancers, others).

17) Debate new national policy and enact laws for the five reasons for an abortion with children's rights, their personhood, and US citizenship in full view. Abortion is not a just a state by state issue in a moderate's view because children are also US citizens first.

18) Debate and architect appropriate reforms for the US institution and industries of education outlined in the Education Transformation Initiative in chapter 10. Provide programs that improve childhood development, health care, and education including parenting skill programs for early childhood development information and positive parenting skill. Consider crafting programs for ages a) minus one to 3, b) toddler to school-age, c) elementary-age, d) middle thru secondary age.

19) Attack as many issues of early childhood trauma, adultism, deprivation, inadequate development, and mental health. Strive to minimize the number of children born to or raised in high-risk parent and household environments that lead to addiction, poverty, poor early life outcomes, abandonment, abuse, and criminality.

20) Hold Mean Street industries accountable to a high moral code and legal standards of care and trust. Repeal section 230 of the Communications Decency Act. Penalize producers and distributors for content and digital manipulation techniques that are inappropriate, damaging, or addictive to toddlers to teens on all screen devices—movies, TVs, computers, iPads, and smartphones.

Pre-Conception to Birth

21) Establish policy and programs to minimize unwanted-unplanned conceptions to reduce the number and outcomes of children born into and raised by single teen/adult-led households – especially for adults under the age 30.

22) Reform, regulate, and restrict commercial fertility retail stores and genetic science further—E.g.,

- Limit sperm and egg donors and recipients to only one pair bond and limit the donation to one or perhaps two transactions (two siblings by same donor for the same receiving pair bond). Eliminate the prospect of multiple perhaps hundreds of siblings any new human so conceived may have and not know about because of unlimited use of individual sperm or egg donors.

- Frozen embryos. There are perhaps a million frozen human embryos in the control of fertility industry providers as of 2020. How do Americans deal with this issue? It has to be fully, humanely addressed devoid of any commercial interests. Prohibit fertility industry practices that create and freeze multiple embryos in most situations. But allow creation, freezing, and implantation of one to two embryos solely for the embryo-creators later use. Should rules for destruction of the embryo(s) be required in the event of death or disablement of both embryo creators? Are embryos property? Who's property/responsibility? Who has the right to decide to bring an embryo into life? Which one(s)?

- Render it impossible for fertility staff to use their sperm or eggs.

- Require fertility industry doctors and courts to record and inform all conceived persons of all of their biological siblings by donors whose DNA was used to conceive in more than one transaction.

23) Provide pre-conception incentives and services for adults to pre-plan parenthood and prepare for positive, successful childhoods.

24) Consider a 'Head Start'-type program for prospective / new parents to provide early-life child development knowledge and skill competency. Include topics not limited to: care, early childhood safety, nutrition, development, and education, bonding, talking to, touching, addiction avoidance, positive character building, growth mindset, hazard elimination, health, medical condition identification, safety, interpersonal communication and language skills, others. Offer through high school, colleges, hospitals, and federally sponsored online and cable TV education channel(s).

25) Provide universally available, low/no cost conception testing/prevention education, products, and services for post-puberty males and females via retail channels and designated government facilities. Products included: conception prevention (birth control and Plan B pills), Thermometers, Home Pregnancy Testing Kits, condoms, IUDs, and others. Consider funding this one program with public funds in place of employer-based health insurance.

26) Protect pre-born child's right to be gestated and born addiction-free (drug-, smoke-, and alcohol-free) with required testing. Provide education services for gestating females and male partners on nutrition and abstinence from smoking, vaping, alcohol, pain/

addictive killer drugs, recreational marijuana, and other behaviors that damage the health or jeopardize the life of the pre-born.

27)   Consider government-funded health care insurance and services to all gestating females to ensure the health and safety of mother and pre-born US citizens as one possible additional public health care insurance option or in addition to any improvements to Medicare/Medicaid or Obamacare programs Americans may create.

28)   Debate the merit of federally supported services for testing of those potentially at genetic risk pre/post conception and embryo for early detection of inherited genetic defects.

Birth to Pre-Kindergarten

29) Debate the merit of federally-funded genetic testing service for detection of serious early life genetic/congenital medical challenges.

30) Issue US-sealed Birth Certificates (in place of or in addition to state birth certificates). Certify the country of citizenship and DNA-identity of both biological parents as one of a set of federal services provided at birthing centers per the next New Deal proposal.

31) Provide a US Birth Certificate, Social Security Number, Passport, and 529 Education Investment Account at birth. For those new persons conceived by a legal US citizen, provide each new-born US citizen a free Passport, Social Security Number, and 529 Education Account issued by federal personnel at the birthing facility. The 529 account, established federally or in collaboration with the newborn's state of residency and biological parents, provides a modest startup endowment (e.g., $1,000 per child) from the people of the United States.[156] There is evidence that a child with education savings is three times more likely to enroll in a two- or four-year college and four times more likely to graduate.[157] Encourage parents, grandparents, and extended family to contribute to the 529 account before birth and onwards. Incent employers to provide an employee benefit at a child's birth for parents working at the time of conception of a contribution to the newborn's 529 - e.g., $500, $1,000, or more. While the author came up with the idea independently others have similar ideas, liberal presidential candidates to state governments. As of the writing of this book five states have instituted this idea in some form. For example, Pennsylvania has Keystone Scholars which is $100 paid by the state treasury to every new-born's 529 account. Imagine every American child starting life with thousands of dollars in an account that will grow and be available for childhood learning, higher education schooling, or vocational training. If the account started with $5,000

by age one and there were no additional contributions, by age 18 a $5,000 balance compounding at 3% annually would be over $8,000. At 9% it would be over $21,000. Today a number of America's households have less than a thousand dollars in savings to cover an emergency let alone to invest in their children. More security, more hope, more choice, more opportunity, more mobility.

32) Produce the prospect of a higher quality of life for each child with legislation that holds both conceiving adults economically and societally accountable for each new US citizen they create, including sperm and egg donors.

- Establish federal statutory obligations on and legal consequences for persons that violate children's conception rights or fail to contribute to or provide for the care of their offspring starting right at birth if not pre-birth.

- Establish strong sanctions on adults who 'conceive and abandon', especially serial conceivers and abandoners – auto-income garnishment at birth or later as determined...and more.

33) Hold federal and state governments and local care providers accountable to high federal standards of excellence for care and education of all children in public care and childcare. Develop a curriculum and credential for federal and state certification of competency for early childhood development care providers and educators as a condition of employment in addition to current requirements of criminal, child, and drug background clearances.

Kindergarten through Higher Education

34) Consider incentives for stay-at-home child caregiver adults for caring for children from pre-birth to milestone age, perhaps 4 or 5.

35) Establish policy and programs for workforce re-assimilation of the adult who is primary stay-at-home early childhood care giver.

36) Minimize drug use/demand by Tweens and Teens. Use demand-side management practices of detection (breathe, urine, blood, and cognitive testing) and intervention if addictive substances and/or behaviors are suspected by parents, school, or law enforcement.

37) Help all children grow positive as best they can. Establish and integrate into pre-K to high school programs that provide positive adult role models and mentoring experiences for children of all colors from low socio-economic and single adult households.

38) Help Military Children. Recognize and honor the service, sacrifice, and disadvantages of children being raised in military life through a Military Children's College Benefit Program. Perhaps, amend the existing GI Bill, Dependent Education Assistance program, a program that would obligate (say the top-half ranked) higher education institutions to provide tuition-free education for qualified military children (include children of active, disabled veterans) as part of the higher education institution's national service duty. Also, help military children avoid the negative issues of growing up in military life during preK-12 years with a tailored Counseling Program accessible at public and private schools.

39) Ensure childhood equality for Disenfranchised Children. Help fostered, orphaned, incarcerated w/wo incarcerated parent, and abandoned children address the negative and trauma issues of being raised in the 'system'. Ensure they are not deprived, disadvantaged, disenfranchised using special federal and state programs to protect their rights and to empower opportunities for them.

- Cut red tape and time to provide universal and specialized services to address the trauma of abandonment, poor parenting.

- Provide mental and medical health, education services.

- Provide good foster guardian certification and accountability.

40) Supplement K-12 education with a set of in-school/through-school Coping Support Services, as introduced in Chapter 10, On Education, that span mental health, social development, dysfunctional family, and other services. The idea is to address and intervene when children are identified at-risk for mental, emotional, physical, drug, trauma, or suicidal problems. Providers would be professionally educated and certified specialist in children's psychology, early development, and other disciplines.

41) Consider fixing high school dropout phenomena by making it illegal to quit school before graduation. Design Special Federal or State Programs to address children under the age of independence who declare they quit or are at risk to drop out. Deliver specially designed recovery curricula to help teens reengage and succeed in tailored formats from 5 day x 8 - 12 hours per day up to 7 days x 24 hours per day (boot camp setting?) locally or regionally as needed.

42) Enlist the wisdom and experience of America's parents and child development experts for their ideas on ways to improve the early lives of children on US soil/Earth.

American Moderate Agenda

6. Labor Markets and 21st-century Jobs and Skills

We have got to stop saying we want to do well by children and invest in education and invest in job training and then essentially withdraw from that.
— Late Paul Wellstone, Liberal U.S. Senator

Moderate's View

Growing up is challenging by definition for every generation. But here in the twenty-first century, for far too many of America's youth, especially those "from families that are deprived or isolated or fractured or all three"[158], entering adulthood with limited preparation and too much debt is a recipe for failure and discrimination. The adverse effects of Mean Street, pop culture, screen-time, and addictions, raised fatherless, or in moderate to low-income single adult-led households all contribute to delaying/derailing youths' passage to adulthood. Moderates would readily agree America must change how we educate our children and how we prepare our youth for economic life so each of us can be the best we can be with the innate talents with which we are endowed. Both are moral and American imperatives for moderates. America cannot build a stronger, inclusive economy or compete in the global economy unless we strengthen America's workforce and lower personal and social costs associated from early life trauma and failure.

Many federal programs already exist[159] but are marginally effective. For example, despite President Obama's $12 billion attempt to reclaim the number one spot on the list of nations with the highest graduation rates rising from American's current number 12 slot, America is still 12th and far behind in preparing American youth for work life and adulthood. President Obama's 2009 America Graduation Initiative was supposed to successfully address the graduation rate issue but fizzled when the Affordable Care Act took center stage. The Moderate Agenda calls for re-engineering federal and state programs that already exist as appropriate and innovating new, highly effective and efficient education, vocational, and skill development programs. The programs would be available for all of our youth of all colors in addition to displaced, unemployed, unmotivated, addicted, and incarcerated teens and adults. The programs: 1) Provide aptitude tests, strengths/weakness assessment, and self-awareness learning that help students acquire an understanding of their natural talents, and interests. 2) Supplement education with focused primary, general, and civic curricula for those who need remedial instruction. 3) Enable the development of vital life, vocational, leadership, adult character, and life competencies. 4) Provide information on current and emerging opportunities, jobs, skill certification programs, careers, professions. 5) Provide training on how and where to look for work (websites, government and commercial services, etc. 6) Provide mentor, apprenticeship, and public-private training programs. 7) Link existing and new job placement processes so that students can enter the workforce prepared, productive, and self-sufficient in their late teens and early twenties without much if any debt. 8) Promote program awareness with TV and online public service advertising/ infomercials to inform public of programs, choices, and things they can do to improve themselves and to find work.

Moderates' Proposals for 21st Century Jobs and Skills

1) **Assessment**. *Middle School through High School and Higher*. Include tests, surveys, and assessment tools in curriculum at appropriate age points. Enable students to go through middle and teen years more aware of what they are good at and not so good at starting in late elementary or early middle school. Use tools and information to develop essential life, vocational, aptitude skills, strengths, and interests. Deliver at public and private schools, community colleges, and additional channels to youth - prisons, immigration services, foster, and others. There is no lack of aptitude and strength assessment tools. What America has lacked is systematic and sustained national focus so all children get a fair chance to succeed.

2) **All Children Grow Positive (ACGP).** *Kindergarten through at least Middle School*. Provide supplemental practice one-on-one or two adults-on-one, etc. in a supervised room (possibly virtual online sessions also) to help children who are below grade-level performance acquire necessary literacy and numeracy education skills from caring and competent adults who are trained in the education method to use for math and the *5Ps positive parenting skills* (see chapter 10). This is a program delivered in Kindergarten to perhaps as far as twelfth grade for any student identified as struggling or behind in the primary languages of life 1) speaking, reading and writing in the English language, 2) numeracy skills - arithmetic and mathematics at a minimum, 3) perhaps several other disciplines like geography, etc. Paid educational assistants and volunteer adults made up of retirees and homemakers would be the ACGP army of mentors. They must be educated, work well with children, be well-balanced, pass criminal, sex, and child clearances, pass drug and alcohol dependence tests. They would work with the children during the school day at school at 'free periods' to help them improve in the skill area that the student is

behind. Perhaps supervised Saturday morning programs at school or virtual online sessions could be additional options. This program is to repair and remediate children of poor parents, poor learning experiences, poor-readiness-to-learn, poor-preparedness-to-learn, or those that can't afford for-fee tutoring services. The goal is to ensure that at least in school, each child is provided everything needed to achieve and stay at grade level or higher in foundational learning skills as measured by testing in 4th and 8th and 12th grades. Imagine offering retirees of appropriate education and temperament the opportunity to earn additional social security benefit, income, or tax savings in exchange for volunteering in schools xx to yyy hours a year in a program like this.

3) **Competency Toolkit.** *Middle School through High School.* To help youth build positive aptitude and attitude, provide tools and programs online and in-school for individual and group development of leadership, character, and necessary social interaction skills among others. Let's engage America's best child and vocational development experts to design this program. Imagine online experiences and videos of great American's from various walks of life sharing their path to leadership and their successful lives. Let them share what they believe a leader and a successful life is? How about a video game that tests an individual's character choices when faced with moral situations and let them compare their answer to what proven leaders and people of strong moral character from different persuasions would say the 'best' choice is. Consider schools hosting programs like the Civil Air Patrol. Civil Air Patrol is an example of a program that does an excellent job of preparing youth ages 12-18 for an adult life of leadership and service with a number of skills built along the way. Many programs like this can be integrated into school life.

4) **Opportunity Awareness and Preparation.** *Elementary through High School.* Of the many issues that limit young people and unemployed peoples' ability to make a living wage or to secure a good livelihood is knowing what opportunities, jobs, and career opportunities are available now and in the future. Our youth need help developing the skills that best match their abilities, strengths, interests with opportunities and jobs. There are around 900 different current occupations tracked by the Bureau of Labor Statistics. How many young people know what even a small fraction of them are? We can fix that. Imagine the federal and state government organizing and building a series of online video and publication libraries of all the current and future tier 1, 2 and 3 economy occupations, jobs, careers, professions, opportunities with summary and detailed information on what is needed and what their lives could be like. Require students to make time in school or online self-study at home to review a basic set of the survey videos (3-5 minutes per occupation) and some number of career-specific videos per year. By the time a student graduates

from high school each student should have a better idea of where they might focus their vocational interests after high school.

5) **Workforce Development and Job Training.** *High School, Vocational School, Community College, Prison, and Industry Training Institutes.* Take advantage of and enhance the existing workforce development programs like the Obama era Workforce Innovation and Opportunity Act (WIOA) of 2014, which was designed to help job seekers access employment, education, training, and support services to succeed in the labor market and to match employers with the skilled workers they need to compete in the global economy. Only problem is who knows about it or how to access and use the program? Provide access to job search services in high school and college for basically anyone that comes out of high school or college without a next step plan or a focus on a job.

Require TV channels, online search engines, and major website providers to play for free government sponsored advertising and infomercial campaigns that inform and encourage users about where to get help and information from various federal, state and local government programs. Some advertising content would be a regulatory requirement on distributors as part of FCC and Internet Use licensing as their patriotic contribution to the people of the United States.

American Moderate Agenda

7. Health Care and Health Care Insurance.

Why exactly are the bills so high?
— Steven Brill, *Bitter Pill*, Time Magazine article on health care costs,
February 2019

Moderate's View

Every American should be able to have access to affordable health care service, not just affordable health care insurance. The cost of health care in the US has more than doubled since 1980 from about 8.5% of GDP to nearly 18%[160] of GDP in 2020. Health care like education and internet service are the three quasi-monopolistic industries that currently have unregulated and somewhat inelastic pricing. They may need to be managed through price mechanisms and regulated more like utilities as they are grossly unresponsive to price competition and equal access to service. How do we make health care and health care insurance affordable and accessible for all Americans? Health care's biggest problem – price – is still getting worse, even under Obamacare which was supposed reduce costs? Until legislators address the 'fee-for-service' price issue, arguing over access to health care insurance is only a partial answer to America's health care challenge.

The Moderate Agenda proposes that we ought to 1) Re-architect the health care industry pricing model to reduce the overall cost of health care. 2) Re-architect health care insurance industry to provide affordable insurance for people in all five quintiles of U.S. income distribution. 3) Enable broader access to prevention, intervention, emergency, maternal and childhood health care, and conception avoidance and planning services. 4) Innovate new highly effective methods to improve and personalize health care access, delivery, quality, and outcomes.

Are you for single-payer universal health care insurance? Are you for 'Medicare for all' with the federal or state government as a single insurance carrier eliminating private insurance carriers and replacing it with one government-run provider? Proponents of 'single-payer' broadly claim insurers are the root cause of the current system, causing high premiums and out-of-pocket expenses. They believe abolishing for-profit insurance companies with a government program will bring down the costs and expand coverage to everyone. Or are you for Obamacare as liberals support? Or are you for free market based health care insurance as some conservatives support? Proponents of the 'free market' believe market forces will drive down the cost of insurance. Moderates like liberals easily agree health care ought to be an universal service like public education but moderates are readily persuaded that neither the conservative or the liberal approach will work for at least three reasons: 1) Health care insurance access and pricing is not the major part of the health care cost challenge. 2) Health care provider list prices of per-service-fees is the critical factor driving everything up. 3) Health care providers (mostly hospitals and specialists) are currently consolidating into regional systems creating dominant regional monopolies that will tend to behave as monopolies, further exacerbating higher prices, possibly lower quality, and fewer choices.

If you believe the real issues start with the unaffordability of the price that doctors, hospitals, equipment, and drug manufacturers/ distributors charge, then you are thinking like a moderate. Obamacare or the liberals 'single-payer system', Medicare-for-all, and the Republican counter-proposal for the free market system are weak choices for a moderate. Neither will reduce prices very well. Liberals and conservatives are not even focused on the central issue, which is the high, inelastic, unbundled and 'hard-to-discover-or-compare-or-shop-or-negotiate' per-service-fee charged for most health care services. You are a moderate if you want a solution that delivers higher quality for a lower price as experienced on a personal level and as measured by percent of GDP on a macro level.

Moderates' Proposal for Health Care Transformation
'Single Price' System for Public and Private Insurance

This moderate believes if Congress were to replace or enhance the current Affordable Care Act and other health care-related legislation with a 'Single-Price' approach for health care and drug coverage that would drive the cost reduction we need in the 2020-2030 timeframe. This would be a better interim solution than Single-Payer or Free Market solutions. The fundamental issue is the high list prices hospitals, specialists, and drug providers set for itemized, unbundled services in the Fee-for-Service delivery model. That issue can be addressed with a localized fee-for-service item price based on a modest mark up over the price Medicare pays a provider which is based on Medicare's Price List. Whether the service is paid for by private health care insurance providers, the government, or a self-insured individual, the price range would be set by value-based standards and metrics by Medicare led procedures. This approach obsoletes the use of list and net contract pricing for each service by each delivery entity, i.e., doctor, hospital, etc. It neutralizes the advantage volume or capitated purchasing power net price private insurance carrier contracts have.

All insurance company volume purchasing power contracts would be eliminated. For critics of price controls, all volume purchase based contracts are legal instruments for price control between private parties, which is what many private insurance carrier deals are with doctors, hospitals, and drug companies. The competitive differentiation for private carriers would move from volume purchase 'in-network' pricing power to personalization and value-added coverage services. Other pricing and quality measures could be accommodated for innovative bundling and capitated pricing models. However, as long as a health care provider prices each service/product delivered, the Single Price model would prevail. Using the Medicare computed/allowed rate as the base price, health care providers may be permitted to mark-up maybe a modest xx to yy percent if the bill is to be paid by private citizens or private insurance carriers. This is compared to current industry pricing practices where prices charged/paid in private insurance and consumer paid bills can be many hundreds of percent higher than what Medicare pays. The government provided coverage (Medicare and Medicaid) would continue to pay the fair market price established on Medicare Charge Master Price List. The net effect would be that the cost of health care should drop from 17-20% of GDP to closer to 12%-15% of GDP over a reasonable period of time while allowing health care and insurance industry administration jobs and plans to stay in place. Health care insurance carriers would be pricing their premiums closer to the premium charged by Medicare for insurance coverage. The model constrains health care and medical equipment providers from overcharging, gouging, or changing the price of services delivered at will. The net effect is to reduce the net margins harvested. Other reforms should be considered, including pay-for-performance, while new business and delivery models are innovated.

Additional Proposals for Health Care Reform

1) **Pre-existing Conditions**. Continue Affordable Care Act feature that disallows a carrier to charge more for patients with pre-existing conditions.

2) **Dependent Coverage.** Continue the Affordable Care Act feature that allows dependents to be covered under the parent's insurance plan until age 26.

3) **Medical Education Institutions.** Consider redesign of how doctors become doctors and how much debt they have to take on to become doctors as part of comprehensive reform. Under the Single Price model, the amount of money some doctors and hospitals make will have to go down. The way they will make more money under Single-Price Proposal is incurring less debt and

more patient interactions, so we should reduce the risk, stress, and debt with which medical professionals start their professional careers. Perhaps we consider having the federal and state governments underwrite the tuition and resource costs for medical and dental schools, so they are tuition-free to those who qualify to be accepted in exchange for XX months of service in an American version of Doctors without Borders type Service Program for national or international deployment. XX stands for the number of months needed to repay the monetary value of the free tuition's estimated worth. For example, if $15,000 equaled the value of each month of service and medical school tuition equated to $150,000, the new doctor would serve ten months in the national service as a medical service provider at some national or international under-served location. With the service obligation met the new doctor has no tuition debt to repay.

4) **Federal and State Governments** underwrite the cost of running Medical, Dental, and Allied Profession Schools, so they are tuition-free to the American students who qualify to be accepted and agree to serve. Students still pay for room & board. Foreign nationals and US students unwilling to serve in the Service Program would pay full tuition unless covered by other funding programs. This has the collateral benefit of getting the cost of Medical Schools out of the cost structure of higher education institutions who may be passing on the operating costs to both their medical school and wider university students.

5) **Equal Opportunity.** Accept more American students in to Medical Schools from the bottom four income quintiles based on calling, aptitude, capabilities.

6) **Delivery Model Innovation.** Provide programs and incentives for R&D and innovative medical service delivery business models - E.g., Telemedicine or factory models that employ Artificial Intelligence assisted diagnostics or genetic testing for defects and quality of life strategies given genetic susceptibilities, other ideas.

7) **Out of Network Services.** Ban 'surprise out-of-network' bills. By definition everyone at a facility serving a patient will be 'in-network.'

8) **Single Patient Record.** Expand the use of a universal single patient record so all providers can receive authorization from the patient to access the patient history for their care.

9) **Medical Malpractice.** Address fair and reasonable lawsuit jury-award caps.

10) **Subrogation.** Address health care liability event subrogation for carrier & self-insured insurance providers that currently benefit insurance and legal industries at the expense of victims.

11) **Federal Health care Insurance Coverage.** Congress and employees of all three branches of government shall be entitled to health care insurance coverage and premiums that are no better than everyday average American households.

12) **Children's Health.** K-12 mental and physical health screening at various ages for development, fitness, addictions, vaccinations, nutrition, testing.

13) **Teenage Pregnancy Prevention.** Determine if local hospitals and medical communities should be part of conception avoidance efforts in conjunction with school health programs where available.

American Moderate Agenda

8. American Service and Volunteerism

Earn this.... Earn it. — Capt. John H. Miller, Saving Private Ryan, Movie

Moderate's View

Americans should appreciate and earn the freedom America offers. Every able American has a duty to serve. The Moderate Agenda calls for a national rebirth of patriotism and civic duty for both citizens and corporations. Moderates are disinclined to have our nation give away anything and everything for free like partisan liberals hold nor are moderates inclined to make each person's life a complete roll of the dice as libertarian partisan conservatives might advocate. Moderates likely believe each able-bodied person should earn a large measure of the blessings of liberty in their lives in America.

Even though there are an estimated 63 million volunteers in the US sharing their time, labor, and expertise contributing in invaluable ways [161], the 18-24 aged cohort[162], among others, is largely disengaged, uninformed, mostly non-voters, non-participants in our democracy. We need to help our young people to care and appreciate our great nation and to respect those whose sacrifice have kept us safe and free.

In the 1998 World War II movie, *Saving Private Ryan*, the Captain that led a squad of soldiers to find Private Ryan, says these words to Private Ryan - *"Earn this ... earn it."* The simple sentence is powerful for those who understand what *'Earn this'* means. During World War II, about 10% of Americans (16 million) were in the armed services serving their country with a substantial percentage supporting the war effort on the home front. Today less than one percent serve in the military. Though Americans are a very humane and giving people, much of our volunteerism is for political, ideological, and civic causes. In general, faith-based and patriotic-duty service are in decline. Young Americans, millennials and younger — particularly those raised in affluent households who have lived in a time of continuous prosperity, may not have ever experienced any serious socio-economic stress. The coronavirus pandemic may be changing that for many including our young Americans. Contemporary Americans, on the whole, have come to expect our federal government to pay for everything and just fix anything that goes wrong — natural disasters, floods, other people's problems, the pandemic response, and more. As well, according to some studies[163] teens volunteering with younger children experience physical and mental health benefits that lower the likelihood they will engage in illegal behaviors and have fewer arrests and convictions between the ages of 24 and 34. Helping our young people, from as early as 5 years old, build service and work ethics benefits themselves and America.

Proposal for an Individual American Service Obligation

"Everybody can be great. Because anybody can serve". Martin Luther King, Jr. Let us collaborate as a people, as a nation, to fix those things we can fix working together. It begins by educating and motivating our young on the obligation of duty to serve others and our nation. Let us embed the 'duty to serve' into the fabric of our society and into the character of the people of the United States by institutionalizing a way to perform humanitarian and patriotic service early in life. Moderates propose the establishment of a programmatic institution of national service and tasking every able-bodied/-minded person with the personal civic duty starting in youth[164] — something like jury duty is a personal civic duty for adults.

The Moderate Proposal calls for the establishment of an American Service Program that morally obligates and incents each person to volunteer 2,000 hours of service between ages 5 to 29 for family, local, regional, national, and international projects. There would be a way to aggregate and recognize volunteering for family projects and many of the estimated 1.5 million volunteer organizations in the US as well as a way to create new opportunities to volunteer.

The American Service Obligation (ASO) is a moral duty of all able citizens and residents under the age of thirty managed through a federally funded infrastructure system (website, time accounting, general administration, and incentive-reward program) that:

- Sets Obligation Fulfillment Goals: E.g., xxx hours by age 12, yyy hours by age 18, 2000 hours by 30 with caps in some categories.

- Records each person's volunteer time. Advertises projects.

- Provides a place for families to define and manage family chores and local projects for their children (school, community, church,) up to a set number of hours and age limit (ends by age 12? 14?).

- Provides a marketplace for non-family projects/programs/events from which the balance of the service obligation would be earned with the individual selecting from advertised local, regional, national, international projects, military service, and select low wage jobs for young people with working papers. Programs would include local efforts like volunteer fire & ambulance first responder companies[165], hospital aid, prep services like Civil Air Patrol, Young Marines, Peace Corp, AmeriCorps, etc.), or global-sponsored projects like Mercy Ships, FeedMyStarvingChildren Peace Corp, many others. Individuals over a certain age could put their names on a *self-draft list*. Self-draft means volunteers can elect to be 'called up' by FEMA or county/state emergency service administrations for certain types of projects and geographic areas—e.g., natural disaster recovery, fight forest fires, pandemic, food insecurity, and weather event response—e.g., emergency snow removal, flood, tornado, hurricane rescue/recovery. Excluded from ASO volunteerism are all sports, academic credit projects, internships, fund raising, and all things political— anything directly or indirectly related to political action or activism (e.g., protests, petitioning, voter registration, canvasing.)

American Incentive-Reward Program. One idea is to enhance American Service with a national incentive/reward program for volunteers. It would provide recognition and financial reward in the form of a modest sum of taxpayer money volunteers earn—say ages 5-18—for meeting or exceeding hours-volunteered age milestones. There would be cap/maximum amounts a volunteer can earn. The federal and/or state government would make a contribution to the volunteer's 529 education funding account as milestones are met. Should Americans also consider other milestone rewards for being drug, alcohol, smoke-free, or arrest-free through high school, and others? Finally, if a person achieves or exceeds their 2,000-hour commitment, consider an additional dollar contribution to 529 or earned income tax credit of some kind in their income tax obligation later in life for a year or two?

Proposal for a Corporate American Service Obligation

Corporations benefit greatly from the strength, vitality, freedom, and protections available to them in the United States. Moderates call on America's corporations as US citizens to repay the American people by providing service to the nation in ways that strengthen our people, institutions, and future. Obligate industries to provide targeted beneficial policies, services, and/or resources to beneficiaries as their American duty. They get a tax benefit for the firm. Though many corporations take on causes already here are examples of what I mean as their duty to the nation:

Higher Education. Best colleges and universities provide free tuition to qualified children of active/disabled military & more ideas.

Financial Lenders. Student loans up to $XX,000 are priced at no greater than x percent (e.g., 3%) no matter current rates or inflation.

Employers over a certain size. Provide an employee new child education benefit of $xxxx 529 account contribution per child birth.

Many others. Crafted by industry/profession to serve the nation.

All numbers and ideas are illustrative, subject to revision and extension in public debate.

American Moderate Agenda

9. Energy Policy And Climate Impact - Manhattan 2.0

The saddest aspect of life right now is that science gathers knowledge faster than society gathers wisdom.

— Isaac Asimov

Moderate's View

We owe future generations due diligence, stewardship, and sustainability of our planet. The Moderate Agenda calls for energy policy and programs to stop the growth and then lower atmospheric carbon dioxide content to as far under 400ppm as rapidly and economically practical. Even though the world just passed through 400ppm in recent years even with very diligent effort it will take decades to get back under that level given our growing world population and fossil fuel consumption. We owe that goal to ourselves and future generations. Moderates will respond positively to proposals that reduce demand for and reduce supply of fossil fuels cost-effectively and pragmatically or any effort to reduce carbon dioxide emission into the atmosphere.

Moderates' Proposals for Energy

To reduce carbon emissions from fossil fuels, America and the world ought to pursue renewable energy, agricultural innovations, and conserve per person energy consumption by or well before 2050.[*] Moderates would likely support a 3- pronged approach to:

1) **Reduce supply-side fossil fuel production** with incentives and actions that reduce forward fossil energy infrastructure lock-in. Establish limits on new exploration and extraction, reduce financial industry investment in fossil fuel use, particularly coal, and remove government subsidies for production.

2) **Reduce demand-side consumption** by blending tactical and long term strategies from science, technology, economics, conservation, education, renewable energy tax credits, and

---

[*] See briefing paper at harrypmartin.com for why 2050 is important target completion date for carbon reduction.

gasoline and carbon tax that lower global demand for fossil fuels. Demand-side strategies put people in charge.

3) **Reduce carbon emissions.** Fast-track two solutions 2020-2030.
- *Displace coal-fired power plant capacity* with renewables – solar and wind as practical. This approach is actively being assessed and applied in key coal-using nations. Solar is now cheaper than coal. Cost of utility-grade solar has decreased by over 80% in the last decade to $.0.068 per kWh in 2019 and may go under $0.040 per kWh by 2021. Wind is also very economical in areas where wind is plentiful, predictable and power storage is not needed.
- *Pursue carbon capture* for the coal, oil and natural gas fired power plants expected to remain in operation for more than a decade. Use a strategic project for carbon capture innovation here in the US. Mobilize the talent, technology, money, and will to get it done on an aggressive timeline. The three Energy Policy strategies, combined, are a concrete, balanced, and economical path to reduce the US and global carbon footprint responsibly and to achieve the 1.5°C scenario with the US in or out of the Paris Agreement. It is far less costly than a Green New Deal approach.

Moderates' Proposal for Carbon Capture Manhattan Project
Moderates are the kind of voters who ask the question, "Why can't we innovate a way to take carbon out of the exhaust of fossil fuel-powered power plants?" We have the theory and the technology today. We put a man on the moon. We won World War II in the Pacific Theater when the United States pursued the Manhattan Project to build the Atomic Bomb. During World War II about 130,000 people and about two billion dollars ($23B in today dollars)[166] were employed in the top-secret, military-led Manhattan Project to build the Atomic Bomb in under six years (1939-1945). An enormous sum for that time. It was almost one percent of the total US WW II investment. Its' success is credited with ending the Pacific theater war with Japan faster and at lower loss of human lives than other options perceived at the time. We should reduce carbon emissions from the most significant source – fossil fuel based power plants – as the one thing we do to as an American imperative. If we reduce the one key source of carbon dioxide emissions while stationary and mobility renewable technologies and infrastructure innovations take hold we buy time and bend the atmospheric CO2 ppm curve.

By comparison, the US response to the 2020 coronavirus pandemic is a Manhattan-like 'whole of government', 'whole of nation' approach. Public-private projects are making sizable investments in science and pharmaceutical firms who have promising treatments and prevention initiatives – e.g., vaccines, virus-killing air filtration systems, and personal-protection equipment. The US coronavirus approach is a 'loosely-coupled' coordination of federal, state, local government and private sector efforts - not quite a 'Manhattan-class' project with tightly-coupled, laser-focused centralized management - but it is in the ballpark.

The Moderate Proposal is a call for the federal government to authorize a program to harness US ingenuity and existing technology to lead the world community on global sustainability with a least-cost critical solution for climate. Let's name it *Manhattan 2.0*. The purpose of Manhattan 2.0 is to focus, fund, and fast-track private-sector work currently underway by industry leaders in hydrogen fuel cell carbon capture technology [ExxonMobil, FuelCell Energy, and others]. The technology can potentially capture up to 90% of the carbon dioxide at fossil fuel-powered electric power plants before it is emitted into the atmosphere and store it underground. We need to accelerate innovation and infrastructure scale technology engineering like America is doing with pandemic vaccines in 2020. In parallel America must organize and commit the utility industry to deploy. The United States can be a leader in achieving the goals of the Paris Climate Agreement whether we are in or out of that agreement.

US Carbon Capture Manhattan Program

Goal: Reduce US emissions of carbon dioxide from many fossil-fueled power plants by 50% to 90% over the next 10 to 15 years.

Mission: Congress authorize policies, funds, and actions to:

- Facilitate final-stage innovation and validation of carbon capture and storage solutions. The federal government would provide coordinating legislation, organize the public-private partnership program and players, and provide funding reimbursed to the taxpayer from various industry and consumer behaviors.
- Establish and co-ordinate fast-track funding, standards, and regulation for large-scale deployment of carbon capture and storage platform solutions across the utility industry.
- Fast-track sale and construction at select national and global coal, gas, and oil-fired power plants planned to be used for the next 10-50 years in a phased manner (cost-benefit prioritized & justified.)
- Report progress and results to Americans and the world.
- Enable global sale and deployment of the American-system.

Funding: Funding would be a cross-industry, cost-sharing approach with contributions from cost-causer and benefit stakeholder industries so the utility and innovating energy industry players are not saddled with all the costs. Why? Everyone in the present and the future benefit from this solution. Cost-causers industries include automotive, airline, cruise, shipping, oil & gas, petrochemical, and other industries. Beneficiary industries who gain from lowering their costs over time would contribute e.g., Property & Casualty and Health care insurance carriers, others. Indirect cost-causer and beneficiary industries could be required to shoulder some of the financial burden – e.g., tourism, Wall Street, Mean Street. Consumers would also underwrite part of the costs through very modest higher highway use tax and/or utility surcharge. Current and future generations of taxpayers could contribute by repaying federally issued Carbon Bonds that have very long term maturity – say 30 to 50 year terms. By spreading the cost and risk over a number of stakeholders and time, a fast, critical-mass deployment is very doable.

Benefits: By attacking carbon emission at root cause at stationary fossil fuel plants, the US and world buy time and flexibility similar to the pandemic 'Economy Shutdown' intended to buy time in preparing a response to the coronavirus. It allows fossil fuel to be used longer with lower climate impact. As the number of Electric Vehicles (EVs) on the road increases the carbon impact of refueling EVs with electricity from fossil powered utility plants decreases. It slows the increase of load on the residential electricity distribution system which will likely require infrastructure upgrades at the neighborhood level as the number of EVs refueled at home increases. It optimizes impact on the economy and the transition from fossil to renewables while new electricity infrastructure, storage, and energy use technologies are innovated. It helps close the carbon emissions gap to achieve the 1.5°C Scenario of the Paris Climate Agreement on a faster timeline than currently forecast. Finally, in addition to untold human costs avoided, the economic cost—in billions—is far less than the trillions of dollars in costs endured and savings not realized over the centuries if we do nothing or wait for large scale use of renewables.

Additional Policy Challenges for Debate

- Enhance industrial policy on renewables and rare earth minerals.
- Upgrade national electric grid infrastructure for economic impact of mass deployment of Electric Vehicles.
- Pursue more effective foreign policy on coal-based carbon emitters (China, India, US, Australia, Indonesia, and others) and absorbers (Brazil-Amazon, US, Africa, and others). If all nations reduce reliance on coal except China over the next 25 – 50 years, total atmospheric carbon dioxide probably continues to rise.
- Address climate change at root causes – 1) total world population, world over-population born into poverty, world population moving from low to moderate/higher energy consumers 2) how we produce energy 3) how we farm the planet to feed the world 4) other actions.
- Innovate a land management program sponsored and funded by the United Nations or a consortium of Nations United that protect designated vital world natural resource areas for water, food, or carbon cycle protection. Should the world buy and conserve the Amazon region of Brazil, parts of Africa, Greenland, or other areas deemed essential for global or human sustainability?

American Moderate Agenda

10. Fiscal Policy - Balanced Budget, Deficit, Debt, Fair Share and New Sources of Federal Revenue

A billion here, a billion there, and pretty soon you're talking about real money. — Late Senator Everett Dirksen,
House 1932-1948, Senate 1959-1969

A trillion here, a trillion there, and pretty soon you're talking about real money and destroying America's future and children.
 - Harry Martin, 2020 update of Senator Dirksen's famous 1960s quip

Moderate's View
Balance the federal budget![167] *We owe ourselves and future generations balanced budgets. We demand that our children's children inherit only the debt and interest obligation on that part of monies spent in our generation that benefits them and their children.*

For America's first two centuries deficit spending was largely investment in the future of America (except for debt incurred during wars) but for the last half century deficit spending has been increasingly borrowing from our children to pay for spending and benefits for adults today. The coronavirus pandemic exacerbates and delays any attempt at fiscal responsibility but as soon as possible moderates call for vigorous national and Congressional action to make the hard choices on all obligations and to balance the federal budget. Moderates call for 1) tax, debt, and entitlement policy relying on pay-as-we-go federal financial policy. 2) Congressional fiscal discipline and accountability for an ongoing commitment to balance the federal budget during times of peace 3) Congressional duty to minimize the National Debt that future generations are responsible to service and repay. Here are five positions on US fiscal matters for you to judge the merit of the American Moderate Agenda on Domestic Policy.

Moderates' Proposals for Fiscal and Tax Policy
1. **Tax Policy.** The federal revenue collected should match or exceed the spending requirements of the nation year to year except in times of declared war, national emergency, or pandemic. Federal spending is over 20% of GDP but revenue is only 16% of GDP. Sources of 2019 federal revenue are 50% Individual, 7% Business, 36% payroll, 7% other, and a deficit of about one trillion dollars per year[168] future generations must cover. Unsustainable. Unacceptable. Individual

Income Tax Policy should reduce federal income collected from individual households' contribution to be about 45% of revenue. Cap individual contribution at that level to incent our labor using a progressive tax rate schedule that roughly reflects a 'percent of income by income tier' or 'percent of wealth by wealth tier'. The current Corporate Income Tax Rate is 21% and federal revenue from the business sector is down to around 7% from 15% in the 1950s. Moderates propose that business contribution shall not be lower than 10% and target a range of 10-15%. A new, higher tax rate would have incentives that enable individual companies to earn a lower tax rate in the low 20's percent by implementing incented America First and American Service Obligation Programs incorporated into individual companies' employee benefits programs and national behavior. The remaining 40-45% of federal revenue shall be collected from payroll tax, any health care tax, excise & estate taxes, and new sources of revenue primarily from the digital economy. The federal government should keep individual income taxes lower to incent self-determination, personal savings, and wealth creation. But America needs to face the fact that the federal government needs new revenue to balance the budget because of decades of Congressional over-spending. That income should come from America's new digital economy and private business value-add created that use government services. Here are ideas for additional sources of federal income:

- Cost-causer taxes. E.g., Recreational drug sales (marijuana), carbon tax via fossil fuel use, and others.

- Online sales tax. State & federal revenue from online transactions. States should be able to collect their sales tax on any transaction originating online in their state. Consider a federal online sales tax – say 1 percent - to defray costs to protect US digital economy, personal identity, and lives on the internet.

- Federal service fees and taxes. New revenue for commercial use of national services like GPS, cybersecurity, space, others, e.g., street address. The internet is a postal road when carrying email within US territory. Should there be an US internet email postal fee?

- Wall Street industry fees or taxes. Revenue from transactional taxes on financial equity and bond market transactions above a certain size and by certain market participants – target big players like high-frequency traders, hedge funds, and others - not retail investors below a certain size or various accounts like pension funds, 401k, 529, Roth, or Coverdale.

- Mean Street industry fees. Revenue from licensing fees for interstate/international image transmission (the more images per show/ad, the more licensing fees paid), substantial fines for children's protection code violations, and penalties for display of visually or cognitively abusive or addictive images on TV, online, social media, entertainment, and advertiser productions – sex, guns, violence, disturbing images, adult themes, others.

2. **Congressional Fiscal Accountability Policy.** As discussed in George Will's *The Conservative Sensibility*, Warren Buffett has proposed an instant fix for budget deficits. For any year (barring war or emergency) the budget does not balance members of Congress would be ineligible for re-election. Not likely to be supported by any member of Congress but Buffett's proposal makes the point. Moderates' would favor some form of accountability by their nature. Consider this? In any year Congress does not pass an official budget or a balanced budget or violates in-force Annual Deficit Policy or National Debt Policy, there be Congressperson accountability in the form of salary and benefits reductions? Ineligibility for re-election... other ideas. In any case how about Congressional term limits?

Since 1970, the federal government has run deficits during every fiscal year for all but four years -1998 to 2001. The last time Congress completed all spending bills on time was in 1996. Instead of the prescribed appropriations process, Congress has resorted to massive omnibus appropriations bills and continuing resolutions that carry over spending from the previous year. The last time Congress reformed the budget process was in 1974. There have been calls for the passage of a Balanced Budget Constitutional Amendment for some time. A proposal from the conservative side by R.G. Hubbard of Columbia and T. Kane of Stanford calls for the limitation of spending to the median annual revenue of the previous seven years with temporary over-spending authorized by congressional super-majorities.[169] A group of moderate House Democrats, the Blue Dog Coalition, is supporting a constitutional balanced budget amendment, proposed by Utah Representative Ben McAdams (D) as they distance themselves from the party's progressive wing, which is pushing dramatic spending increases for social programs and infrastructure.

3. **Moderate's Balanced Budget Policy Proposal.** If neither factional proposal is acceptable, consider the following moderate idea for either Congressional rules or Constitutional Amendment. *The higher the Debt to GDP ratio over a set Target Ratio%*[170]*, the shorter the period of time over which Congress must balance the total spending and total revenue by a Balanced Budget Rule, a Maximum Annual Deficit Rule, and a conditional Wealth Tax Rule that invokes until the Debt to GDP ratio declines to the Target%.*

- Balanced Budget Rule: The federal budget must balance during every 'X'-year rolling window not to exceed 6-years. 'X' is set dynamically based on the size of the National Debt as a percent of GDP. If Debt to GDP for the prior year is less than the Target Ratio% (say 50%) then the window for the accumulated spending and revenue for the previous 6-years would have to balance. If the Debt to GDP ratio is 1 to 10 points over Target Ratio% (e.g., between 51-60%) in the previous year the window would be 5-years. If the Debt to GDP ratio was between 61-70% the window would be 4-years. And so on for each additional 10% increase in size of the Debt to GDP ratio until the window would limit at every two years.[171] If the Budget does not balance then each member of Congress (active & retired), the President, Vice President, and others are accountable with reductions in salary and benefits.

- Maximum Annual Deficit Rule. Congress will be accountable to manage the federal deficit in peacetime such that the federal budget proposed spending bills cannot project a deficit that exceeds Z% of prior X-years' Rolling Window Rule' total revenue. Z% might be set by statute somewhere between 1.5 percent and 3.0 percent of the Rolling Window's total revenue. This rule makes it harder for Congress to create a runaway deficit and an ever-increasing National Debt like America has in 2020.

- Wealth Tax Rule. When the Debt to GDP ratio exceeds the Target Ratio% a conditional tax[172] on the wealth of households whose wealth exceeds $X00 million or annual income exceeds $Y million (including interest and dividends) will be computed on total measurable wealth over $X0 million. This tax would be collected in addition to the household's income tax. Revenue from this tax would be applied solely to reduce the Federal Debt starting with debt tranches that are being carried forward irresponsibly to future generations of tax payers until the Debt to GDP ratio is below the Target Ratio%.

4. **Debt Repayment Policy.** The principal of the National Debt that may be carried forward for more than 30 years payable by future generations of Americans shall not exceed the amount that calculates as xx percent of the Debt to GDP ratio (e.g., 30 percent). Debt above 30 percent of Debt to GDP must have a repayment schedule and payable from federal revenue sources of 30 years or less.

(All numbers and metrics are illustrative and are subject revision and extension through public debate).

Chapter 13: Are You A Moderate?

Here is the <u>Are You a Moderate?</u> Self-Assessment. Scale is 0 to 10.

	Are You A Moderate?	Points
1	I believe in or identify with or substantially live the beliefs, values, world view, philosophy, morals, character, goals, and principles of a moderate described in Chapter 3? *If yes, give yourself one point.*	_____
2	I substantially believe in or subscribe to the importance of the issues, questions, solutions, and the ideological principles of: 1) Children's rights and futures first before adults'.............. 2) Family first among national institutions........................... 3) Country first among the nations of the world................... 4) Solutions first before political party interests.................. *For each of the four principles discussed in Chapters 4-7, you believe in or will support give yourself one point. Up to 4 points on Moderate Ideology.*	_____ _____ _____ _____
3	I agree substantially with or am willing to subscribe to moderate solution ideas and proposals like those outlined in this book to solve America's problems on these issues: 1) Guns .... 2) Immigration .... 3) Education .... 4) Climate .... *For each of the four issues discussed in Chapters 8 through 11 for which you support a moderate stance, give yourself one point each. Up to 4 points on Moderate Solutions.*	_____ _____ _____ _____
4	I believe in or would support half or more of the partial Moderate Agenda outlined in Chapter 12. I would vote for candidates that promise these kinds of ideas in their political campaign, platform, or vote for in legislation? *If you do, then give yourself one point.*	_____
	'ARE YOU A MODERATE' TOTAL SCORE > *10 points maximum*	_____

If your score is six or more on the ten point scale, then consider yourself a moderate more than a liberal or conservative. Stop identifying yourself as a liberal or conservative. Start calling yourself a moderate. You're not undecided or independent. If you score 7 or 8 you are a solid moderate. If you score 9 or 10, you are a true moderate with partisan moderate politics — ready to advocate, debate, lead, campaign, and serve in opposition to liberals and conservatives.

Invitation to help reunify American Politics

Now that you have heard the voice and conscience of a true moderate, is this book a call to action for you? Or has it read as the eulogy for the beliefs, values, hopes, and dreams of Middle America—discarded in the last century? Has this book helped you put your finger on why you react negatively to both conservative and liberal positions and media? Or are you as committed as ever to liberal or conservative ideology and parties? If you are a moderate or want to become a moderate, start 'the long walk to freedom' from party loyalty toward the middle where many Americans want to welcome you and debate, civilly, the issues of the day. Accept this invitation to find the moderate voice inside of you and engage politically with others as a moderate. Help find the moderate-minded among us who are ready to serve our nation. Be part of a peaceful movement of American conscience. Be part of America's solution for extreme politics.

Here is partial take of a moderate solution to: 1) rebalance rights to include children and the future; 2) rebuild key national institutions to improve the prospects and prosperity for our Republic, especially the bottom half; 3) prescribe new solutions for national defense and interests that enable the United States to remain a positive global power in the emerging multipolar world China may dominate. What would your version of the following solution be if it were your call?

An American Moderate Political Solution

More moderates and moderation in politics. More root cause problem-solving, less rent-seeking in government. More disciplined focus on the future and the long view of global systems and nations. More fair and balanced reporting. Undo bias and indoctrination in media. More focus on diversity of ideas, children's rights, family, and common needs of all people. More patriotism, less partisanship. More good paying jobs. More economic and social equality, opportunity, and mobility. More American common bond of trust, respect, responsibility, integrity, and civility. More policy that eliminates, and less policy that perpetuates, poverty, inequality, adultism, racism, and injustice. Less tribal and radical group identity ideology. Major reforms in select institutions and industries, including elections, law, and criminal justice. New secure nationally uniform voting system. Transformative reforms in education, health care, and housing. Take foreign and domestic dark money out of politics. Grow and rebalance Americans' wealth using capitalism not socialism. Action to balance the budget, reduce the national debt, and authorize new sources of federal revenue especially from digital economy sources. Manage dangerous people, immigration, and other critical issues better. A New Deal for children. A new civic obligation of American Service for citizens and businesses. New citizen advocates for the many moderate issues such as Planned Childhood v Planned Parenthood, Anti-adultism, conception control, Children's Bill of Rights, Congressional leadership, and fiscal accountability. Continually strengthen and grow America's economy. Ensure national security. Establish new defenses for undeclared cyber & biologic war. New foreign policy to address the reality of global population, climate, the new China, and evolving world order. Balanced energy policy and a carbon capture Manhattan Project to lower carbon under 400 ppm for global sustainability. Reform Mean Street, K Street, and Wall Street...for real.

And finally, for you, *new politics* to...

Plan A **Depolarize both Parties with more moderate politics.**

Talk, act, and debate civilly as a moderate with others in both parties. Mobilize and organize other moderates. Challenge both parties to nominate moderate candidates, and craft platforms that advocate moderate principles. Vote for moderate candidates. Run for political office as a Party moderate. Collaborate with Congressional 'problem solver caucus' participants and other advocates.[173] Get moderates on TV and social media platforms to engage in on-air, on-line, on-stage discussions. Challenge hosts, moderators, pundits, and guests with hard questions on the many moderate root cause issues. Go for a career in any of the Mean Street industries to advocate for children's rights and other moderate agenda issues. Call out and root out dark-moneyed interests. And add your ideas to create *new politics*.

Plan B **Mobilize Independents and all moderate-minded people.**

If party elites are unresponsive to Plan A, work to mobilize voting and non-voting eligible voters with a 'virtual' 3rd political party using the internet. Give your Party a name. How about American Moderate Party—'American' for short. Drive a wedge through the political landscape with a new, keystone coalition of 'gold-colored' moderate legislators in the middle of the 'blue-red color-coded' seating chart of both houses of the Congress and other elected bodies. Stop donating time or money to either Party. Run candidates with moderate sensibilities who are committed to America and the American Moderate Agenda. Help your candidate beat the Democrat and Republican candidates at the polls. Run those candidates as Independents if the standing parties block their candidacy. Incorporate all of the elements of Plan A. Also build a platform and legislative agenda that empowers solutions that matter to our nation without increasing income taxes or debt. Infiltrate media, government departments, and politically motivated non-profits as a moderate. Liberals have made a fine art of infiltration and take over from within. Build or buy media TV, news, and social media companies. Commit them to moderatism. And your voice ideas to elect *new politicians*.

It will take an enormous amount of moderate energy to reverse the incredible damage and debt created by all of the generations of liberal and conservative politicians who followed *The Greatest Generation*.[174] The Greatest Generation saved the world from the evil of the Third Reich in World War II and built a path forward for democracy and freedom. The Third Reich is an example of a mega-turning point in Human History that did not happen because the incredible, collective determination and sacrifice of freedom-loving people of the Allied Nations united in common cause to deny the Nazis that path. America's fate is not sealed. Americans can pull America back from the current mega-turning point conservatives and liberals have set us on. Be among those who believe we can create a better future if we are willing to become a moderate nation.

Have you had enough predatory politics and divisive media ruining our nation and destroying our children's future? If you have, imagine an America if moderates led the nation from both ends of Pennsylvania Avenue? It is time for moderates to push back on both parties, the media, and bring back America's core values, peacefully. The current generation has no right to deny future generations of Americans the freedom and opportunity to experience the miracle of life, flourish, prosper, coexist peacefully, and enjoy the blessings of liberty in our great nation on our beautiful, blue planet just like we have.

It is time for *New Politics*. There are enough of us if you are '*In*'.

Are you '*In*'?

About the Author

The author is retired, married, living in Pennsylvania. Industry experience spans over 35 years in technology sales, systems, software, and management in defense, banking, healthcare, communications, manufacturing, and Silicon Valley industries. Education includes degrees in Philosophy, Engineering, Organization and post-graduate studies in a number of other subjects.

Watch for the author's future projects in the *Conscience of a Moderate Series* on children's rights, moderate policy solutions for national issues, and other topics from the moderate point of view.

Author's website, harrypmartin.com for briefing papers and more.

Bibliography

Adams, H. (2018). *Dialogues on the Refugee Crisis*. Minneapolis: Sparkhouse.

Ball, M. (2014, May 15). Moderates: Who Are They, and What Do They Want? The American center is alive and well—and up for grabs by both political parties. *The Atlantic Magazine*, p. Politics Section.

Bell, R. G. (Many). Courses on History, Law, Science, and Climate. *TheGreatCourses.com*. Chantilly Virginia: The Teaching Company.

Bitecofer, R. (2020, February 26). Hate is on the ballot. *The New Republic*.

Brokaw, T. (1998). *The Greatest Generation*. Random House Trade Paperback.

Brook, D. (2020, February). The Nuclear Family Was a Mistake. *The Atlantic*.

Drutman, L. G. (2018). Spoiler Alert - Why Americans' Desires for a Third Party Are Unlikely to Come True. *Democracy Fund Voter Study Group*.

Drutman, L. G. (2019, Sept 24). *The Moderate Middle Is A Myth*. https://fivethirtyeight.com/features/the-moderate-middle-is-a-myth/.

Hacker, A. D. (2010). *Higher Education?* . New York: Times Books Henry Holt and Company LLC.

Hibbing, J. R. (2013). *Predisposed Liberals, Conservatives, and the Biology of Political Differences*. New York: Routledge, Francis and Taylor.

Killian, L. (2011). In *The Swing Vote* (p. 20). St. Martin's Press.

Livi Bacci, M. (2017). *A Concise History of World Population*. John Wiley. Kindle Ed 3017.

Quinlan, J. P. (2011). *The Last Economic Superpower*. New York: McGraw Hill.

Rothstein, R. (2017). *The Color of Law*. New York: Liveright Publishing Corporation, Division of W.W. Norton & Company.

Sawhill, I. V. (2014). *Generation Unbound*. Brookings Institution Press.

Tough, P. (2019). *The Years That Matter Most* . New York: Houghton Mifflin Harcourt.

Will, G. F. (2019). *The Conservative Sensibility* . New York: Hachette Books.

Index

A

abortion, 16, 28, 59, 60, 61, 62, 63, 64, 134
Abraham Lincoln, 7, 10
addiction, 28, 41, 42, 43, 44, 63, 68, 73, 74, 99, 104, 114, 134, 135
addictive drugs, 41, 43, 97
adultism, 13, 14, 16, 17, 46, 52, 53, 64, 160
Adultism, 52
Affordable Care Act, 139, 144, 145
Alexander Wiseman, 97
All Children Grow Positive, 140
American Moderate Party, 129
American Moderte Party, 161
American Service Obligation, 149, 150
American way of life, 2
And-focused, 25, 30
Andrew Jackson, 10
Andrew Johnson, 11, 12
Annie E. Casey Foundation, 94, 131
ATF, 69

B

Balanced Budget Policy Proposal, 157
Barbara Jordan, 77
Barry Goldwater, 1
Ben McAdams, 157
birthrights, 36, 38, 39, 132
Black Codes, 11, 12, 48, 91
Blue Dog Coalition, 157
Both/Neither, 26

C

carbon dioxide capture, 123, 126
Children first, 34, 44
children's rights, v, 14, 17, 22, 27, 28, 31, 35, 36, 38, 39, 40, 41, 44, 52, 53, 57, 60, 64, 87, 132, 134, 160, 161, 163
Children's rights, 35, 159
China, 4, 41, 56, 64, 117, 119, 120, 121, 123, 125, 126, 154, 160, 161
China Syndrome, 56
Citizens United v. Federal Election Commission, 15
Civil Rights Act of 1964, 49
climate, 2, 17, 21, 22, 28, 31, 63, 117, 118, 119, 120, 121, 122, 123, 125, 126, 127, 154, 161
Common Core curriculum, 92
Compromise of 1877, 12
confirmation bias, 21
Congress, 7, 11, 12, 20, 23, 36, 47, 49, 67, 72, 75, 82, 83, 107, 132, 133, 144, 147, 153, 157, 158, 161
Conservative philosophy, 28
cost-causers, 29, 30, 99, 130, 131
Country first, 34, 159

D

David Brooks, 45
Deferred Action for Childhood Arrivals, 82
Democrats, 9, 11, 23, 50, 55, 100, 119, 120, 129, 157
Dietrich Bonhoeffer, 35
Digital life, 115
Disenfranchised Children, 138
disintegration of the nuclear family, 45
Diversity of ideas, 26
DREAMers, 82, 84
Dred Scott, 10, 11

E

economic inequality, 1, 4, 14, 17, 28, 46, 48, 53, 64, 98
Education Act of 1965, 91
Education Transformation, 101, 102, 116, 134
Educational Testing Service, 98
Eglantyne Jebb, 131
emotive capture, 21
Everett Dirksen, 155
ExxonMobil, 153

F

Family first, 34, 53, 159
first principles, 34

five positive parental competencies (5Ps), 114
FuelCell Energy, 153

G

Gallup Poll, 68, 81, 119
GDP, 32, 33, 78, 85, 91, 143, 144, 145, 155, 157, 158
George Washington, 9, 67
George Will, 157
Germany, 56, 78, 123
GI Bill, 91, 138
Giffords Law Center, 68
Gilded Age, 48
graduate education, 93
Green New Deal, 125, 126, 127, 152
gun laws, 68, 69, 73
gun violence, 41, 68, 69, 73
Guns, 65, 67, 130, 159

H

Harriet Beecher Stowe, 10
Harry Blackmun, 61
Health Care Reform, 145
Health Care Transformation, 144
Henry Clay, 10
higher education, 33, 48, 91, 92, 93, 94, 95, 96, 97, 99, 100, 101, 106, 107, 108, 109, 110, 111, 113, 136, 138, 146
Hollywood, 69, 73

I

India, 78, 120, 121, 122, 123, 125, 126, 154
Isaac Asimov, 151

J

James Heckman, 91
Jeff Flake, 1
Jim Crow, 12, 48
Jim Crow laws, 11, 12, 48
John Adams, 10
John Locke, 35
John Quincy Adams, 10
Joseph P. Quinlan, 56

K

K Street, 14, 49, 161

Keystone Scholars, 136

L

Lee Drutman, 8
liberal humanism, 4, 16, 29
Liberal philosophy, 28
Linda Killian, 55
Lyndon Johnson, 49

M

Manhattan Project, 126, 130, 152
Marbury v. Madison, 10
Margaret Chase Smith, 23
Mark Twain, 55
Martin Luther King, Jr, 149
MEAN Street, 13, 16, 19, 21, 38, 41, 43, 73, 103, 114, 115, 131, 134, 139, 154, 156, 161
Medicare, 49, 136, 143, 144, 145
Megatrends, 16
Middle Passage, 47
Military Children, 137
Military Children's College Benefit Program, 138
military-grade weaponry, 72, 75
militia, 72, 74
misinformation, 14, 20
Missouri Compromise, 10
Mobility, 90
Moderate philosophy, 29
Moderatism, 17, 24
moral reasoning, 29
Morrill Act in 1862, 92
multiversities, 107

N

Nation's Report Card, 104
National Debt, 33, 155, 157, 158
National Skills Coalition, 90
Nations United, 58, 132, 154
natural birthrights, 29, 37, 38, 39, 60, 62
Nelson Mandela, 35
New Deal, 60, 102, 112, 125, 126, 127, 130, 131, 132, 136, 160
No Child Left Behind Act, 91
Non-school factors, 97

O

Obamacare, 143, 144

Obergefell v. Hodges, 15

P

Paris Climate Agreement, 117, 118, 127, 153, 154
Paul Krugman, 1
Paul Tough, 87, 96
Paul Wellstone, 1, 139
Pell Grant, 110
Pew Center, 23
PISA, 95, 104
Planned Childhood, 22, 62, 133
Plessy v. Ferguson, 12, 91
President Clinton, 94
President George Bush, 91
President Obama, 81, 82, 139
Presidents Wilson, 49
private sponsorship, 83
pro—all, 60
pro-children, 60, 62, 63
pro-choice, 59, 60, 61, 62
pro-life, 59, 60, 62, 63
propaganda power plays, 21
Public education, 91, 94

R

R.G. Hubbard, 157
Rachel Bitecofer, 7
Rachel Carson, 117
racism, 13, 16, 17, 40, 44, 46, 48, 52, 53, 64, 90, 101
Raj Chetty, 96
Reconstruction, 11, 12
reference dependence, 21
Refugee Act of 1980, 83
Reinhold Niebuhr, 59
relativism, 4, 16, 34, 51, 52
Republicans, 9, 11, 12, 23, 50, 119, 120, 129
Roe v Wade, 61, 133
Roger Taney, 10, 11
Rutherford B. Hayes, 12

S

sacred scrutiny, 38
Sandra Day O'Connor, 61
SAT, 95, 107
Saul Alinsky, 19
Saving Private Ryan, Movie, 148

School factors, 97
scrutiny doctrine, 38
Second Amendment, 70, 71, 74, 75
Second Middle Passage, 47
silenced majority, vii
Silicon Valley, 97, 114, 115, 163
skill gap, 89, 105, 106
Skills, 89, 102, 106, 130, 139, 140
slavery, 10, 11, 17, 46, 47, 48, 53, 132
socialism, vi, 4, 14, 16, 17, 160
Solutions first, 34, 65, 159
Steven Brill, 143
Supreme Court, 10, 11, 15, 38, 59, 60, 84, 91, 132, 133
systemic improvement, 30

T

T. A. Frank, 15
T. Kane, 157
Thad Polk, 41
the UN Treaty on the Rights of the Child, 88
third political party, 7, 8, 9
Third Reich, 162
Thomas Jefferson, 9, 10
TIMSS, 95, 96, 104
Treaty of Westphalia, 55
turning point, 3

U

UK, 39, 78, 123
Ulysses Grant, 12
UN Convention on the Rights of the Child, 40, 57, 132
UN High Commission on Refugees, 81
UN International Panel on Climate Change, 117
UN Universal Declaration of Human Rights, 40, 57, 132
United Nations, 40, 58, 80, 118, 120, 132, 154
unwanted/unplanned conceptions, 41, 62
US v. Carolene Products, 38
US v. Cruikshank, 12

V

Vietnam War, 14
Voting Rights Act of 1965, 49

W

Wall Street, 14, 20, 49, 97, 154, 156, 161

Warren Buffett, 49, 157
wealth inequality, 17
Workforce Innovation and Opportunity Act, 142
World Economic Forum, 90, 117

End Notes

---

[1] This paragraph benefits from the scholarship of Professor Edward O'Donnell, PhD, The College of the Holy Cross, TheGreatCourses.com, *Turning Points in American History*, lec. 1 and others.

[2] Rachel Bitecofer is an election forecaster and analyst, a senior research fellow at the Niskanen Center, and a political scientist at Christopher Newport University. Source: "Hate is on the ballot," The New Republic, February 26, 2020.

[3] 68 percent, as polled in 2018 by the Democracy Fund Voter Study Group.

[4] Drutman, Lee, Galson, William A., Lindberg, Tod, *Spoiler Alert—Why Americans' Desires for a Third Party Are Unlikely to Come True*, Democracy Fund Voter Study Group, 2018. Both Gallup and the VOTER Survey asked the question: "In your view, do the Republican and Democratic parties do an adequate job of representing the American people or do they do such a poor job that a third major party is needed?" (Lydia Saad, "Perceived Need for Third Major Party Remains High in U.S.," *Gallup News*, Gallup, September 27, 2017.

Retrieve at: https://news.gallup.com/poll/219953/perceived-need-third-major-party-remains-high.aspx.). Pew Research Center asked a different variation: "Some people say we should have a third major political party in this country in addition to the Democrats and Republicans. Do you agree or disagree?"

[5] Drutman, Lee, Graphics by Ella Koeze, *The Moderate Middle Is A Myth*, Sep. 24, 2019 https://fivethirtyeight.com/features/the-moderate-middle-is-a-myth/.

[6] See previous footnote.

[7] *Marbury v Madison* was the court case that established the principle of judicial review, meaning that American courts have the power to strike down laws, statutes, and some government actions that, in the judgment of the court, violate the Constitution of the United States. The case involved Marbury, an appointee of John Adams for a judicial position, who needed to receive his appointment papers by midnight of the last day of Adam's presidency from Secretary of State John Marshall, who was also the chief justice of the Supreme Court. The new secretary of state, James Madison, at the instruction of the new president, Jefferson, to not deliver the appointment, did not. Thus Marbury sued for his appointment directly to the Supreme Court.

[8] This paragraph benefits from the scholarship of Professor Gary Gallagher, PhD, University of Virginia, TheGreatCourses.com, *The Civil War*, Multiple lectures.

[9] Candidates were: Abraham Lincoln (Republican), John Breckinridge (Southern Democratic), Stephen Douglas (Northern Democratic), John Bell (Constitutional Party).

[10] Scandals during the Grant presidency included the Credit Mobilier which involved corruption in the building of the transcontinental railroad; the Whiskey Ring which involved distillers paying off high ranking administration officials to avoid paying a seventy cent per gallon tax on whiskey production; and the Indian Affairs scandal which involved bribes by companies licensed to sell goods to Indians on Reservations. Source: O'Donnell, Edward, Phd., TheGreatCourses.com, *Turning Points in American History*, multiple lectures.

[11] For an understanding of residential segregation see Richard Rothstein's comprehensive and compelling history of twentieth century discrimination by the US government in housing and real estate in *The Color of Law*, (2017), Liveright Publishing Corporation, New York.

[12] *Citizens United* was a landmark US Supreme Court case concerning campaign finance. The ruling effectively freed labor unions and corporations to spend money on electioneering communications and to advocate for the election or defeat of candidates.

[13] The makeup of the top 1 percent is shifting from the traditional profile of predominantly Republican, conservative, and White to one that is much more diverse, Democratic, and liberal as the economy moves from physical, manufacturing, and extraction based to virtual, service, information, and technology based. See articles like Lee Drutman, "Democrats are replacing Republicans as the preferred party of the very wealthy," https://www.vox.com/polyarchy/2016/6/3/11843780/democrats-wealthy-party, Michael Baron's "Which Party Is the Party of the 1 Percent?" https://capitalresearch.org/article/party-one-percent/.

[14] The Fairness Doctrine of the United States Federal Communications Commission (FCC), introduced in 1949, was a policy that required the holders of broadcast licenses to both present controversial issues of public importance and to do so in a manner that was—in the FCC's

view—honest, equitable, and balanced. The FCC eliminated the policy in 1987 and removed the rule that implemented the policy from the Federal Register in August 2011.

[15] This point is informed by the scholarship of Scott Huettel, PhD, Duke University, TheGreatCourses.com, *Behavioral Economic: When Psychology and Economics Collide*, Lecture 23. The *framing effect* is a cognitive bias wherein people decide on options based on whether the options are presented with positive or negative possible outcomes—as a gain or a loss. People tend to avoid risk when a positive frame is presented but seek risks when a negative frame is presented.

[16] Senator Margaret Chase Smith represented the state of Maine. For more than three decades, she served as a role model for women aspiring to national politics. As the first woman to win election to both the US House and the US Senate (four terms), Smith was known as an independent and courageous legislator. Though she believed firmly that women had a political role to assume, Smith refused to make an issue of her gender in seeking higher office. Margaret Chase Smith's defining moment in the US Senate came on June 1, 1950, when she took the Senate floor to denounce the investigatory tactics of the red-baiting Wisconsin Senator Joseph R. McCarthy. In a speech she later called a "Declaration of Conscience," Smith charged that her Republican colleague had "debased" Senate deliberations "through the selfish political exploitation of fear, bigotry, ignorance, and intolerance." She said, "The American people are sick and tired of being afraid to speak their minds lest they be politically smeared." In the Senate, Smith remained more independent than a party-line Republican. In 1989, President Bush(43) awarded her the Presidential Medal of Freedom, the nation's highest civilian honor. Wikipedia.

[17] Of the 2016 eligible votes 27.3 percent (62,984,828) voted for Trump, 28.5 percent (65,853,514) for Clinton, 2.9 percent (6,674,811) "other" and 41.3 percent did not vote. Source: 100MillionProject full report, page 6. Additional statistics provided at USAFacts.org.

[18] Bitecofer, Rachel, *Hate is on the Ballot*, The New Republic, February 26, 2020. Pew Research at https://www.pewresearch.org/fact-tank/2019/05/15/facts-about-us-political-independents/.

[19] Drutman, Lee, 2018, *The Moderate Middle is a Myth*, Democracy Fund Voter Study Group.

[20] The Knight Foundation conducted the survey and reported findings at 100MillionProject.org. The 100MillionProject is a comprehensive national study of the nonvoting adult population in the United States and aims to understand citizen disengagement from the political process.

[21] Ball, Molly, "Moderates: Who Are They, and What Do They Want? The American center is alive and well—and up for grabs by both political parties." Politics Section. The Atlantic magazine, May 15, 2014, According to that survey summarized in The Atlantic, 44 percent of Hispanic and non-White voters and 42 percent of the millennials identify themselves as moderate.

[22] For a sense of left-right assessments, see tests on political orientation at https://www.idrlabs.com/ and research by Hibbing, John R., Smith, Kevin B., Alford, John R., (2013), *Predisposed Liberals, Conservatives, and the Biology of Political Differences*. Routledge, Francis and Taylor, New York.

[23] This section highlights scholarship in George F. Will's *The Conservative Sensibility*.

[24] Moderates offer limited support for the administrative state (bureaucracy) prescribed by liberals to pursue efficient governance. Our skepticism aligns us with conservatives also who remind us all of the Constitutional non-delegation doctrine that the power to legislate is solely vested in the Congress, not judges or bureaucrats.

[25] This point relies on the scholarship from George F. Will's *The Conservative Sensibility*, which credits other political thought leaders.

[26] *Harm* is used here to mean 1) rent-seeking and 2) negative externalities as an economist uses these terms. 1) *Rents* identify economic or social benefits extracted from others in a transaction or systemic way via law, regulation, entitlement, power, positional advantage that either harvest some benefit (money, right, etc.) from or impose negative outcomes or costs on others outside of the transaction, the contract, the system. 2) The term *negative externality* describes damage or negative outcome from a transaction or system for parties that are not part of the transaction or system.

[27] Source: https://www.bea.gov/system/files/2019-04/digital-economy-report-update-april-2019_1.pdf

[28] This chapter benefits from the scholarship and lectures of Professor John E. Finn, PhD, Wesleyan University, *Civil Liberties and the Bill of Rights*, Father Joseph Koterski, SJ, PhD,

Fordham University, *Natural Law and Human Nature*, Lauren, Paul G., *The Rights of Man: Great Thinkers and Great Movements*. TheGreatCourses.com.

[29] First in vitro fertilization (IVF), developed by Dr. Patrick Steptoe, MD, Dr. Robert Edwards, PhD and Jean Purdy (nurse) in England. Support for IVF and assisted reproductive technologies for legally married opposite-sex pair-bonds is defensible with some stipulations on these grounds: 1) natural human rights, 2) the UN Declaration of Human Rights, and 3) the US Constitution. No claim can be supported for any other transactions.

[30] For instance, there is a new public corporation that specializes in supporting all forms of human creation for anyone. It is a vertically integrated benefits management entity providing insurance benefits management and access to a network of fertility providers for traditional and nontraditional paths to parenthood. It also provides services and access to fertility drugs.

[31] What are rights? Rights are the fundamental normative rules of civil society about what is allowed of people or owed to people, according to some legal system, social convention, or ethical theory. Wikipedia. What is a human right? Every person is entitled to certain fundamental rights, simply by the fact of being human. "Human rights," rather than privileges (which can be taken away at someone's rule), are "rights" because they are things you are allowed to be, to do, or to have by the natural world or natural order because one is genetically a human. Civil rights are the rights of citizens to political and social freedom and equality.

[32] *Strict Scrutiny* is the highest standard of Judicial Review for a challenged policy in which the court presumes the government policy to be invalid unless the government can demonstrate a compelling interest to justify the policy. The two lower tests of constitutionality ... 1) Rational Basis 2) Heightened Scrutiny 3) Strict Scrutiny. I hold that if the Supreme Court can claim these are doctrines for deciding a case then there ought to be a 4th doctrinal test I name as *sacred scrutiny* whereby the court presumes all parties positions are invalid and the Court requires itself and all parties to a case including Amicae to demonstrate no position of any party denies children as a protected class (and perhaps other defenseless groups - mentally disadvantaged?) their constitutionally protected natural rights

[33] *United States v. Carolene Products Company*, 304 U.S. 144 (1938), was a case of the United States Supreme Court that upheld the federal government's power to prohibit filled milk from being shipped in interstate commerce. In his majority opinion for the Court, Associate Justice Harlan F. Stone wrote that economic regulations were "presumptively constitutional" under a deferential standard of review known as the "rational basis test." But it was footnote four that began changing how the court adjudicated cases involving minority interests. The case is most notable for "Footnote Four", wherein Stone wrote that the Court would exercise a stricter standard of review when a law appears on its face to violate a provision of the United States Constitution, restricts the political process in a way that could impede the repeal of an undesirable law, or discriminates against "discrete and insular" minorities that are denied effective access to the political process. Footnote Four would influence later Supreme Court decisions and establish the higher standard of review now known as "strict scrutiny." Wikipedia.

[34] The United States by allowing these industries to serve others beyond opposite-sex legal marriages are likely violating the 1st, 4th, 5th, 9th, 10th, 13th, and 14th Amendments.

[35] Estimates of 82 billion by Massimo Livi Bacci and 108 billion by Carl Haub. Both are population scientists. See Livi Bacci, Massimo, (2017) *A Concise History of World Population*, Kindle Location 3917. John Wiley. Kindle Edition and https://www.prb.org/howmanypeoplehaveeverlivedonearth/.

[36] Review a copy of the Universal Declaration of Human Rights (UNDHR) at https://www.un.org/en/universal-declaration-human-rights/.

[37] Children's rights appear not to be recognized by the Supreme Court. A moderate would hold the people and government of the United States are obligated to honor rights available to children as enumerated in a number of the human rights stated in the UN Universal Declaration of Human Rights to which the United States is a signatory. See human rights 1 through 8, 15, 17, 29, and 30 of the UNUDHR.

[38] The solutions are based on the science finding about "precommitment"—keeping young people from being in dangerous and risky situations in the first place.

[39] Author Shreeya Sinha, *NY Times*, online story, December 18, 2018.

[40] Polk, Thad, PhD, University of Michigan, TheGreatCourse.com, *The Addictive Brain*, lec 4/5.

[41] Though there is not one "addiction gene," of the ninety or so genes possibly involved addiction inclination, one gene may play an outsized role. Any individual born with the D2 version of the dopamine receptor (DR) gene may be at heightened risk. The dopamine receptor gene designs the proteins that define how the dopamine receptor is shaped in the ventral tegmental and the nucleus accumbens areas of the brain. The author's understanding of the current hypothesis is that the DR-D2 gene increases the likelihood of addiction.

[42] Survey results of Knight Foundation, the100MillionProject Study at www.100Million.org.

[43] Visit FixFamilyCourt for heartbreaking statistics: https://www.fixfamilycourts.com/single-mother-home-statistics.

[44] See D. Pager, "The Mark of a Criminal Record," *American Journal of Sociology* 108, no. 5 (2003): 937–75; and Devah Pager, *Marked: Race, Crime, and Finding Work in an Era of Mass Incarceration* (Chicago: University of Chicago Press, 2007) and Stiglitz, Joseph E., *The Price of Inequality: How Today's Divided Society Endangers Our Future* (p. 69). W. W. Norton & Company. Kindle edition.

[45] Neuroscience and psychology conclude teens are about as good as adults in understanding risks associated with making choices that have substantial risk. They overweight the positive consequences and underweight the risks of negative consequences of any behavior. They prefer a sense of belonging, experiencing some perceived benefit more than they fear the risk, so they make poorer judgments at times than adults based on the immaturity of their prefrontal cortex, which may not finish myelinating until their midtwenties, according to neuroscience.

[46] Many sources. E.G. Olson, S. (2013), Men Mature After Women—11 Years After, To Be Exact—A British Study Reveals, Medical Daily.

[47] 72 percent, Sawhill, Isabel V. (2014) *Generation Unbound*, Brookings Institution Press.

[48] Brooks, David, "The Nuclear Family Was a Mistake," *The Atlantic*, Online edition, February 2020.

[49] As an aside, smartphone and digital-device video chat and video conference capabilities are enabling extended families to stay connected or reconnect visually virtually, almost as well as if extended family lived under the same roof. The new capabilities are eliminating barriers of time, distance, continents, and even languages (translation apps), enabling extended family members to stay connected and relationally engaged.

[50] "Forged families" is a term created by Daniel Burns, a political scientist at the University of Dallas. To describe households of unrelated people who choose to act as a family, according to David Brooks in "The Nuclear Family Was a Mistake," published in *The Atlantic*, February 2020.

[51] In 1949, 79 percent of all households contained married couples. Seventy years later, that number is just 48 percent: fewer than half of American households have a married couple. Source: USAFacts.org.

[52] This section is based on the scholarship of Richard Bell, PhD, professor of history, University of Maryland, TheGreatCoursesPlus.com, *America's Long Struggle against Slavery*, Lecture 17.

[53] See Richard Rothstein's excellent work on institutional racism in housing, (2017), *The Color of Law*, Liveright Publishing Corporation, New York.

[54] Loss of hope, interpersonal abuses, and conflict associated with the prospects of failure, realities of poor choices, inadequate job benefits, inabilities, and disincentives or inability to earn a living wage, job loss, disability, addiction, illness, and loss of wage earner, among many other potential reasons for one or more family members to quit or disengage from the family.

[55] Stoler, Mark, PhD, Univ. of Vermont, TheGreatCourses.com, *Skeptics Guide to American History*, Lec.10, 4:30 min.

[56] Business Insider: chart from source: Saez and Zucman, QJE, May 2016, DB Global Markets Research.

[57] This trend is validated by the increase in America's GINI coefficient since 1970 (from 35 in 1970 to over 41). The GINI coefficient is an economic measure of concentration of wealth. "0" means everyone gets an equal share of income or wealth. "100" means one household holds all of the income or wealth of the population measured. The world average is around 41 and ranges from low 30s in Northern Europe nations to 70s in very autocratic/impoverished nations.

[58] Even now during the pandemic of 2020, government policies are picking winners and losers, further increasing the wealth of the wealthiest. A news story published by CNBC in May

of 2020 reported that US billionaires' wealth increased by nearly half a trillion dollars in the first two months of the pandemic, while many in the bottom half of our economy are facing Depression-era realities. "American billionaires got $434 billion richer during the pandemic," CNBC.com published May 21, 2020, 12:43 p.m. by Robert Frank. Fortunes of America's six-hundred-plus billionaires grew from $2.95 trillion to $3.38 trillion. In the last half of 2020, the wealth of the 651 US billionaires grew to $4 trillion.

[59] Richard Rothstein's scholarship and writing informed this section from his book *The Color of Law* (2017), Liveright Publishing Corporation, New York.

[60] George F. Will's scholarship and writing informed this section from his book *The Conservative Sensibility* (2019), Hachette Books, New York. See chapter 8, "Culture and Opportunity."

[61] Mollie Orshansky, American economist and statistician who, in 1963–65, developed the Orshansky Poverty Thresholds, which are used as a measure of the income that a household must not exceed to be counted as poor.

[62] Blood family means people who are genetically related within a nuclear family and as part of an extended genetically related family (ancestry).

[63] Killian, Linda, (2011) *The Swing Vote*, St. Martin's Press, 2011, page 20.

[64] Quinlan, Joseph P. (2011) *The Last Economic Superpower*, New York, NY: McGraw Hill.

[65] Quote from Keith Martin, director of Homeland Security Pennsylvania, brigadier general (PA), retired, 2003–2004 and senior adviser to the governor of Pennsylvania in 2005.

[66] There are rare instances of multiple male sex-partners close in time leading to multiple new humans conceived in the female by different males. Science has also enabled the ability for two mothers with the replacement of genetically defective mitochondrial DNA of the biological mother with that of a non-defective DNA female to address genetic defects in the new person. Neither case should be the foundation for societal policy.

[67] According to the March of Dimes, as many as 50 percent of all pregnancies end in miscarriage—most often before a woman misses a menstrual period or even knows she is pregnant. About 15–25 percent of recognized pregnancies will end in a miscarriage. More than 80 percent of miscarriages occur within the first three months of pregnancy.

[68] Rape and incest are about 1 percent of abortions, as estimated in the *New York Times*, Tamar Lewin, Oct. 13, 1989.

[69] There are several sets of estimates: the US CDC and Guttmacher Institute. As of the late second decade of the twenty-first century, Planned Parenthood performed about 345,000 abortions in 2019, nearly nine million in total over time. The Guttmacher database estimates well over sixty million performed since *Roe v. Wade* of 1973 in the United States. The website http://www.numberofabortions.com/ estimates the number of abortions worldwide since 1980 is over 1.5 billion with over 42 million in 2019 alone. It is the largest single cause of death, nearly three times higher than the next three leading causes of death (cancer, 8.2 million; smoking-related, 5 million; and HIV/AIDS, 1.7 million). The number of abortions in the United States increased gradually from 1973, then peaked in 1990 and since has declined. According to the CDC, 65.5 percent were performed at the eighth week or earlier, and more than 91 percent were performed at or before thirteen weeks. About 7.7 percent were performed between fourteen and twenty weeks, and the remaining 1.2 percent were performed at or above twenty-one weeks.

[70] FBI *Crime in the United States Report*.

[71] The six countries in the Americas accounting for half of all firearm-related deaths in 2016 are Brazil (43,200 deaths [over 60,000 in 2019]), United States (37,200), Mexico (15,400), Colombia (13,300), Venezuela (12,800), and Guatemala (5,090). Institute for Health Metrics and Evaluation (IHME) at the University of Washington website.

[72] 2017 Small Arms Survey of the Graduate Institute of International and Development Studies in Geneva.

[73] John Lott, "Concealed Carry Permit Holders across the United States," 2019, Crime Prevention Research Center.

[74] Study of Thomas Abt, research fellow, Harvard University, as reported in American Rifleman Oct. 19, 2019, p. 73.

[75] Giffords Law Center, Source: https://lawcenter.giffords.org/wp-content/uploads/2019/05/Giffords-Law-Center-Facts-about-Gun-Violence.pdf.

[76] Survey review of 2019 polls of Americans on the gun issue by Gallup Poll, Quinnipiac University, Suffolk University/*USA Today*, Marist/NPR/PBS, ABC/*Washington Post*, NBC/*Wall Street Journal*, CNN, others.

[77] History of laws on firearms: While over 280 gun safety laws have been enacted in forty-five states and DC since the tragedy at Sandy Hook of 2012, federal laws starting in the 1930s are the core of the regulations regarding firearms. In addition to the Second Amendment to the Constitution, there are at least ten federal laws and three notable Supreme Court rulings (*U.S. v. Miller*, 1939; *D.C. v. Heller*, 2008; *McDonald v. City of Chicago*, 2010). The ten major congressional acts on guns in force starting with the National Firearms Act (NFA) of 1934, which prohibits certain firearms used by criminals and a transfer tax and the Federal Firearms Act (FFA) of 1938 that requires licenses to make or sell weapons, prohibits felons from buying guns, and requires seller sales records. Congress enacted a "repeal and replace" of FFA in the Gun Control Act (GCA) of 1968 following the assassinations of President Kennedy and others with net improvements, including a prohibition on mentally ill, set ownership age limits, required serial numbers on guns, and stricter gun industry regulations. The sweeping changes in the Violent Crime Control and Law Enforcement Act (VCCLEA) of 1994 included a ten-year ban on nineteen different assault weapons and limited the sale of high capacity magazines (never renewed) was the last major gun control legislation. Gun laws of 1986 (prohibiting the establishment of a national gun registry), 2003 (Tiahrt Amendment prohibiting disclosure of where criminals bought their weapons), and 2005 (prohibiting victims from suing gun manufacturers) would by today's perspective be seen as unfavorable by most who are not strong gun advocates. Taxation of firearms is covered in the Pittman-Robertson Act of 10 percent on handguns and 11 percent on rifles, shotguns, and ammunition.

[78] The 1934 National Firearms Act was first federal law to require certain weapons be registered.

[79] Neuroscience has amply studied that one of the large cognitive effects of even marijuana use is *impaired judgment* (a response to the impacts on the dopamine pathway between the ventral tegmental area (the wanting function), nucleus accumbens (the liking function) and the prefrontal cortex (between/above the eyes - front of the brain) where self-control is managed.

[80] Barbara Jordan was a lawyer and educator who was a congresswoman from 1972 to 1978—the first African American congresswoman to come from the Deep South. In 1994, President Bill Clinton appointed Jordan to head up the Commission on Immigration Reform.

[81] Stearns, Peter, PhD, George Mason University, TheGreatCourses.com, *A Brief History of the World*, lectures 2–4.

[82] Federal Reserve Economic Data (FRED) website. Q1 2020 is down to $57,581 from Q4 2019 of $58,392.

[83] *Assimilation* is the label used to describe immigrants who strive to live as a member of the receiving country's culture, and *integration* describes the political accommodation a receiving nation's people are expected to make so immigrants can live in a new country as they did in their home country and culture.

[84] Whaples, Robert, PhD, Wake Forest University,TheGreatCourses.com, *Modern Economic Issues*, lecture 21 on Immigration.

[85] Whaples, Robert, PhD, Wake Forest University, TheGreatCourses.com, *Modern Economic Issues*, lecture 7 on Economic Inequality.

[86] Whaples, Robert, PhD, TheGreatCourses.com, *Modern Economic Issues*, lecture 7 on Economic Inequality

[87] US BLS. Source: https://www.bls.gov/news.release/forbrn.nr0.htm/labor-force-characteristics-of-foreign-born-workers-summary.

[88] Pew Research Center, Jynnah Radford, Key findings of US Immigration. https://www.pewresearch.org/fact-tank/2019/06/17/key-findings-about-u-s-immigrants/.

[89] The United Nations High Commission of Refugees (UNHCR) created in 1950 oversees the global movement of displaced people. UNHCR authority and agency was set in its Convention of 1951 and Protocol of 1967. Refugees are displaced people who live outside of their homeland and can't or won't return due to a well-founded fear of reprisal. Asylum seekers are refugees who have traveled to the border of or reside in the country they hope will permit them to live legally. A migrant is a person seeking a better life away from their homeland that does not meet

the UNHCR definition of a refugee. Nearly 85 percent of refugees are living in developing nations, and about half of them are children. Many children are unschooled.

[90] Pew Research Center, Jynnah Radford, Key findings of US Immigration. https://www.pewresearch.org/fact-tank/2019/06/17/key-findings-about-u-s-immigrants/

[91] Adams, Halima Z. and others, (2018) *Dialogues –on the Refugee Crisis*, Sparkhouse, Minneapolis, MN.

[92] *Arizona v. US Court* ruled federal law preempted state law on immigration enforcement.

[93] Tough, Paul, (2019) *The Years That Matter Most*, Houghton Mifflin Harcourt, page 328. This chapter relies on the scholarship and thought leadership of Paul Tough from his book cited above in a number of areas.

[94] Source: Measuring human capital: https://www.thelancet.com/journals/lancet/article/PIIS0140-6736(18)31941-X/fulltext measuring education attainment, learning, health, and survival (longevity).

[95] For a copy of the *UN Treaty on the Rights of the Child refer to* https://www.unicef.org/child-rights-convention/convention-text.

[96] Material in this paragraph relies on the scholarship of GreatCoursesPlus.com Program on *Adult Education in the Age of AI*, presented by Dr. Ellen Scully-Russ, associate professor of human and organizational learning at the George Washington University Graduate School of Education and Human Development.

[97] Conclusion of T. M. Cottom research on for-profit education firms as summarized by Paul Tough in his *The Years That Matter Most*, pages 262–264.

[98] See NationalSkillsCoalition.org.

[99] Dr. Heckman's research concludes that the return on investment in early childhood education is 7 to10 percent per year when computed against the lifelong earnings of an individual provided with early childhood education.

[100] *Plessy v. Ferguson* was reversed in *Brown v. Board of Education* Supreme Court 1954.

[101] Federal direct spending while briefly over 1 percent in period before 1980, federal spending has been about .6–.8 percent of GDP 1980 to present. Summary of graphs at https://www.usgovernmentspending.com/education_spending.

[102] US Bureau of Labor Statistics. The proportion of the foreign-born labor force age twenty-five and over that had not completed high school was 20.4 percent in 2019, much higher than the figure for the native-born labor force, at 3.9 percent.

[103] Some facts in this paragraph from USAFacts.org.

[104] See National Center for Education Statistics. https://nces.ed.gov/programs/digest/current_tables.asp.

[105] Source: National Science Foundation. https://nsf.gov/statistics/2018/nsb20181/report/sections/higher-education-in-science-and-engineering/graduate-education-enrollment-and-degrees-in-the-united-states.

[106] There are more than 1 million international students at U.S. colleges and universities, and they contributed $38.7 billion to the U.S. economy in 2019-20. That financial contribution is down more than 4% from the prior academic year, the NAFSA report found, marking the first drop since the nonprofit association began collecting data more than 20 years ago. For years, there has been a steady influx of students studying in this country, particularly from China. Prior to the coronavirus outbreak, the number of Chinese students in America was roughly 370,000, according to the latest data. Source:https://www.cnbc.com/2020/11/17/fewer-international-students-cost-the-country-1point8-billion-last-year.html

[107] STEM stands for science, technology, engineering, and mathematics.

[108] Source: educationdata.org website

[109] Per Pupil Spending By State Population. (2020-02-17). Retrieved 2020-03-07, from http://worldpopulationreview.com/states/per-pupil-spending-by-state/.

[110] Annie E. Casey Foundation "KidsCount" 2019 Data Book: www.aecf.org/resources/2019-kids-count-data-book.

[111] Source: https://www.pewresearch.org/fact-tank/2017/02/15/u-s-students-internationally-math-science/.

[112] Wiseman, Alexander W., PhD, Lehigh University, TheGreatCourses.com, *How the World Learns*.

[113] Mullis, I. V. S., Martin, M. O., Foy, P., & Hooper, M. (2016). *TIMSS 2015 International Results in Mathematics*. Retrieved from Boston College, TIMSS & PIRLS International Study Center website: http://timssandpirls.bc.edu/timss2015/international-results/.

[114] The Pew Research Center, FactTank. https://www.pewresearch.org/fact-tank/2017/02/15/u-s-students-internationally-math-science/.

[115] Research by economists Tim Bartik and Brad Hershbein conclude if you grow up in a lower-income family, your BA will add about $355,000 in lifetime earnings. But if you grow up in a higher-income family, your BA will add an average of $901,000 to your lifetime earnings. Source: *The Years That Matter Most*, page 256.

[116] Will, George F. (2019) *The Conservative Sensibility*, Hachette Books, New York, page 316 summarizing the work of Paul Barton of the Educational Testing Service.

[117] Republican 2016 Platform, p 41. https://prod-cdn-static.gop.com/media/documents/DRAFT_12_FINAL[1]-ben_1468872234.pdf

[118] Ditto

[119] Democratic 2016 Platform p 27. https://democrats.org/wp-content/uploads/2018/10/2016_DNC_Platform.pdf

[120] NAEP is the National Assessment of Education Progress, which collects and analyzes test data from tests administered in America's fourth, eighth, and twelfth grades.

[121] Multiversity is a term attributed to Clark Kerr, president of University of California 1958–67. "Multiversity" is an institution that provides services to accommodate knowledge creation of any kind like institutes, centers, and areas of the study compared to the institution of university that is primarily focused on teaching. Hacker, Andrew, Dreifus, Claudia (2010) *Higher Education?*, Times Books, Henry Holt and Company LLC, pg. 37.

[122] College endowments. In 2016, the value of the endowment funds of colleges and universities was $542 billion. The 120 institutions with the largest endowments accounted for about three-fourths of the national total. The five institutions with the largest endowments were Harvard University ($36 billion), Yale University ($25 billion), the University of Texas system ($24 billion), Stanford University ($22 billion), and Princeton University ($22 billion).

[123] Term from Paul Tough's *The Years That Matter Most*.

[124] Tough, Paul (2019), *The Years That Matter Most*, Houghton Mifflin Harcourt, NY pg.171.

[125] Source: Education Department's National Center for Education Statistics. https://nces.ed.gov/ipeds/search/.

[126] Source: National Center for Education Statistics. https://nces.ed.gov/programs/digest/d17/ch_3.asp.

[127] A credit is usually fifteen to eighteen hours of classroom/online instruction, so a three-credit course amounts to forty-five or more hours of instruction in a fifteen- or sixteen-week semester.

[128] According to a survey by CNBC TV in 2020, 53 percent of households have no savings for their children. Eight percent have savings bonds, cash, or CDs, 3 percent custodial accounts, 13 percent 529 accounts, 7 percent IRA/Roth IRA, and 32 percent savings accounts.

[129] Absence of a stable male role in an adolescent's life, especially males, can lead to wild and self-destructive behavior in teen years. Tough, Paul (2019) *The Years That Matter Most*, page 242.

[130] The scholarship of Paul Tough informs this section. Source: Tough, Paul (2019) *The Years That Matter Most*, Houghton Mifflin Harcourt, New York, page 217. Some colleges like the University of Texas–Austin have programs in which they proactively pursue "teach and support." As articulated by David Laude, chief graduation officer at UT, Austin, "If you do this right then during the period of time between 18 and 22 you can arrest the damage that 18 years of mediocre academic preparation has done to the student."

[131] For more information see the works of Angela Duckworth, University of Pennsylvania, Carol Dweck, Stanford University, and Eileen Kennedy-Moore at TheGreatCourses.com.

[132] Would the rewiring of the brain in cognitive addictive behavior be similar to the neuro-rewiring that occurs with repeated use of addictive drugs like heroin or opioids? Or is it more like social rewiring that occurs for social acceptance, which was used to capture our youth to tobacco use, not unlike the way adoption of smoking was promoted to young people through product placement in the twentieth century in movies and TV shows?

[133] For a primer on the science of climate change before reading the politics of climate change, go to the author's website.

[134] USAFacts *Report on the State of the Earth*. 2016 temperature higher by 1.71° F/0.95°C.

[135] G20 includes nineteen countries and the European Union. The nineteen countries are Argentina, Australia, Brazil, Canada, China, Germany, France, India, Indonesia, Italy, Japan, Mexico, Russia, Saudi Arabia, South Africa, South Korea, Turkey, the United Kingdom, and the United States as of 2019. www.international.gc.ca

[136] One estimate is China may produce 70% of all human-generated CO_2 in coming years.

[137] Source: USAFacts Report on the State of the Earth.

[138] SEI, IISD, ODI, Climate Analytics, CICERO, and UNEP. (2019). The Production Gap: The discrepancy between countries' planned fossil fuel production and global production levels consistent with limiting warming to 1.5°C or 2°C. http://productiongap.org/. This analysis shows that in aggregate, countries' planned fossil fuel production by 2030 will lead to the emission of thirty-nine billion gigatons of carbon dioxide (GtCO2). That is 13 GtCO2, or 53 percent, more than would be consistent with a 2°C pathway, and 21 GtCO2 (120 percent) more than would be consistent with a 1.5°C pathway. This gap widens significantly by 2040. This production gap is most significant for coal. By 2030, countries plan to produce 150 percent (5.2 billion tons) more coal than would be consistent with a 2°C pathway, and 280 percent (6.4 billion tons) more than would be consistent with a 1.5°C pathway. Oil and gas are also on track to exceed carbon budgets, as countries continue to invest in fossil fuel infrastructure that "locks in" oil and gas use. The effects of this lock-in widen the production gap over time until countries are producing 43 percent (thirty-six million barrels per day) more oil and 47 percent (1,800 billion cubic meters) more gas by 2040 than would be consistent with a 2°C pathway.

[139] According to the Production Gap report cited above, national projections suggest that countries are planning on 17 percent more coal, 10 percent more oil, and 5 percent more gas production by 2030 than would be needed to achieve the 1.5 °C goal.

[140] Source:CarbonBrief at https://www.carbonbrief.org/mapped-worlds-coal-power-plants

[141] SEI, IISD, ODI, Climate Analytics, CICERO, and UNEP. (2019). The Production Gap: The discrepancy between countries' planned fossil fuel production and global production levels consistent with limiting warming to 1.5°C or 2°C. http://productiongap.org/. The study examined how national plans and projections of fossil fuel production steer expectations, policy, investment, and, ultimately, infrastructure toward fossil fuel reliance. The study looked at these ten key countries: seven of the top nine producing countries (China, United States, Russia, India, Australia, Indonesia, and Canada), and three significant producers with emphatically stated climate ambitions (Germany, Norway, and the United Kingdom).

[142] "Climate change now sits alongside only four other mainstays—health care, the economy and jobs, immigration policy, and Social Security," *The Atlantic, Voters Really Care About Climate Change*, Robinson Meyer, February 21, 2020.

[143] Source: USAFacts Report on the State of the Earth 2020.

[144] Norman Borlaug, PhD, University of Minnesota, Nobel Peace Prize 1970 for life-saving work in agriculture.

[145] David Sadava, PhD, TheGreatCourses.com, *Understanding Genetics: DNA, Genes, and Their Real-World Applications*, Lecture 23, Genetics and Agriculture.

[146] FuelCell Energy (FCEL), a US-based corporation, has world leading technology for producing power while capturing carbon. At present, it is likely the best technology to achieve the Paris Climate Agreement 2050 goal by mitigating carbon emission. R&D, engineering, and validation need to accelerate to decisively make 2020–2030 the turning-point decade.

[147] CarbonBrief.org: https://www.carbonbrief.org/mapped-worlds-coal-power-plants.

[148]

Country	Operating (MW)	Share	Country Pipeline (MW)	Share
China	972,514	48%	China	198,600	35%
United States	261,037	13%	India	93,958	16%
India	220,670	11%	Vietnam	42,215	7%
Russia	48,463	2%	Turkey	37,466	7%
Germany	48,275	2%	Indonesia	24,691	4%
Japan	45,568	2%	Bangladesh	21,364	4%
South Africa	42,281	2%	Japan	15,308	3%
South Korea	37,064	2%	South Africa	14,192	2%
Poland	29,625	1%	Egypt	13,240	2%
Indonesia	29,307	1%	Philippines	12,618	2%

[149] "Existing Electric Generating Units in the United States." Energy Information Administration. 2009. Retrieved 2010-07-27."Inventory of Electric Utility Power Plants in the United States 2000." Energy Information Administration. March 2002. Retrieved 2008-06-19.

[150] See Moore, M., Gibbs, J., documentary titled *The Planet of the Humans*. Retrieved at https://youtu.be/Zk11vI-7czE.

[151] Photosynthesis. But reforestation is inherently land-intensive: scenarios assembled for the IPCC Fifth Assessment Report assumed that between 245 million hectares and about 1.5 billion hectares of agricultural land would be dedicated to bioenergy crops, compared to the approximately 1.5 billion hectares currently devoted to agriculture (Popp et al. 2017).

[152] Concentration as measured at the US NOAA Mauna Loa Observatory 8/22/2020 412.6 down from 416 April 2020, as the world is likely to see a pause in the growth of CO_2 in 2020 due to the dramatic reduction of economic activity caused by the coronavirus pandemic economy shutdowns many nations have temporarily put in place.

[153] The proposals in this chapter are illustrative and not a complete set of proposals. All numbers are for illustration and are subject to change with better information and public debate.

[154] Eglantyne Jebb (1876 - 1928) a British social reformer who founded the *Save the Children* organization at the end of WW I. Among the earliest and most influential advocates for children's rights she drafted the Children's Charter that became the Declaration of the Rights of the Child at the meeting of the International Union in Geneva in 1922. It asserted the rights of children and the duty of the international community to put children's rights in the forefront of planning. Later it was adopted by the League of Nations in 1923. It became the foundation of an expanded version adopted by the United Nations in 1959 which evolved into the United Nations Universal Declaration of the Rights of the Child in 1989 which became an international treaty with 196 signatories as of 2015 - not including the United States. The US signed but did not ratify the Treaty so it is not bound by it.

[155] The ten Children's Rights are enumerated in Chapter 4.

[156] Pennsylvania, Nevada, Rhode Island, Connecticut, and Maine have higher educational savings plans as of 2020.

[157] This finding is sourced at the PA Department of Treasury Keystone Scholars website at www.pa529.com/keystone / with original reference from Elliot, W., Song, H-a, & Nam, I. (2013). Small-dollar children's savings accounts and children's college outcomes by income level. Children and Youth Services Review, 35(2013), p. 560-571.

[158] Quote from *The Years That Matter The Most* by Paul Tough.

[159] The Obama era **Workforce Innovation and Opportunity Act** (WIOA), signed into law on July 22, 2014, is an example. Designed to help job seekers access employment, education, training, and support services to succeed in the labor market and to match employers with skilled workers, they need to compete in the global economy.

[160] Federal Reserve data from 2018. FRED data.

[161] Source: https://independentsector.org/value-of-volunteer-time-2020/

[162] Documented by the '100MillionProject' study

[163] Several examples of studies on the linkage of volunteering and personal well-being, see 2013 study https://jamanetwork.com/journals/jamapediatrics/fullarticle/1655500 and 2016 study https://www.ncbi.nlm.nih.gov/pmc/articles/PMC5197933/

[164] The author has worked with children as young as five in mission work with their parents, grandparents, and school mates and people from the community in projects like a charity called FeedMyStarvingChildren.org (FMSC). FMSC prepares and provides food for international shipment to starving children. Great way to introduce children to the importance of service to others and something beyond themselves.

[165] For example, in the author's home state of Pennsylvania there used to be about 300,000 volunteer fire fighters in 1970. Today there are almost an order of magnitude fewer fire company volunteers at 40,000. Many volunteers are needed. Source: PA-01 District. Congressman Brian Fitzpatrick's Weekly Update, August, 2020.

[166] Figures from a study by Brookings Institute in 1998 summarized at https://www.brookings.edu/the-costs-of-the-manhattan-project/

[167] The Coronavirus Pandemic, Stock Market Crash, Economic Recession of 2020, and the explosion of the national debt and Federal Reserve Balance Sheet make it nearly impossible to start fiscal responsibility in the early 2020s.

[168] Tax Policy Center. https://www.taxpolicycenter.org/briefing-book/what-are-sources-revenue-federal-government

[169] Will, George F., (2020) *The Conservative Sensibility*, Hachette Books, New York, New York, page 143.

[170] Americans can debate the Debt to GDP Target Ratio% – I am initially proposing that it should be 50% as fiscally responsible. The current ratio in 2020 is over 100%.

[171] The U.S. debt-to-GDP ratio for Q3 2020 was 127%. That's the total U.S. debt of $26.9 trillion at the end of September divided by the nominal GDP of $21.2 trillion. Source: https://www.thebalance.com/u-s-gdp-5-latest-statistics-and-how-to-use-them-3306041

[172] The statutory tax rate must be set either progressively or single fixed rate that is adequate to comply with the rules that enable the national debt to decline as prescribed in the Balanced Budget and Maximum Deficit Rules.

[173] Organizations like nolabels.org, newpolitcs.org, nationalskillscoaltion.org, moderatevoters.org. I am sure there are many others.

[174] Title of a book by Tom Brokaw, "*The Greatest Generation*," Random House Trade Paperback, 1998, where he describes the incredible contributions of leaders and ordinary Americans who survived the Great Depression and fought and won World War II.